# GRIZZLY

# GRIZZLY

## MY LIFE AND TIMES IN CRICKET

### CHRIS ADAMS

First published by Pitch Publishing, 2015
Paperback edition, 2018

Pitch Publishing
A2 Yeoman Gate
Yeoman Way
Durrington
BN13 3QZ
www.pitchpublishing.co.uk

A CIP catalogue record is available for this book
from the British Library.

ISBN 978-178531-408-7

Typesetting and origination by Pitch Publishing

Printed in India by Replika Press

# Contents

In loving memory of my
brother David and our
beautiful friend Victoria

# Acknowledgements

'IT'S not where you start nor where you end that matters, it's the journey that counts.' When Peter Moores left to become the England academy director in 2004 he gave me a framed selection of pictures showing the two of us enjoying and suffering many moments together at Sussex. Below it he had those words inscribed in bold letters. They really struck a chord with me and have stayed with me ever since.

Writing this book has reminded me not just of the many triumphs and disasters that are experienced through any life or sporting career but just how many people contribute and assist you on that journey. It would be impossible to personally acknowledge everyone who helped me on my way but rest assured there is a place in my heart for every one of you and I cannot thank you enough.

I do, though, wish to say thanks to a few very special people and organisations to which I will always be eternally grateful. Mum, Dad and David. We may not have had the fairytale family but I could not be more proud to be part of it. All of you have given me all the love and support any son or brother could ever need and without it I know I would not have got as far as I have in my journey.

Special thanks, as always, to Staveley Miners Welfare, Chesterfield Cricket Lovers, Repton School, The Rank Foundation, Derbyshire County Cricket Club and, of course, my beloved Sussex for giving me the platform and support to fulfil my dreams. And to Paul and Jane Camillin and everyone at Pitch Publishing for their help in putting the book together.

To all the coaches who worked with me on the way and all my team-mates in every team I represented, thanks. The camaraderie of a dressing room is unique and cannot be replicated in other walks of life. Great times!

To Bruce Talbot, who not only had to sit and watch me play for 11 years at Sussex through all the agony and ecstasy, but has had to endure hours and hours of me talking and reminiscing for my book. There was only ever one person who could have and who I would have wanted to write it. You are a champion, mate.

To Michael and Sandra, my wonderful in-laws. You took me into your family and made me feel very much part of your lives from day one. And Michael, you were right about Samantha!

Finally to Samantha, Georgia, Sophie and Mollie. You are my world and the most important people in my life – thank you. The next chapter in our lives is the beginning of a new exciting journey and I cannot wait. Onwards and upwards.

**Chris Adams, West Sussex, August 2015**

# Foreword by
# Peter Moores

IT'S a pleasure to write a few words by way of introduction to Grizzly's story – and what a tale it has been. I've been fortunate to share some wonderful times with him when we worked together at Sussex.

Before we linked up in 1997, I'd come across him a few times during his time at Derbyshire. I remember quite early in his career when they came down to Eastbourne in 1992 and Chris stationed himself at short extra cover during a one-day game, bravely diving around like a goalkeeper with those big hands and stopping everything. I thought then that he had something about him.

As a batsman I always felt he was at his best when he played aggressively. When he was in form he had a front-foot pull shot that he would play to respectable, good-length balls. And when bowlers were forced to adjust their length, he would drive them down the ground.

Chris is at his best when he is instinctive, allowing his intuition to guide his decision-making. We saw that during his time as captain of Sussex but also as a batsman. He always seemed to be able to spot the danger ball and when it was in his area he found a way of scoring runs. He had the ability to hit the ball hard, though more importantly a competitive instinct that more often than not found a way of winning the situation. It was a proud moment for everyone at Sussex when he got his opportunity with England in 1999. We were all willing him to do well and although it didn't work out at Test level he perhaps deserved more opportunities in one-day international cricket.

That, of course, worked to our advantage as he grew into the captain's role at Sussex. At Hove it was a classic combination of a new captain and a new coach finding things out together and, though occasionally we made mistakes, we saw the game from the same perspective and realised to be successful we needed to be a united front. We decided early on that we wanted to play aggressive cricket and create an environment where we enjoyed ourselves, while working hard to keep improving every day. Chris was fiercely ambitious right from the start and though he started as an inexperienced captain he always had presence as a player and led from the front. The goal to win trophies was always strong, though we both realised that to achieve this we needed a culture and an environment that would allow this to be sustainable. In many ways winning would be a by-product of how we went about our business.

We had some great times together at Sussex, most memorably of course the County Championship win in 2003. It was fitting that when Murray Goodwin hit the winning runs, Chris was at the other end. He led us magnificently that year, most notably for me after a tough loss at Old Trafford in the penultimate game. This was a time for certainty, to have no doubts and to believe in yourself and the team. These traits came naturally to Chris and he duly led from the front as good leaders do. It had actually been a tough summer for him with the bat and I remember countless hours in the nets as he searched for the form that was eluding him. In the end, like all good players, he worked out a way. In his case, he freed himself up, trusted his ability and allowed his talent to shine through. This sounds easy, though in the pressurised environment of a title challenge it is far from it. He wasn't afraid to make tough decisions and often trusted his instinct which served him well in many pressure situations. This was a time when many players emerged together and we all felt excited about what was happening and what we might achieve. Chris finished on 11 seasons as captain which will be a tough record to match for anyone in the future. To lead for that length of time requires a strength of character and a resilience that is rare, along with a desire to build a legacy of sustainable success. Chris had these qualities and an ability to let the non-important stuff go and focus on the things that really mattered.

Coaching is no different though the challenge now is to create opportunities for others to lead and believe in their ability as a player. This brings its own challenges with coaches often watching for many hours waiting for the window to help a player clarify the way forward. My advice to young coaches is normally the same, 'You watch a lot to say a little.' He could not have had a much harder first challenge than at a big club like Surrey with its tradition and expectation. He will have learned a lot through the experience and, like playing, will be better for it.

It's been a pleasure to play some part in Grizzly's life in cricket and remember some wonderful days at Sussex. Anyone who loves the English game will surely enjoy this book and like you I'm looking forward to reading his story.

**Peter Moores**

# 1

# The Pinnacle

Fast. Full. Straight.
Fast. Full. Straight.
Fast. Full. Straight.
As I made my way down the long tunnel on to the outfield at the Wanderers to play my first Test innings my senses were somewhat scrambled. Number six in the England order and already going out to face the world's best two bowlers with the match just 17 balls old. I knew where I was and I knew what I was going to be up against but that was about it.

We were 2/4 with four England captains – Mike Atherton, current incumbent Nasser Hussain, Mark Butcher and Alec Stewart – all out to a combination of Allan Donald and Shaun Pollock, two fiercely competitive athletes at the top of their game and harnessing conditions that could not have been any better for fast bowling, or seam bowling of any sort to be honest.

Fast. Full. Straight. Fast. Full. Straight. Fast. Full. Straight.

As I reached the edge of the outfield and adjusted my eyes to the Johannesburg light that's what I kept repeating to myself, again and again and again. Fortunately, there had been a drinks break when the fourth wicket fell so I had a few extra moments to compose myself and try and block out the sledging that had already begun, led by Mark Boucher – the archetypal chirpy wicketkeeper. Oddly, though, the verbals were all in Afrikaans which none of us understood. Only Donald sledged in English.

My fellow debutant Michael Vaughan was already out there, prodding the pitch and eyeing the skies suspiciously. Like me, he was probably hoping that it would get a bit darker and the umpires might offer us the light.

Me, 'What's happening then Vaughany?'

Him, 'I don't really know. I haven't faced a ball yet!'

What else could we do but laugh at the absurdity of the situation. Two England Test debutants together facing one of the best pair of fast bowlers the game has ever seen. It actually helped relax us a little.

The sight of us trying to take the heat out of things seemed to rile Donald. Now he was in my face. I'd faced him before, of course, in county cricket. I'd even had a beer with him after play when Derbyshire played Warwickshire but at that moment I don't think he remembered the social niceties of our previous encounter at all. It was probably the last thing on his mind.

I knew exactly what he would bowl – or at least I hoped I did. So as I took guard I settled just a touch deeper in the crease than I normally would. Grizzly the aggressive front-foot batsman always looking to take on the opposition bowlers would not be coming out to play, for a while anyway.

Donald in his pomp was one of the most fearsome and impressive sights in the game. There was the blond hair, the slash of white zinc cream across his nose and the aggressive intent, even as he walked back to his mark. Then he turned. There weren't many people in the vast Wanderers stadium that day – no more than 5,000 – but they made the noise of ten times as many as he charged in on a hat-trick, sniffing the blood of another hapless English batsman. No wonder they called this place the Bullring. I wasn't scared but I knew the next few minutes would not be a pleasant experience. I was about to find out just how big the step was from the cosy confines of county cricket to the Test arena.

Up to the wicket, into his delivery stride and down came the ball.

Full. Fast. Straight.

An in-swinging yorker hurled down at around 92mph, aiming for my toes. Just what I expected and, fortunately, I had a response. The bat jammed down in time and the ball dribbled off the toe-end and trickled down the pitch. I'd survived. For now.

\* \* \* \* \*

South Africa 1999 was supposed to be another fresh start for English cricket, and there had been a few of those in that decade. Earlier in the year we'd lost a home series to New Zealand for the first time and were officially the worst Test team in the ICC rankings. Bowled out for under 200 in both innings of the decisive Test at The Oval. Lower even than Zimbabwe in the standings. In came a new coach –

the former Zimbabwe all-rounder Duncan Fletcher, who had been a success in our domestic game with Glamorgan – and a new skipper in Nasser Hussain, who replaced Alec Stewart.

Stewart had led England to an unlikely 2-1 series win against South Africa in 1998, a few months after I had made my debut for my country in the one-day series which preceded the Tests. There was a fresh look to the squad. As well as myself and Vaughan, Graeme Swann and Gavin Hamilton were also chosen. Darren Maddy, who'd made 14 and five on debut in our last Test against New Zealand, got another opportunity.

The squad had been announced on August Bank Holiday Monday. When my name came up on Teletext I was elated, of course, but also pleasantly surprised. I scored more than 1,000 one-day runs in 1999 and had performed consistently in limited-overs cricket for a few years. I had duly got my chance in the series against South Africa the previous year, but played just twice.

A separate one-day squad for the series against South Africa and Zimbabwe, which would take place after the Tests, was also unveiled, featuring the likes of Nick Knight, Mark Alleyne, Mark Ealham and Ashley Giles. In the days leading up to the announcement I thought it more likely I would be included among the one-day specialists. That summer I averaged a modest 33 for Sussex in four-day cricket, against Second Division attacks, and didn't even get to 1,000 runs. There seemed to be players with stronger claims to be part of Fletcher and Hussain's new world.

The day after the squad was announced Sussex played Essex at Eastbourne. The TV cameras were there and a few journalists were keen to talk to me about my selection.

I was happy to oblige, Nasser less so. When asked for a comment he told the media he was playing for Essex and wouldn't talk about England. Fair enough, I thought. It showed his professionalism.

I don't think Nasser felt my technique was good enough for Test cricket. At the time I thought my selection owed more to Fletcher, who'd seen me play a couple of good innings when he was coaching Glamorgan, and nothing since has made me change my mind. But I really enjoyed playing under Nasser. During the warm-up games we had a few chats and some of the things he said definitely helped build my confidence. I had my own doubts as well. Players embarking on the start of what they hope will be a long Test career have. I cannot remember now much of what Nasser said at the time. It was all probably pretty standard stuff about playing my natural game and going out there trusting my technique and being mentally strong to deal with Donald, Pollock and a pretty strong supporting cast as well. I felt as if I was playing for him *and* England and as a captain myself I knew that was a pretty strong position for Nasser to be in. It took him a while to really put his own stamp on the team but he went on to become an outstanding England captain. I wish I'd had the opportunity to play under him more.

In many ways, though, you were on your own. We had a lot of experience in our batting line-up but Atherton, Butcher, Hussain and Stewart all had their own personal battles with form to overcome. I sat next to Atherton on the flight out to South Africa (we were placed in alphabetical order on the plane) and we barely talked about cricket. It was only after the series had finished with England winning the controversial Test at Centurion, for which South

Africa captain Hansie Cronje had received £5,000 from a bookmaker to ensure a positive result, that Atherton and I had a proper chat. He pointed out things that he felt I had to work on and where I needed to adapt my game. Who knows if having that conversation before the series would have made any difference, but I wish we'd spoken a few months earlier. Perhaps I should have approached him but there was a definite hierarchy in the dressing room and, as a new boy – even one who'd been in the game for more than a decade – I guess I knew my place.

These days players can turn to any manner of support staff for advice and help, physical, mental or on the nuts and bolts of their own game. Fletcher eventually instigated something of a revolution in the way England prepared but back in 1999 it was still a bit basic. The back-up staff consisted of Fletcher, bowling coach Bob Cottam, physio Dean Conway, fitness expert Nigel Stockhill – who didn't do the whole tour – scorer Malcolm Ashton, a couple of lads handling the media and Phil Neale, the tour manager. Four people with cricket-specific skills to handle a Test squad of 16, which was later augmented by Chris Silverwood and Mark Ramprakash, who came in as cover for injuries.

Duncan brought along videotapes of South Africa's recent one-off home Test against Zimbabwe. Analysis like this is easily available now but back then we thought it quite innovative. He had noted that Donald seemed to be falling out of his action, that his wrist position was wrong and he couldn't get his out-swinger going. Few bowlers in world cricket at the time used the crease as well as he did, but the footage Duncan showed us did suggest that he might be struggling. In 33 overs he'd taken just one wicket. It was encouraging to see but I think we all knew that Donald could easily get his mojo back very quickly. All the best bowlers could.

I did well in the warm-up games. Against Western Province at Cape Town I scored 89 and then made 84 a few days later against Free State in Bloemfontein. On both occasions I batted at six, the position I thought, heading into the tour, the selectors had earmarked for Maddy, who clearly wasn't going to be opening as he'd done on his Test debut a few months earlier. Right up until a few days before the Test I still regarded myself as the spare batsman in the squad.

No one else was in great form though. We didn't score a century in the three first-class matches prior to the opening Test but I'd knuckled down although I didn't feel my technique was being tested. The attacks we faced were county standard at best. None of the South African Test bowlers played. They kept their powder dry.

Duncan and Nasser pulled Vaughan, Hamilton and I aside two days before the Test to tell us we were playing. What a moment that was. I knew I'd be nervous but I was now able to prepare in the knowledge that I was going to make my debut. There would be no disappointment on the morning of the game or the day before when you discovered you'd been left out. It was an excellent decision by the management to let us know early, one we all appreciated.

We practised in glorious sunshine and I felt good. So did Vaughan. Gavin, though, went into his shell a bit. In fact, from the moment he knew he was playing until the evening of the third day when he knew he'd made his contribution to the Test (a pair and 0-63) it was difficult to get a word out of him, he was that badly affected by nerves.

Then when it was all over it was as if a pressure valve had been released and amiable, likeable Gavin was back. I'm sure the moment that happened, on the bus going back to the hotel, Duncan and Nasser noticed this transformation. His Test career was already over.

I slept well the night before but when I peeled back the curtains on the first morning I looked out to skies that could easily have been Derby in early season or Hove when the sea fret rolls in and you can hardly see your hand in front of your face. The clouds were as dark as they could be without it actually raining, although it clearly had rained heavily during the night.

When we got to the Wanderers there seemed little prospect that we'd start on time. I prepared as if we would but the experienced guys were convinced there would be a delay. Did that contribute to what subsequently happened? Possibly. Even when the umpires, Sri Venkataraghavan and Dave Orchard, called out Nasser to toss-up with Cronje some of the guys still weren't convinced we were going to play. But they were happy with the light and the outfield was dry enough. Nasser called incorrectly and Cronje not surprisingly stuck us in. We'd have done the same. The overheads and a slightly damp, underprepared pitch were perfect for bowling. I put my whites on and cleared out of the dressing room so the guys at the top of the order could get ready. I felt good. I was nervous, but I was ready.

The next 20 minutes was a surreal experience and even now, all these years later, I occasionally find myself asking, 'Did that really happen?' I remember getting a cup of tea and sitting in one of the big, comfy armchairs they have in the viewing gallery. Of the senior batsmen, Atherton was the only one with any semblance of form going into the game with a couple of 80s and, of course, it was on this ground that he had batted for nearly 11 hours four years earlier to save the Test with one of the most courageous innings by any English batsman.

Third ball of the match, Donald bowled a perfect in-swinger and as Atherton groped forward, the ball cannoned into his off stump. Hmmm, 1/1. This could be testing for a while. Next over Pollock bowled one just short of a length that reared up off the top of Nasser's glove and into Lance Klusener's hands at third slip, 2/2. Time to head back to the dressing room.

Donald could hardly wait to get back to his mark at the start of the third over. His personal duel with Atherton was seen by many as key to the outcome of the series and, having landed the first blow, he sniffed more English blood. Sure enough Butcher was next, caught behind off the fourth ball of the over for a single. At that stage it looked like a wicket might fall with every ball.

I was changing next to Stewart and, amid the pandemonium, he seemed to be the calmest man in Johannesburg. A check of the pads, a tug of the shirt sleeves and a twirl of the bat. Everything had to be just so before Alec went out to bat. He was in his own little world while, next to him, I was trying to gather together as much of my kit as I could find. In the corner of the TV screen the match was on. I remember glancing up at Alec as he prepared to face his first ball. Next thing I knew there was a huge guttural roar. I looked up at the screen, which was a split-second behind the live action of course, in response and Alec was a goner, plumb lbw for a golden duck. We were 2/4 after 17 balls and had made the worst start by an England team in Test history.

When Stewart began walking back I still hadn't got my pads on. While I was strapping on the right, Darren Gough, while trying to suppress his giggles, was putting the other one on. Hardly ideal preparation but despite the turmoil I still had clarity about one thing. I knew what Donald would bowl at me first-up.

The tunnel at the Wanderers is like nothing else I'd ever experienced in cricket, before or since. There's a slight incline on to the outfield but the Perspex cover makes it feel like you're walking through a greenhouse. And then there are the kids who appeared from nowhere to bang out their welcome to the new batsmen with their fists like hundreds of drummers at a convention of heavy metal bands thumping away simultaneously to the same beat. I felt slightly intimidated before I had even stepped on to the outfield.

Once I'd negotiated the hat-trick ball I felt marginally better. I didn't face Pollock in the next over and when Donald came back I collected my first Test runs. He bowled just short of a length outside off stump and I carved it over gully for a one-bounce four. Perhaps not the stylish cover drive or clip off the toes with which I'd necessarily have liked to have launched my England Test career but at least it doubled the score. Cronje immediately took one of his four slips out and posted a third man, thus revealing the plan he and their coach, Bob Woolmer, had worked out for me which remained in place throughout the series. He was going to cut off my runs in the area behind square on the off side with three slips and a third man. Jonty Rhodes was at cover which was like having three fielders in one so anything in front of square on the off would invariably go to him. There was an extra cover as well and if I wanted to take on any short stuff Gary Kirsten was waiting for any mistake under the lid at short leg.

My first Test innings lasted 50 minutes and 31 balls. My 16 runs meant I was our third-top scorer but I never felt in any way fluent or settled. This was the most intense cricket I had ever experienced. Of course I'd faced quick bowling before many times in county cricket and I relished the challenge. Back then, nearly all the counties had a world-class quick but if you were facing Donald for Warwickshire there would generally be relief at the other end in the form of someone like Tim Munton, a fine English-style seam bowler but not someone looking to knock your block off or bowl consistently upwards of 90mph. You could normally get runs and keep the strike ticking over.

But this was something else. Pollock was not much slower than Donald but just as challenging. He was accurate, had great seam variation and always bowled that nagging length that made him very difficult to score off, a bit like Glenn McGrath but slightly quicker. And when he did bowl something I could attack outside off stump the chances were that Rhodes would stop it.

I hit a couple more boundaries as Vaughan and I put on 30 runs in ten overs. Donald worked me over a bit and I got hit a couple of times but that didn't worry me. It was almost like a badge of honour. He knew my record in England was decent and may well have seen me as a threat. The wicket was underprepared, but nothing worse than some of the surfaces I'd played on in county cricket. But the quality of the bowling was something I'd certainly never experienced in England. The ironic thing is that when I did get out to Donald in the 13th over I didn't do myself any favours.

He got the ball to jag back off the seam and I got myself in the wrong position to defend it. My hands were in front of my body and the ball took the glove and deflected off the top of my bat handle on its way to Boucher. He was up celebrating straight away but Venkat wasn't sure and Donald only belatedly joined in the celebrations. During my career I had always walked and took a couple of steps towards the dressing room, which seemed to make the umpire's mind up for him. If I'd had a longer Test career perhaps my attitude might have hardened and I would have waited for the umpire to make the decision in marginal cases. I'm not sure Hussain or Atherton were impressed with my honesty.

Andrew Flintoff hit 38 and Vaughan looked a bit more assured than I for his 33 but 122 was still under-par and when the sun came out on the second day South Africa batted themselves into a strong position. We went in again 281 behind and although Stewart counter-attacked well for 89 we were dismissed for 260 and lost by an innings. My contribution in the second innings was a single before the Donald–Boucher combination did for me again. Between them Donald and Pollock took 19 of the wickets to fall and South Africa had won their tenth successive home Test.

My first experience of Test cricket had been a real eye-opener. I thought that with more experience I would be able to adapt and eventually play my natural game. Fletcher had told the press that he wanted to give myself and Vaughan a run in the side to see if we could make it. If I thought Test cricket would be tough, little did I realise just how tough.

# 2

# Bed Of Nettles

I AM proud of my Derbyshire roots, but Christopher John Adams might easily have been an Essex boy like my elder brother David. Although my Dad, John, was born in Huddersfield he migrated south to teach PE, first in Gravesend, Kent and then at Hornchurch Grammar School, where he was head of the PE department from 1964–67. As he arrived my Mum Eluned (Lyn) had recently left to study PE at a training college in Dartford. Mum had been born in Essex although her mother, Joan, hailed from Derbyshire. When she qualified, Mum got a post at a school in Shenfield, Essex, before becoming a head of department herself at Dagenham County School.

With their teaching background I suppose there was always a chance that I would follow the academic path. But, more importantly as it turned out, they were also sports-mad. Not only did they teach it but they also played it. Dad had been on Huddersfield Town's books as a youngster and had been approached by their manager Bill Shankly, who cut his teeth with Huddersfield before going on to greatness at Liverpool, to become a professional. Dad could play on the left wing or as a centre-forward and was considered a good prospect. Unfortunately for him, his father Alf, who had played for Tranmere Rovers as a very quick winger, told John he had to concentrate on his education. Alf, incidentally, had quite a varied working life. At the time he ran a fish and chip shop and later became a cinema manager. His own father had been stud groom to the Earl of Derby, so there's another Derbyshire link!

Dad was a more than useful club cricketer and played at a good level for many years as a left-arm spinner and lower-order batsman, more Boycott than biffer, with various clubs, notably Staveley Miners Welfare. He had played his first league game in Huddersfield aged 12, coincidentally the same age I won my first cricket trophy, the single wicket competition at Staveley. Mum played netball, hockey and tennis while my enduring love of golf was probably fostered by her parents, both of whom ended up captaining Maylands Golf Club near Romford. I can still remember, as an eight-year-old, hitting a ball with an adult's club about 150 yards to the utter astonishment of the professional there.

Dad had ambitions beyond the classroom, though, and in 1967 applied for a job with the Football Association. They were expanding their coaching operation and were recruiting coaches for the four regions. Dad recalls going to the FA's old headquarters at Lancaster Gate for his interview and being offered the job a few days later. Once the formalities were completed he was led down to the basement that was full of training kit left over from the 1966 World Cup. He was told to help himself, which is why for years I always associated Dad with Sir Alf Ramsey because both of them wore that famous blue tracksuit with 'Admiral' emblazoned across the front. He became one of the youngest qualified FA coaches in the country, qualifying at Lilleshall with the likes of Don Revie, Bertie Mee and Ron Saunders, all of whom had long and successful managerial careers. One of his proudest achievements was being unbeaten in two games in charge of the England women's team, against France and Scotland.

His patch included Yorkshire, Nottinghamshire, Lincolnshire and Derbyshire and he decided to move the family – David had been born in Essex in 1967 – to Harrogate. It was a real wrench for Mum to move away from her friends and family. She was only 23 and it wasn't long before they were on the move again. Having been gazumped on a house they fancied on the Nottinghamshire–Derbyshire border, they settled on another in Whitwell, a couple of miles from Yorkshire just across the border in Derbyshire.

The house was a mews cottage that only had two bedrooms, but there were two large barns as part of the property and a big back garden. They paid £4,500 and renovated the barns to make it five bedrooms. It was there, on Wednesday 6 May 1970, that I was born with the midwife's help while two-year-old David and my Dad kicked a football about in the front garden.

By all accounts David was a bit of a handful. He had a stubborn streak and would run off at every opportunity. With Dad away for a lot of time because of his job and David proving such a difficult toddler, bringing up two young boys must have been very hard for Mum.

Although there were farms and fields at our end of Whitwell, it was a pit village and everything in the community revolved around the mines. Mining in Whitwell dated back to 1894 and when I was born the pit still employed just under 800 miners and was producing nearly 500,000 tonnes of coal a year. The bowls club, tennis courts and Miners Welfare social club in the village were all inextricably linked to the pit. I had moved to Chesterfield by the time Margaret Thatcher's government began to dismantle the coal industry but I would go back to Whitwell to visit Dad at weekends, after my parents split up, and can clearly remember picketing going on outside the entrance to the pit during the miners' strike of 1984.

Two years later the pit had gone and, it seemed to me at the time, a large aspect of village life went with it. I remember a few years later wandering through the village and discovering that the bowls club had closed and the tennis courts were overgrown with weeds. With the pit shut down and so many people out of work the village simply could not sustain the leisure facilities which had been an integral part of life in Whitwell for nearly 100 years. A similar thing was happening all across the coalfields of the north Midlands and Yorkshire as a once-great industry slowly disappeared. It was very sad.

My earliest sporting memories are of playing football in our sloping back garden at 38 High Street. Mum loved village life and was very community-spirited. She was soon part of the playgroup and coffee morning crowd. Saturday mornings were always spent at our house. The mums would be inside drinking coffee and gossiping while five or six of us would play football outside. Being the smallest and the youngest I would invariably be shoved in goal while the others played a game called Cup Tees until there was only one person left, usually David.

Dad's job with the FA took him away a lot which is why weekends at home were so important to him. He played cricket for Staveley Miners Welfare in the Bassetlaw League. Staveley had several pits and a flourishing sports set-up, a bit like Whitwell but on a larger scale.

On Friday nights he would head off there for a pint or two while outside David and I dragged the mini roller across the outfield to use as the stumps so we could play cricket using Dad's bat. It was one of those old-fashioned blades with the manufacturer's name burned on to the front. A few years later I had it framed for him and he has still got it. It was on the vast outfield at Staveley where David and I began to love the game.

We would play until it got dark, go inside for a shandy and bag of crisps, and return for the next two days for more games on the edge of the outfield while Dad rolled out his left-arm slowies a few yards away from us. Back at home, when we set up some stumps in the back garden, we had no alternative but to play straight. If we hit anything square the windows of the house would be in range so it was a case of back and across and presenting a straight bat all the time. I don't think we ever broke a window, although I nearly caused David a serious injury during one of our games at my birthday party.

He was bowling and struggling to get me out. I warned him that he was bowling too fast but he cranked up the pace and cracked me on the leg with the ball. As he scarpered around the corner of the house I threw the ball as hard as I could and saw it whistle past his ear. If it had struck him heaven knows what might have happened. Dad reckons that was the first time he realised I wasn't the shy, introverted type he thought I was. Among the fielders that night was my pal Matthew Root, father of the England batsman Joe.

By then I had become a somewhat reluctant pupil at Whitwell School where even walking from the infants' playground into the junior one always felt intimidating for a shy five-year-old who, even then, had little interest in academic subjects. What I also remember about the place was how cold it got in winter. With all that coal on our doorstep you would have thought they could have heated the building. Back at home, I soon became friends with the Burgess brothers across the road. Like us, Simon and Giles – who was the same age as me – were football and cricket mad and we would spend hour after hour all year round playing in either our back garden or across the road.

It sounds like an idyllic upbringing and in so many ways it was but things changed when I was seven years old and my parents split up. I will never forget the first time I realised all was not well between Mum and Dad. I had gone across to the Burgesses' place where we had set up a rope swing from a huge tree next to their house which swung across a big bed of nettles. That was the challenge of course, to swing across the nettles to the other side. When it was my turn I lost my grip on the rope and ended up face down in the nettles. I made my way home covered in nettle stings and in some distress. Mum was getting ready to go out but she settled me down, applied some dock leaves and waited for the babysitter to arrive.

When Dad got home later that night I was still in a bit of a state and he was upset when he realised that Mum had left me with the babysitter. That night I sat there listening to their argument about whether she should have gone out or not. A few days later they sat us down and told us they were splitting up. I thought it was all my fault – my parents were going their separate ways because of what had happened when I fell in the nettles. I carried the guilt around for a long time but, as I got older and things became clearer, I realised that their personalities had been incompatible, even though they had been married for 13 years. They had been happy for a while but I suppose it was a split waiting to happen. Back then, in the mid-1970s, divorce was still relatively uncommon. We didn't know of any parents who were not together although the Burgesses split up soon after Mum and Dad. Michael Burgess remarried a woman called Sandra and his stepdaughter Samantha was to become my wife. Small world, I suppose.

Dad remained at the house in Whitwell but Mum got a job teaching PE and human biology at a technical college in Clowne, near Chesterfield. We moved to a semi-detached house in Brimmington Common and enrolled at Calow Church of England School. For someone who loved the village life we'd had at Whitwell and hated any sort of change it was a traumatic time but kids adapt and we quickly built up a new circle of friends.

I was nine when I was first introduced to Benita White, a woman who had as big an influence on my career as anyone else. These days, coaching youngsters in any sport has a proper structure to it. Young talent is identified at a very early age and nurtured through various age groups. Back then the Chesterfield Cricket Lovers' Society, which is still going strong today, recognised that there was a lack of even basic coaching for youngsters in the area, apart from the sessions that local clubs would run on Saturday mornings during the summer. Dad saw an advertisement in the local paper and to help persuade us that it would be a good idea he bought David and I our first proper bats. Mine was a Gunn and Moore with red and blue stickers.

Dad remembers my full 'debut' for one of the Chesterfield Cricket Lovers' teams at Hathersage in Derbyshire's Hope Valley. There must have been 60 or 70 kids playing there that day and Dad was so worried his presence might disturb my concentration that he hid behind a stone wall. He does recall me touching gloves and patting my batting partner on the head after every run we scored. He thinks that was the first time he thought I had leadership qualities.

Every Thursday we would go to the local polytechnic where Benita and a small army of willing parents would teach us the basics. Benita's analogy that holding a bat was like rocking a teddy bear stayed with me throughout my career.

When you are a kid you remember things like that and it was simple really. If you visualise how you hold your bat you've got your arms in a round with your elbows sticking out and when you're batting the action that you do is rock your bat backwards and forwards as if you are rocking your teddy bear to sleep.

The first time we met her Benita came across as someone with a lot of self-confidence. 'We'll make cricketers of you,' she told David and I. And she did. At the time it certainly did not seem odd that a woman was teaching us cricket skills. Benita had so much charisma and energy and we soon started to look forward to Thursday nights in the polytechnic gym. When I went on my England tour in 1999 Benita was there in Cape Town for the fourth Test and to watch the young player whose love of the game she had helped to nurture. She was extremely proud. I wasn't the last either. A few years later Ian Blackwell, who has had a fine career with Somerset and Durham and played a Test match and 34 one-day internationals, learned the game with Benita.

If it sounds like cricket was taking a hold on me it wasn't the case. By now Dad had left the FA and began working for a chap called Ken Stanley, who was one of the first football agents and whose star client was George Best. It was through that connection that he worked with George and Geoff Boycott on coaching books designed to teach the rudiments of football and cricket to youngsters. After a couple of years he became disillusioned and after helping a pal of his at Plymouth Argyle raise £40,000 in sponsorship so that they could sign the former Liverpool player Brian Hall he took a job at Rotherham United as their commercial manager, combining the role with football reporting duties for the BBC's Saturday sports programme *Sport on Two*.

I think Dad found his true calling in life when he got that job and for the next few years every Saturday for David and I during the winter involved watching the Millers. We must have visited every lower-league boardroom in the country during those years and a few at a higher level when Rotherham got promoted under Emlyn Hughes, an iconic figure during Liverpool's glory years who joined the club as player-manager in 1981.

I developed a soft spot for Rotherham and loved being part of the fabric of the club, albeit in a small way, but I was an Arsenal fan. That might seem strange for a boy being brought up in Derbyshire whose father supported Huddersfield Town so let me explain. Ian Elliott, one of my pals back in Whitwell, was a big Arsenal supporter and when he had a growth spurt I got Ian's hand-me-downs. In 1978 Rotherham played Arsenal in a League Cup tie at Millmoor.

By then I had got quite attached to them and their players, guys like Ronnie Moore, Tony Towner and Gerry Gow, a Scot they had signed from Bristol City whose ferocious tackling shook the ground. That night they pulled off a surprise 3-1 win over the Gunners. Dad was delighted of course; I didn't know whether to laugh or cry.

I hated school, not least because I was occasionally bullied. When I was 11 I moved to Tapton House School on the other side of Chesterfield, whose alumni included Robert Louis Stephenson, inventor of the steam engine. It was a very old-fashioned place. They still used the cane for instance. I was still essentially a shy lad and hated being taken out of my comfort zones. David and I, as brothers do, would fight like cats and dogs and because he was a couple of years older he would invariably get the better of me.

The bullying always started when I began to run into a few boys who had been on the receiving end of some beatings in the playground from David. I remember one instance when I was travelling home on the bus one afternoon, sitting there minding my own business, when another lad got up to get off and whacked me in the eye as he passed. I got home and when David and Mum confronted me I blamed it on a cricket injury. I think I told them I'd been hit in the nets. David was protective of me although he wasn't necessarily sympathetic. But when I eventually confessed what had really happened he gave my assailant a real thumping.

Bearing in mind the reputation I earned, unfairly or not, as a bit of a hot-head myself when I began playing professional cricket, it might come as a surprise to discover it wasn't me doing the bullying as a kid. It went on a lot then of course as people who grew up in the 1960s and 70s will remember.

Teachers didn't necessarily turn a blind eye but we are talking about a time when exam results and the performances of individual schools were starting to attract scrutiny so scrapes in the playground tended to be ignored until they got totally out of hand, which rarely happened.

But it was an unhappy time for me. Our idyllic life in Whitwell before Mum and Dad split up seemed a long time ago. These beatings continued occasionally for a while but I began to toughen myself up and filled out a bit physically although it wasn't until I went to Chesterfield Boys' School when I was 13 that I began to settle down.

I did not play much cricket there – in fact I can only remember one game because they concentrated on athletics in the summer – and academically I was still struggling but they played football and I was soon progressing into the first team.

I also joined a youth team called Somersall Rangers in Chesterfield. The manager was a guy called Roger Woodhead and under his guidance I began to turn myself into a decent schoolboy centre-half. I didn't have the physical attributes perhaps but I could read the game well, I enjoyed organising those around me and I relished a tackle. Pride of place in our house in Whitwell was a picture of the 1966 World Cup winners and I modelled myself on Bobby Moore. One or two clubs began to come and watch me play for Somersall and Chesterfield seemed the most keen. The plan was for me to leave school at 16 after I had taken my O Levels and be taken on to their YTS scheme.

I came under the wing of Frank Barlow, who had played for Chesterfield for eight years and was a terrific coach. He took over as manager for three years in 1980, somewhat reluctantly, before going back to coaching.

In a trial game for their youth side there was a mix-up in communication between Frank and the team manager and I ended up playing as a striker in two games against Scunthorpe United and Derby County, and scored in both matches. There were four YTS places up for grabs and Frank thought I had a chance.

Scunthorpe must have liked what they saw in that game because they offered me a trial as well and so did Barnsley while Sheffield Wednesday, who were a First Division club in those days, wanted to take me for a month to see how I measured up.

The trouble was I still loved my cricket and was starting to do very well. When I was 14, I took 3-24 and Dad 7-21 in a match for Staveley and I remember scoring 145 not out against Clipstone when I batted for much of my innings with Michael May, who was on the Derbyshire staff at the same time as me a few years later. I was captain of Derbyshire Schools Under-14s, having played for them since the age of 11, but back then I always regarded cricket as something I might take a bit more seriously if I didn't become a professional footballer.

It all seemed to be mapped out for me. I was going to leave school as soon as I could and start out on a life in professional football. Then a chap called Mike Stones, who ran the Derbyshire Cricket Association, came into my life and things were never the same again.

# 3

# Repton

THE year I was fortunate enough to spend at Repton College was the making of Chris Adams, as a professional sportsman and as a person. Even now, nearly 30 years later, I consider myself very fortunate to have been able to spend some time there. It was the happiest period of my pre-adult life.

I am in the fortunate position financially to have been able to have all three of my girls, Georgia, Sophie and Mollie, privately educated. When we got married and started thinking about having a family we made a conscious decision that, if it were financially possible, we would try and provide a private education for our children. If they didn't like it then we'd have no problem if they switched into the mainstream state system. We just wanted to give them the opportunity to have the sort of chance I had been fortunate to receive.

Initially, I wasn't sure that I wanted to go to Repton. It was a conversation with my grandmother, Joan Jones, which persuaded me, 'If you don't try it you will always think what if I had. And if it doesn't work out you can always go and join the YTS scheme at Chesterfield Football Club.'

I left Chesterfield Grammar School in the summer of 1986, having just celebrated my 16th birthday, with two O Level passes in English Language and Economics. I failed the other five subjects, including French. Not only was there little sport that interested me at CGS, particularly in the summer when the focus was mainly on athletics, academically it wasn't an environment where I felt I was making any sort of progress. I wasn't thick. I loved projects and course work in a range of subjects from natural history to science and I was very creative. I liked art and I enjoyed drawing. But when it came to studying and the actual exams themselves I struggled and back then whether you passed or failed depended pretty much entirely on how you did in the exam. You weren't judged to any extent on how you had done during the year. I enjoyed trying to work things out but then I would spend so much time theorising on what to actually write on the exam paper that I would invariably run out of time.

During my final year at Chesterfield Grammar the teachers were regularly on strike. For weeks I remember the school shutting down at lunchtime and gangs of us roaming the streets of Chesterfield during the afternoon before it was time to go home. Even in class the teachers were working to rule so they spent most of the time marking course work and not actually imparting their knowledge. More often than not we would turn up for a class and the teacher had written on the blackboard the instructions on what to study and a few references from textbooks to help us. We would be left to get on with it. Basically, for most of my last year there we were effectively self-taught and I certainly didn't have the discipline to study hard.

I couldn't wait to leave. The subject that gave me particular nightmares was French. I loathed it but I was determined to try and pass the exam because I could not stand the teacher, Mr Staniforth, at all. Towards the end of my final term there he caught me daydreaming in class one day. I must have been staring out of the window watching some athletics on the sports field. I wasn't that keen on running and jumping but at that moment I'd rather have been doing that than learning French verbs. He asked me a question that, of course, I hadn't even heard so he made me come out and stand in front of the rest of the class. I was being made an example of. I was still quite shy back then and I hated those sorts of situations where I was being put on the spot. He asked me what I was going to do with my life. I told him I was going to be a professional sportsman. He just laughed and the others joined in. 'I'll make one prediction now,' he said. 'You'll never pass your French O Level and you will never, ever, be a professional sportsman.' I remember skulking back to my seat feeling about two feet tall.

My parents were both teachers and if they felt let down with my academic achievements they never let on. I remember Mum driving me to school to pick up my O Level results. She was trying to be positive but I knew deep down how poorly I'd done. To actually pass two subjects came as a pleasant surprise. To add to my humiliation, as the deputy headmaster passed me the envelope containing the grim news he couldn't stop himself. 'So I guess you won't be coming back next year...' Mum was sympathetic.

'You did your best,' she said, but she must have been disappointed. I was as well, but I knew it had been coming.

We talked about what I would do for the next few months. I was going to play cricket for my village team, Whitwell, another club side, Staveley, and the Derbyshire Under-17s and Under-19s. Then, in August, I would join Chesterfield FC on their YTS scheme where my weekly wage was going to be £25. Frank Barlow's son Matt was also offered a place, but he declined so he could concentrate on a career in sports writing. A wise move as I'm reminded every time I read Matt's football reports in the *Daily Mail*!

For now I could concentrate on my cricket. By then I was on the radar a bit, certainly in Derbyshire. That summer I played for Derbyshire Colts along with David, my elder brother, as an all-rounder normally batting in the lower-middle order where I would give it a whack and bowl respectable off spin.

We would play various other counties and took part in a festival in Oxford. That summer I had a bit of a growth spurt and John Brown, who had been coaching the youth groups in Derbyshire for years, offered me some advice. As I started to shoot up I was struggling with my bowling. I couldn't get my trajectory right and would bowl lots of full tosses. Before then I could give the ball a real rip. It wasn't a case of the yips although it did feel like it. John told me to knuckle down and concentrate on my batting. He felt there was a bit more to my game than simply going in down the order and trying to hit the ball as hard as I could.

Mike Stones also saw some latent talent. He coached Derbyshire Under-17s at the time and I must have had a couple of good games. Mike was also in charge of cricket at Repton and contacted my parents. There were some assisted scholarships available at Repton and he enquired whether I would be interested in going to the sixth-form college. My immediate reaction was extremely hostile. I'd had enough of education. All I wanted to do was play cricket and then join the YTS at Chesterfield, but I eventually agreed to go to a testing day knowing full well that I had little chance of passing any sort of entrance examination. I turned up and there were 20 other kids there, all girls, the majority of whom had passed 10 or 11 O Levels with A or B grades. I sat the exam and quite enjoyed it but there was no chance of me getting accepted based on my academic record.

I'll always be grateful that Mike persevered. Another option was a scholarship entirely funded by the J. Arthur Rank Foundation; a charity set up in 1953 by Joseph Arthur Rank, a man synonymous with the film industry. As well as promoting his Christian beliefs, the foundation helped gifted potential leaders. I'm not sure if he had me in mind as a future captain of industry but the bottom line was that my school fees for the year would be funded by the foundation. My parents would have to find money for uniform but it was a spectacular offer.

I would have to retake my O Levels and, all being well, I would then start an A Level syllabus. I wasn't keen on going there to repeat a year. I remember the stigma attached to those in the remedial class at Chesterfield Grammar School and I thought that this could be a lot worse because I can't imagine there were too many other pupils at Repton who were less academically gifted than me.

Mum and Dad were keen but it was only after that chat with my grandmother that I decided to give it a go. Frank Barlow told my Dad that if it didn't work out the YTS scheme at Chesterfield would still be an option and they played football at Repton as well. I'd played representative cricket there a couple of times for Derbyshire and knew it was a stunning place. The school had been established in the 16th century and a lot of the magnificent buildings were strung along the village itself deep in the Derbyshire countryside. C.B. Fry, the former Sussex and England captain, was among its former pupils.

I remember my first day vividly. Fortunately, there was another cricketer in the sixth form whom I knew from Derbyshire Colts, Robin Williamson, and during the hour-long drive from Chesterfield I took comfort in the knowledge that I would know at least one of the hundreds of other pupils there. One of the first things that struck me was how mature I was compared to the rest of the sixth formers. I'd been on nights out in Chesterfield a few times with David, drinking underage of course. I knew when trouble was brewing and how to avoid it. Towards the end, life at Chesterfield Grammar became a daily routine of trying to stop yourself getting beaten up and avoiding scraps and scuffles.

This, of course, was a totally alien environment and for the first couple of weeks I struggled to adapt. I was put in Priory House and allocated into a ten-bed dormitory. We weren't allowed to go home for the first four weeks and I was homesick. There were five of us in a study room of varying ages. I was second in age to a lad called Charlie Henry, who lived in the village and was a really big help to me in those first few weeks. When we were on a break or preparing in the evening for lessons the following day we'd be in the study. Eventually I settled into the routine. Lessons in the morning, sport in the afternoon and study in the evening.

I soon began to reap the benefits academically. For the first time I felt the teachers actually cared. They made me understand what a good education could do for me. Class sizes were smaller so you got more attention and specialist tuition and I started to make progress, although after six weeks I was told it would take longer than they had envisaged for me to pass my O Levels. The chances of me starting an A Level syllabus towards the end of my first year quickly receded.

The only thing I disliked about Repton was the ingrained hierarchy whereby the older boys would subject the younger pupils to a lot of misery through the system of fagging. It was basically a form of slavery and I hated seeing the young lads literally trembling with fear when this daily list of menial tasks would be posted up on the dormitory wall as punishment for often-ridiculous indiscretions. I know it has gone on for centuries at public schools like Repton and I'm sure if I'd been there from a young age I would have just had to accept it and fallen into line. But I was a bit more streetwise than a lot of my peers and when I started to stick up for some of the young lads they didn't know how to take it.

Charlie Henry would sit down at the start of the week with the younger boys in our study and give them their orders. I don't think Charlie felt that comfortable with fagging either but that was how things were done. The youngest member of our study was a gifted young Chinese boy called Kenneth Wong. He was unbelievably talented in a whole range of subjects but possessed limited social skills and struggled to interact with the other pupils in that environment. I know things are totally different at schools like Repton now judging by the feedback I get from my kids but back in 1986 it could easily have still been 1886 and just like *Tom Brown's Schooldays*.

Anyway, Charlie's instruction to Kenneth was that after morning lessons he had five minutes to get from his own class, get in the queue for the toaster and have a couple of rounds of nicely buttered toast on the table ready for when Charlie and I got back to the study. One of my strongest memories of Repton is young Kenneth sprinting past me one morning to make sure he was first in the queue for the toaster. In fairness to Charlie, if the toast wasn't sitting there when he got back he wasn't too bothered but some of his peers treated the young lads like slaves. I didn't see any physical violence so I guess things had moved on a bit from the Victorian era but in its own way it was a fairly brutal regime. Boys were routinely picked on and I ended up becoming something of a champion of the oppressed boys of Repton.

Most of the boys in the sixth form and upper sixth didn't know what to make of me, especially when I started telling a few of them that they couldn't go on treating the younger lads like they did. But it was a tradition as old as Repton itself and they had all been subjected to it when they had arrived. For some it was payback time and who cared about the psychological damage it was undoubtedly causing. One night things came to a head. A couple of the young lads in our dorm started mucking around in the corridor after lights-out, a punishable offence. I quickly sorted things out in front of one of the house prefects who had arrived to see what was happening but next day their names were on the fagging list. So was mine. I took umbrage, grabbed the prefect by the scruff of his neck and put him straight on the matter. After that none of the boys in our dormitory found themselves running errands, tidying up or cleaning shoes.

I went to the football trials and was a bit disappointed to find when the selections for the opening game went up that I was in the second XI. Our first match was against a men's team who had travelled into school and we beat them 3-0 with C.J. Adams scoring a hat-trick. The third goal was still being talked about months later. I got possession in our box – I was playing centre-half – and ran the length of the pitch before hitting a shot from outside their box into the top-right corner. That day the first team centre-half got injured and the following week I was in and stayed there and was awarded my colours within the first few weeks. The English Public Schools' team selectors came to watch me play and I was keen to impress. But on the day of the match I felt really tired and struggling for energy and although we didn't lose the game I played pretty averagely. A couple of days later I came out in a rash. I'd contracted chicken pox and with it went my chance to be selected for the team.

I really enjoyed the football though. Our captain was a lad called Des Anderson and on one infamous trip to Charterhouse, Winston Churchill's alma mater down in Surrey, Des decided that on the evening before the game we'd wander down to the local pub for a spot of team bonding. That environment wasn't a new experience for me but for the other lads this was something else. We marched in, bold as brass, and all ordered a pint. The landlord didn't bat an eyelid. I guess a lot of his passing trade came from groups of spotty teenage schoolboys experiencing pub culture for the first time. We didn't go overboard. We had about four pints then made our way back. The next day we played the game, won 2-0 and headed back on the bus to Repton. No harm done, or so we thought. When we got back the deputy head was forming a one-man welcoming party on the steps of the school entrance and we were told to report to the headmaster David Jewell straight away.

Unbeknown to the rest of us, a very talented young winger called Anthony Jordan had not handled his four pints as well as the rest of us and had been sick in his bed. But instead of cleaning up, he'd rolled his bedclothes in a pile and left it for the cleaner to discover. By the time we'd got back to Repton the six drinkers had already been identified. Apparently, the landlord at the pub had been on the phone to Charterhouse while we'd been sitting in his snug discussing tactics for the following day's game. Mr Jewell addressed us all together and gave us five minutes to get our stories straight before he would start to interview us individually. I thought we were all going to be expelled and my first thought was what my parents would think of me. I was petrified. As we sat there, fearing the worst, Des said he was going to take the rap. We would all tell the head that it had been his idea and we'd been coerced against our will. I knew what the head's reaction would be, 'Is that the best you could come up with?' So before he even began talking to me I spoke out that we all knew what we were doing and that if we'd known that Anthony Jordan had made a mess we would have cleaned it up. He was quite sympathetic and gave us a suspended punishment, the nature of which escapes me three decades later. Des lost his prefect and head of house status so in a way he did take the rap, but he was allowed to captain the first XI cricket team next summer and ended up with 56 wickets.

The second term at Repton was pretty boring from a sporting perspective. Hockey was played and it wasn't a game I enjoyed so I spent most of the time learning a new sport on the Fives court. I knuckled down and concentrated on my academic work, especially French. After the Charterhouse incident I stayed out of trouble, was 'upgraded' to a study of four and felt I had fully come to terms with the environment. I also won a Texaco Cricket Scholarship after being nominated by Derbyshire, an award which went to 78 of the country's most promising young cricketers. We spent a week at Lilleshall in Shropshire learning the game from a quartet of hoary old pros comprising Alan Oakman of Sussex, Nottinghamshire's Mike Bore, Maurice Hallam of Leicestershire, and Lancashire's John Stanworth. Back at Repton we had the odd indoor net during the winter term before cricket began in earnest in April 1987.

On the first day Mike Stones brought us together and promised any player who scored a hundred that he would buy them a new bat. Another Mike – Mike Kettle, who was also Repton's groundsman – assisted him. Mike produced some wonderful pitches and that, allied to the fact that it was a pretty dry summer, were perfect for me. Sure enough, in our first game when I opened I scored a hundred. Mike kept his word and on the Monday afternoon we drove to the sports shop in Derby where I picked out a top of the range Gunn and Moore before eagerly showing it off to the rest of the team. The following Saturday I scored another hundred against Oundle School but sadly Mike's offer was only for one bat. I would have cost him a fortune otherwise because in my first four games I scored three centuries and 80-odd not out in the other match. I reached 1,000 runs before the end of June – one of only six schoolboys to achieve that during the summer of 1987.

We won six of our 12 games and I finished with 1,242 runs with a highest score of 158 and an average of 73.05 from 19 innings. I broke the school record that had been held by Richard Hutton, grandson of the Yorkshire and England legend Len, since the 1950s and which, I'm proud to say, still stands to this day. I also got selected for a couple of representative matches, firstly for the North Schools against the Midlands at Bowdon near Manchester. The captain was Mike Atherton, who batted at number nine – one place below me. David was also in the side along with Peter Martin, who played for England and Lancashire, and David Leatherdale, who had a terrific career at Worcestershire. Then in July, once we'd finished school, I took part in the Oxford Festival, playing for The Rest against a Southern Schools team that included a future England team-mate, Alistair Brown. I opened and top-scored with 65 and put on a few with Nick Knight, who went on to play for Essex, Warwickshire and England.

At the end of term we went on tour to Barbados which was memorable for two things. In one of the games – a semi-final I think – we ran into a left-hander called Brian Lara, who scored a spectacular century against us, and I got my exam results. I'd passed them all and the person who gave me this good news in his hotel room in Bridgetown was Mike Stones, quite appropriate really because without his help and guidance I wouldn't have gone to Repton and I certainly wouldn't have left with a handful of O Levels. I even passed French. If I'd been at school that day rather than Barbados I would have run all the way back to Chesterfield Grammar School and waved the sheet of paper in front of

Mr Staniforth. Not only had he been proved wrong about my ability to master the French language, young Adams was about to become a professional sportsman as well.

Back at Repton, my housemaster Barry Downing collared me one afternoon. He was an intimidating character when you first met him, as most schoolteachers tended to be, but once you got to know him he was a lovely bloke. I'm still in touch with him 30 years later. As we walked to his office I was trying to think of the indiscretion that had necessitated this meeting. Outside his door he turned to me and said, 'There are two guys here from Derbyshire Cricket Club, the chairman Guy Willett and the captain Kim Barnett, who want to talk to you.'

I knew about Kim of course. He had been appointed Derbyshire captain in 1983 and although I always preferred playing I used to watch him and the county when they played at Queen's Park, Chesterfield. I can remember several occasions at Chesterfield Grammar when David would appear at the classroom door and I would be dragged out of class on the pretence of visiting an elderly relative who was at death's door and unlikely to make it through the rest of the day. Once out of the gates we'd head up to Queen's Park instead to watch Derbyshire play. I can vividly remember a game there early in my last year at Chesterfield Grammar when Ian Botham, then playing for Somerset, and Viv Richards had their own spectacular hitting contest. Botham scored 61 off 50 balls – which was some going back then – before going off injured. For someone who liked to hit the ball as hard as he could it was wonderful to watch.

My exploits for Repton had been noted. In those days schoolboy cricket was reported quite extensively in the broadsheet papers and there were always scouts and coaches from county clubs watching our matches. I remember chatting to a Lancashire scout when we played Manchester Grammar – Atherton's school – and someone from Worcestershire when we visited King's School. Hard to believe now, but back then if you wanted to offer a trial to someone from another county you had to seek permission first. Derbyshire knew they had to act quickly to stop me slipping through the net and within a few minutes of the meeting Guy Willett had produced a three-year contract they wanted me to sign. I could sign it there and then and join Derbyshire in the spring of 1988 or I could defer it for a year so I could complete sixth form at Repton.

Derbyshire hadn't even spoken to my parents. They had hoped that the presence of the club captain at our meeting would swing it and they were correct. I didn't sign there and then but I knew it would only be a matter of time. A part of me still wanted to stay at Repton and do A Levels but Mike nudged me in the right direction. He told me I would struggle to have a better year than the one that was just about to end and that I would need two more years to complete my A Levels. After years of underachievement at Chesterfield Grammar I had certainly caught up academically but I was still behind my peers. The course work involved lots more essays and less problem-solving. My parents were thrilled, of course, that I had achieved my ambition although Dad later admitted that he had been furious that Derbyshire had made contact with me without talking to them first. All that remained was to contact Mr Staniforth. I wrote him a letter with my news, not in a 'told you so' tone but actually thanking him for teaching me a valuable lesson about not wasting the opportunities you had and working hard to prove people wrong.

He responded with a lovely letter and when I bumped into him at Queen's Park when I was playing for Derbyshire a couple of years later he told me he could not have been more proud.

The rest of that summer was spent playing as much as I could, whether it be for Staveley or Derbyshire's age group teams. Some weeks I played five or six times. I was full of confidence and I could feel I was improving steadily. By now I'd more or less stopped bowling the off spin. I would bowl some medium pace if necessary but my priority was my batting. John Brown and Mike Stones continued to coach me and I was more and more involved with Derbyshire, acting as 12th man for the second XI. David played three games for the seconds that year and I was just glad to be part of the scene, working on my game and trying to glean as much information as I could.

Towards the end of the season I was sitting at home one afternoon thinking about how I might earn a few quid during the winter when Phil Russell, the Derbyshire coach, rang.

He said that the second XI was playing Hampshire at Southampton in the final of the Bain Dawes one-day competition. My heart missed a beat. I thought he was going to call me up. Instead, he explained that the first team were committed to playing in something called the Asda Challenge at Scarborough, a one-day competition which didn't carry first-class status involving Yorkshire, Hampshire and Lancashire. Because they wanted to field a strong side in the seconds' match Frank Griffith and I were required at Scarborough for 12th man duties. Phil picked us up in his green Mercedes, stuck his jazz cassette on and we trundled up to Scarborough, Frank and I sitting in the back seat scared to say a word.

We got to the hotel and the first shock was that because there weren't enough rooms I would have to share with the coach. The other three teams were staying there as well and when we made our way down to the bar a party was already in full swing. The place was buzzing but any thoughts I had of joining in were tempered by the realisation that I was sharing a room with the coach and how it wouldn't look very professional if on my first trip I was up until the small hours carousing around Scarborough.

It was then that I encountered John Morris for the first time. I'd seen 'Animal' play of course and we'd probably said hello at the County Ground a couple of times but here he was in front of me, looking to a wet-behind-the-ears 17-year-old from Chesterfield like something off a Hollywood movie set. Trendy suit, slicked-back hair and smelling like a million dollars. He shook my hand and then turned to Phil, who'd just ordered a half of lager. 'Phil, Chris and Frankie are coming out with me. Is that okay?' It wasn't a request, more an instruction. Phil smiled and we went and joined the throng. Phil had explained on the journey up that the scorer would give us our expenses the following day but that was no good to me now. I only had a couple of quid in my pocket. 'No worries,' said Animal. 'We'll look after you.' We ended up in a nightclub until very late with 40-plus other professional cricketers letting their hair down at the end of the season.

I crept back to the hotel room at about 2am, trying desperately not to wake Phil. After getting undressed and slipping under the covers I lay stock still for a few seconds before finally relaxing. I thought I'd got away with it when the bedside lamp came on and Phil turned round, 'Night Grizz!'

Next morning I felt fine and Phil, Frank and I set off for the Scarborough ground. It must have been early because the gates weren't even open, although we were somewhat surprised to see a Derbyshire CCC sponsored car in the car park. When the gates opened we went over to investigate. As we got closer we could see that the windows were down and loud music was playing on the stereo. We looked inside and discovered one of our players, slumped over the driver's seat, shivering and shaking, a half-drunk bottle of wine in his lap. He had been out all night and had decided to cut out the hotel bit and head straight to the ground.

He wasn't the only one in a dishevelled state. While I pleaded unsuccessfully with the coach for a net he stood by the door conducting a roll call as the other lads arrived and got stuck into the tea and toast Frankie and I had prepared. Just before Kim Barnett went out for the toss, and with only nine other players in the dressing room, Phil told us we had to play. It was a strong Lancashire side too, although judging by some of the bowling their lads had enjoyed the previous night as much as ours. Kim got a big hundred as the others slept off their hangovers in the dressing room and I came in at number eight and made ten runs in my first professional innings before I gave John Abrahams the charge in search of quick runs and was stumped by Warren Hegg. It started raining just after Lancashire began their reply and in those pre-Duckworth/Lewis days Kim and his opposite number David Hughes stood under an umbrella and tossed a coin to see who got to the final. We lost and headed home that night. Twenty-four hours in Scarborough – my introduction to professional cricket.

With the season over I needed to pay my way for the winter. A friend of the family fixed me up with some labouring at Staveley Works, a chemical plant in the village. I turned up on a chilly Monday morning in October and was pointed in the direction of the foreman. We went outside and there were 40-odd metal pipes that needed coating in bitumen. I lasted one day. As we drove home that night I told Mum I would find something else. By then I'd become friendly with Samantha although we weren't going out as such. But her stepfather Michael had a small logging business in a local forest and I worked there for a few weeks, using the cash to pay for driving lessons, pass my test and take ownership of my first car, a blue Vauxhall Chevette.

David had gone off to New Zealand to coach at a club in Auckland called Takapuna. We spoke on the phone and he told me that if I could get myself over there I could sleep in the spare room in the accommodation he was using that was owned by a lovely couple called Bill and Sue Kapea. Dad paid for the ticket and gave me £150 spending money so I headed off to New Zealand in the first week of 1988. Because Takapuna were only allowed to play one overseas player I had to play in the second XI but they were a social bunch and I enjoyed myself straight away. On the first full day I was there we spent the evening with the Takapuna players in the hotel opposite the ground that also sponsored the team. I'm not sure how much I had to drink but I was sober enough to drive us home in David's sponsored car. A few yards down the road a police car pulled up behind me, lights flashing. Shit. All sorts of thoughts crossed my mind as the policeman got me out of the car and went to find his breathalyser equipment. I then became aware of a queue of vehicles behind the police car, the occupants sounding their horns wildly. It turned out that the policeman was one of the Takapuna players and it was all an elaborate wind-up.

I had nine weeks out there and it was a fantastic experience. I ended up becoming the hotel handyman, a job that involved nothing more strenuous than cleaning up bottles and glasses, changing light bulbs, cleaning the pool and hoovering up leaves. For that I was paid $250 a week in cash, way more than David and the other English pros out there were earning. Bill and Sue and their two kids were a fantastic family and looked after us as if we were their own. We explored the countryside, although David made a tactical error the night he started chatting up some local girls in a remote bar in the Bay of Islands. A few moments later the place was full of the local chapter of the Maori Mongols, a sort of Kiwi version of the Hell's Angels looking for a scrap scenting English blood. We beat a very hasty retreat in David's sponsored car as they gave chase on their motorbikes.

When I got back to England I couldn't wait to get started at Derbyshire. There was a letter from Phil waiting for me informing me that pre-season training would start on 4 April, two weeks before the first game which was against Cambridge University at Fenner's. I was one of 24 professionals on the staff expected to report for duty. Except I didn't.

# 4

# Proving Myself

MONDAY 4 April 1988 was also Easter Monday. I thought it strange that we'd be reporting back on a Bank Holiday so I rang John Brown. 'Oh that will be a mistake,' was his response. 'You'll be in on the Tuesday.' So while the rest of the lads spent Monday sweating cobs on one of Phil Russell's infamous running sessions I was with Sam and her mates enjoying a blissful afternoon at a country fair at Chatsworth House! The following day I drove to the ground where the first mistake I made was trying to get changed in the first team dressing room. Needless to say, the public school-educated big shot, with his Don Johnson jacket and boat shoes looking for all the world like an extra from *Miami Vice*, was ever so politely pointed in the direction of the away changing facilities where the young pros were housed.

A few moments later I realised I had started my career as a professional sportsman a day late and boy did Phil make me pay. For the first two weeks I didn't get near the nets and certainly didn't pick up my bat. While the rest of the senior pros headed to the nets youngsters like myself, Frank Griffith and Tim O'Gorman acted as glorified dressing room attendants.

We joined in during the afternoon for physical training. There were no sports scientists back then, no strength and conditioning coaches. Most players reported back overweight and spent the first couple of weeks sweating off excess pounds by running around swathed in as many layers as they could find. Phil had brought in what he called a 'physicality expert' from Manchester University and it was his job to get the lads into shape and satisfy the coach's sadistic pleasure for watching the players pushed to the point of physical exhaustion. In my 22 years as a player in the game I have never run as much as I did during those first three weeks at Derbyshire. We ran long distances, longer distances and even longer distances mixed in with torturous shuttle runs. We ran and ran until we physically collapsed and for the players who were a bit woolly, and I include myself in that, it was horrible.

There was the dreaded racecourse run that we did most days. Two laps of the old Derby racecourse, which was about three miles and completed as a squad. We had some good athletes so even for youngsters like me it was hard to keep up with the pacesetters and avoid getting yourself isolated at the back. On my first day Paul Newman put his foot down a rabbit hole about 15 seconds in and had to be helped back to the ground by two volunteers who couldn't believe their luck that they would be able to miss the run. Bernie Maher was the speedster. He'd do it in about 18 minutes while ten minutes later Ole Mortensen would bring up the rear. I was somewhere in between. Phil would then get us doing shuttles, often on the grass bank at the ground, and then sprint sessions on a grid he had got the groundsman to mark out on the edge of the outfield. To be fair to Phil if he felt you were putting the effort in he'd go steady. But the moment he thought anyone was coasting you would do more. Kim Barnett was a proper old-school trainer who would run, run more and then even more. He was a tough individual who set the example to the rest of the lads.

Not only had I never felt more tired, but I was burning up so much energy, both physical and mental as I tried to create the right impression. We refuelled, if that's the right word, at lunchtime on cheese and ham rolls – two maximum – and bowls of soup. There was water, which you normally glugged down from the tap in the changing rooms between runs, and I seem to remember Gatorade had just come into the market from America so we would gulp down vast quantities of this orange, strange-tasting liquid without having the slightest idea if it was doing us any good. By the time I got back home to Chesterfield each evening I would literally fall asleep eating my tea.

That remained the pre-season routine for the next few years, until the arrival of Les Stillman as coach and Dean Jones as captain. There was no winter fitness programme, although Phil did put on a session every Thursday during the off-season for the players who were still at home in the indoor school at Derby, a narrow building with a corrugated roof which had room for two lanes and a 50x20 grid at the back where Phil would test us with various sprint and shuttle drills.

Paul Newman chose a good day to turn his ankle over. If you picked up an injury it was best to do so on a Tuesday or Thursday, which were the only days when we had a physio on site. That remained the situation throughout the season as well. If you were injured on any other day you'd be bundled into a club car and driven to the physio's practice in Derby. If you were crocked during a game the St John's Ambulance first-aiders who were on the ground carried you off. Eventually Derbyshire employed a full-time physio called Ann Brentnall who did a fantastic job, but when I started her appointment was still some way off.

A few days after we started the secretary, Ian Edwards, gave me two Derbyshire sweaters, one short-sleeved, a cap, blazer and a tracksuit. You were asked to provide your own whites. A family friend was one of the owners of Gunn and Moore, who were based up the road in Nottingham, and they helped me out with shirts and trousers, a bat, two pairs of batting gloves, two pairs of pads and a thigh guard. That was expected to last you the whole season. I remember being perched on the back row of my first Derbyshire pre-season photo a week or so after we'd reported back. We all looked pretty smart in our Derbyshire blazer and sweater but if you look carefully at the shirt lapels there are various different manufacturers' names.

Compared to modern cricket it was all ridiculously unprofessional of course, but then again we weren't paid what a professional sportsman might expect either. My first year's salary was £3,000 and for the following two years of my contract it went up £250 every April. Kim Barnett would have been earning around £9,000 at the time so there wasn't a massive gulf between the captain and the youngest pro and remember we were only employed for six months, from 1 April. On 1 October you were on your own and had to find work, whether that be at home or, if you were fortunate, playing and coaching overseas.

Some of the senior pros were a bit wary of me when I arrived, a public school-educated – even if it had only been for a year – batsman who had established quite a reputation the previous season. Back then it was quite rare for a 17-year-old to be taken on as a professional and there had been quite a cull of players at the end of the previous season, so much so that I was the only Derbyshire-born player on the staff. Apart from that game in the Asda Challenge I hadn't been around the club at all. I hadn't even played any second-team cricket. I was barely on nodding terms with the likes of John Wright, who was in his final season at Derbyshire, Michael Holding, Peter Bowler, who had joined us from Leicestershire, John Morris and even Devon Malcolm, who hadn't been on the staff for long but of whom much was clearly expected.

The first time I saw Kim in the nets at Derby I was in awe. He was facing Devon and had the quickest hands I had ever seen. He would hit the ball so hard, generating considerable power from his strong upper body. As well as being a hard trainer Kim was also mentally tough and a man of few words. Towards the end of his career he developed an odd stance where he would take guard outside leg stump and move across and into the ball, a bit like Mike Yardy when he remodelled his all those years later when I was captain of Sussex and it transformed his career. These days that technique would be coached out of Kim at an early age but it served him well. He became Derbyshire's leading run-scorer and, of course, played Test cricket as well. I was to have some difficult days with him during the rest of my Derbyshire career but I will always be grateful to him. He gave me my opportunity when I started and he didn't mess with my game at all.

For the first couple of weeks my cricket activity was restricted to bowling a few overs of off spin as the senior pros prepared for their first game at Fenner's against Cambridge University. There was no gym where you could work out your frustrations and it was only once the squad had gone off to Cambridge that Phil allowed the youngsters to practise in the nets. By the time we headed off to Worcester for the opening second XI fixture at the beginning of May we hadn't even had an outdoor net.

I made 26 in my first competitive innings for Derbyshire before being bowled by Stuart Lampitt, who I'd socialised with the previous winter in New Zealand. I batted at number three and sometimes went in down the order that season but in the second XI you never really knew from one game to the next what your role would be. Just as it is now, the team was comprised of junior pros, more experienced guys seeking to find some form and the odd trialist. Even though we carried a squad of 24 there was always the need for a player or two to make up the numbers because of injuries.

Our coach was a wily old pro called Alan Hill, or 'Bud' to those who knew him. He could be a bit full-on at times and a few of the lads weren't keen on his style but he was brilliant for me at that stage of my development. If I wanted to work on something in the nets Bud would quite happily throw balls at me, whether it was to improve my batting or make me a better close catcher. As the junior pro I started my professional career fielding at short leg, or boot hill as the older players called it. A couple of years later, when I took two catches there fielding as a substitute in a Test match, it was to provide me with my first exposure as a cricketer outside Derbyshire. But starting out I quickly realised I didn't like being so close to the action and worked hard to turn myself into a decent slip fielder by catching hundreds of balls thrown at me via a catching cradle by Bud Hill.

Bud tried to make the environment as happy as he could, bearing in mind that each player would have his own agenda. There were some lovely characters including Mark Beardsall, a Yorkshireman who had been a coal miner and who bowled medium pace but with a fast bowler's mentality. He would charge in all day and I formed a friendship with Mark, who taught me some of the dos and don'ts of being a county pro. I was still fairly wet behind the ears and if Bud or one of the senior players had asked me to go and buy some waterproof matches or borrow a left-handed screwdriver from the groundsman I would happily have agreed. Mark took me under his wing a bit.

I had a decent first season in the second team. I finished with 724 runs, including my maiden century against Northamptonshire at Chesterfield early in June. I'd played at Queen's Park many times during my teens and back then the pitch was great for batting on with good bounce and carry and very little sideways movement. I could pull off the front foot with impunity whereas at Derby, where the wickets then tended to be slower and lower, that was a shot fraught with risk.

As well as the runs I scored, I think Bud and Phil Russell, who would watch as much second team cricket as his first XI commitments allowed, could see that I could handle fast bowling. Back then, even in their second XI, most counties had a decent new-ball bowler. In my first couple of years I faced Chris Cairns at Nottinghamshire, Ricardo Ellcock on my debut at New Road, Patrick Patterson, the fearsomely fast West Indian who would occasionally be sent to the second team to find form and fitness, and Wasim Akram, who was just starting to emerge at Old Trafford. I tried to soak up as much information as I could and to keep on the right side of the umpires.

I remember during one game walking when the ball deflected off my pad and touched my glove on its way to the wicketkeeper after Allan Jones had given me not out. As I wandered past him he said, 'I'll see you later.' I thought I was going to get a bollocking but Allan praised me for my honesty. 'I'll remember that,' he said. And he did. For the next 20 years when Allan was umpiring I got the benefit of the doubt on so many close lbws that I lost count!

My big problem wasn't pace bowlers but left-armers. We had none on the staff at Derbyshire and I'd come across very few during my formative years. I tended to commit myself to playing on the front foot quite early and was prone to falling over to anything which swung late, making me a prime lbw candidate. I wasn't the only one. Kim Barnett, magnificent player that he was, hated left-armers. We didn't have bowling machines in those days either so you were left to learn how to adapt in game situations.

A left-armer who I'd often struggled against was my brother David. Back then he was trying to forge a career having not really made any headway at Derbyshire. I don't think he ever connected with Kim, who either didn't think he was good enough or didn't feel that having brothers on the staff was a good thing. Lots of players went on trial back then and even though counties didn't pay much it was quite rare to be taken on based on performances in second team matches. David had also been at Somerset for a few games when he pitched up at Bristol to play for Gloucestershire against Derbyshire.

I opened, batted through the morning session and then half an hour into the afternoon David came on and bowled me for 88! He was a left-arm spinner who bowled quite quickly, a bit like Derek Underwood. That day he picked up five wickets and I guess if I was going to get out to anyone I'd have preferred it to be my older brother. David was a good cricketer and these days, when there is so much emphasis on one-day cricket, he would be a considerable asset. Not only was he a good, economical bowler he could also score runs quickly down the order.

We played against each other many times of course, starting in the back garden at Whitwell, and culminating in that second team fixture. I reckon it was pretty much even-stevens in our personal duels.

The first team were not having a great season. Although we made it to the final of the Benson & Hedges Cup at Lord's, only to lose convincingly by seven wickets to Hampshire, our County Championship form was modest. We only lost three games but a surfeit of draws meant we finished 14th. We relied heavily on Kim, John Morris, John Wright and Peter Bowler for our runs and apart from that quartet none of our batsmen really nailed down a place. We didn't have a great deal of strength in depth. Having said that, when Bud Hill took a call in the pavilion at Crosby Cricket Club, during a second team game against Lancashire in late June, I never expected to be pulled aside a few moments later to be told there was every chance I would make my Championship debut the following day against Surrey at The Oval.

Phil drove up from Derby to pick me up in his green Mercedes and we then motored down to London. As I'd experienced on the trip to Scarborough a year earlier, Phil was a man of few words, although now and again he'd turn the jazz down, take his pipe out of his mouth and offer a few home-spun philosophies. Surrey's best bowler was Sylvester Clarke, a West Indian who generated astonishing pace from a fairly languid run-up and front-on delivery that was certainly not something he'd picked up in the coaching manuals.

Phil, 'Now if you do play, do you promise me you'll play Sylvester Clarke in the appropriate way?'

Me, 'What does that mean?'

Phil, 'Well, if you jump on the front foot against him it won't work. He is quicker than anything you have ever faced and if you rile him he's liable to slip himself and bowl even quicker. Don't wake him up.'

Don't wake him up. It's a phrase I still use these days when I'm coaching and we're discussing the opposition's main bowling threat. Back then every side had a bowler best left to his slumbers. My first captain wasn't Kim, who missed the Surrey game because of a back injury, but Michael Holding, later to be replaced by Ian Bishop. There was Andy Roberts at Hampshire, Patterson at Lancashire and Wayne Daniel of Middlesex. Clarke, though, was reckoned to be the quickest and nastiest.

I can still remember walking into The Oval that day, 25 June 1988. I was so excited. Everything felt special, from the autograph hunters asking for your signature – a novelty for me – to the groundstaff getting the pitch ready for play. The big away dressing room, later to become the committee room and a place I had to fight a few battles as Surrey coach, was twice the size of anything I'd experienced. Phil told me I was making my debut just before we went off to the nets and shortly after tea I was walking down the pavilion steps to play my first innings in the County Championship at number eight, walking past my Dad, who was there with Vic Jobson, the chairman of Southend United where Dad was working as the club's chief executive and vice-chairman.

Peter Bowler was at the other end, on his way to scoring 158, and Clarke was bowling. Pete offered me a few words of encouragement, told me to get into line and try and be positive but all I could think about was Phil's advice the previous evening. 'Don't wake him up.' I let the first couple of balls go past outside off stump but the third wasn't as short as I'd expected and as I ducked the ball struck me flush on the helmet. Apart from a ringing noise in my ears I felt fine. Clarke just stood there, hands on hips, wondering what all the fuss was about. At the end of the over I strolled down the wicket where Pete was struggling to suppress a smile. 'It's much easier down this end!' was his somewhat unhelpful but amusing response.

I actually enjoyed facing Clarke. I even scored a few runs off him and began to settle. I remember smashing a full toss from Keith Medlycott straight at David Ward, who was fielding at short leg. It cannoned off his backside and dropped in front of him. He picked it up and tossed it back to the bowler as if nothing had happened. Pete and I put on 50 of which I contributed 21 before I got carried away and tried to sweep Chris Bullen, who didn't turn his off breaks an awful lot, and top-edged it to Graham Thorpe.

The game petered out into a draw after rain on the last day but I was up and away.

At the end of the season I expected to be hauled in by Phil, Bud or Kim for a debrief but nothing happened. After a game it was rare for anything to be said, whether we'd won or lost, by coach or captain. In the era of three-day cricket your first thought as you came off tended to be how long it would take to get to the venue for the following day's match and where you might stop off for some food on the way. Feedback? That was whether you were in the team or not. If you were, you must have been doing okay.

A few days before I played at The Oval, Sam and I became an item, having been best friends for a couple of years, most of which we spent trying to pair each other off with our mates! Sam's family lived opposite our home in Whitwell, which my Dad still owned and which was being looked after by my grandfather and during the winter of 1988/89 I would spend four or five nights a week there. Her step-dad Michael hired me again for his logging business and I spent the next few months working with him and Sam's uncle, Neville, extracting timber. It was a very happy time. Neville would cut the logs and I would load them on to the back of a truck and deliver them all over Derbyshire. I felt myself getting fitter and stronger every day, allied to the long runs I went on three or four times a week to improve my stamina. Spending so much time with Michael and his wife Sandra I fell into a cosy, family-orientated routine, something I'd missed at home when my own parents' marriage ran into problems.

I don't think I'd consider 1989 my breakthrough year, that was still some way off, but I made progress. I played in seven Championship games and felt I should have played more. I also averaged nearly 40 in the second XI. The highlight came at Chesterfield when I made my maiden first-class half-century against a Lancashire attack led by Wasim Akram. It gave me massive self-belief and I think reinforced Kim's view that I had a future. Mind you, that didn't stop me incurring his wrath during my innings. Just before lunch they brought on an off-spinner called Dexter Fitton who I'd enjoyed facing in second team cricket and had some success against. Having survived some testing overs from Akram and Phil DeFreitas I decided to go on the attack and hit Fitton for a couple of big sixes. When I got back to the dressing room I felt fantastic but Kim had a face like thunder. 'What do you think you were doing?' he asked. 'You were batting so well and then decided to risk it all by going after the off-spinner!' Kim shook his head but I don't think he was expecting my response either. 'Well, I was thinking that in 40 minutes' time Fitton's not going to be bowling again so I'd better make the most of it!' Even Kim smiled at that. Sure enough, on 79, I was caught behind off Akram!

A few weeks earlier I'd made a less-than-auspicious one-day debut in the Sunday League against Somerset at Derby. We were only chasing 156 (in 40 overs in those days) and I went in at number five with overs in hand and only 19 runs needed. My partner Reg Sharma met me as I got to the crease. 'Just watch Roebuck,' he said. 'He's lightning in the covers.' I pushed my first ball quietly into the covers and the next thing I realised was Reg hurtling down the pitch. I was short of my ground by about four yards, run out by Roebuck of course. A few weeks later, though, I made an unbeaten 46 in a victory over Gloucestershire at Cheltenham that helped us to victory. It was another milestone ticked off.

So was playing for England Under-19s for the first time. There was a three-match Test and one-day series against New Zealand towards the end of the summer and I was desperate to be picked. Later in my career the ambition I had to play for my country coloured my judgement and caused me problems but back then it was something I wanted more than anything. A couple of years earlier I had been chosen for the inaugural Junior World Cup in Australia only to be de-selected a few days later when the organisers changed the age criteria. Several members of the England team who had reached the semi-finals were team-mates for that New Zealand series and eight of us went on to win Test caps. I scored 38 at Edgbaston in the first match of the one-day series, which we won, and 71 not out at Canterbury in the second game of the Test series, which we lost 1-0 after Chris Cairns had bowled us out in the first match at Scarborough and they had protected their advantage in the subsequent games.

I made friends with Matthew Hart, the New Zealand all-rounder who went on to play 14 Tests, and managed to fix up some winter employment as coach of his club, Te Puke, near Auckland. I had already done a few coaching courses so the opportunity to go over there, play, coach in the local schools and help out around the club really appealed. We sorted things out and a couple of weeks after the season finished Sam and I headed to the other side of the world. It was a big step for us in our relationship. For the first time we'd be relying on each other.

Matthew's parents collected us from the airport and drove us to the accommodation, which was inside a tin-roofed barn on their kiwi fruit farm. It was a bit basic and not at all what we expected, just a partitioned space in the corner containing a sink, toilet, bed and a couple of chairs. Plush it was not and certainly not what we'd been expecting. Sam sat on the bed, burst into tears and said she wanted to go home. I managed to persuade her that it wasn't that bad and we set off to explore Te Puke which was about 15 minutes away on foot. On the outskirts of the village the Harts pulled up and when I explained Sam was unhappy with the accommodation they whisked us off to their farmhouse. We stayed there for a few nights before I managed to negotiate a room on a long-term basis at a lodge cum hotel in the village. I wasn't getting paid much by the cricket club so Sam had to earn a few quid. And that's what she did – getting up at 6am to pick kiwi fruit on the Harts' farm while I stayed in bed for a couple of hours before heading to the school to coach the kids. I don't think Sam has even picked up, far less tasted, a kiwi fruit in the years since but as an experience we both got a lot out of it and it certainly made us stronger as a couple.

In 1990 it was a great year to be a batsman. It was dry and the authorities experimented with the Dukes ball that had a much less pronounced seam. There were 428 first-class hundreds scored that summer, 180 more than in 1989 and 14 more than in any previous season. Thirteen players scored seven centuries or more and Graham Gooch got 12 of his own. At Derbyshire, 21 hundreds were scored which was a county record, two of them by me. It was my third year on the staff and although I had begun to feel more established and played much of the season in the first team I didn't do that well. I was still inconsistent, liable to get out once the hard work had been done, and prone to lapses in concentration as 800 runs from 21 innings attests. These days I might have struggled to get another contract but I always felt confident that I would be kept on and at the end of the season I was offered a deal until the end of 1994. Kim spoke encouragingly about the progress I and a few others were making and there was even a modest pay rise, £500 per year.

By then my Dad had begun to look after my interests, in the loosest possible sense. He would read over contracts, having gained experience of that at Southend, but it was pretty much a case of take it or leave it and I was having too much fun to turn my back on cricket after just three years.

It turned out to be one of the best years in Derbyshire's history. We won the Sunday League for the first time and the club felt sufficiently confident about its long-term future that it announced plans for a £10m, and much needed, improvement to the facilities at the County Ground, which had been lagging behind other clubs for some time and were starting to get us a reputation for all the wrong reasons.

I started the season by scoring my maiden first-class hundred, 111 against the Cambridge University students at Fenner's. Their bowling attack was pretty modest but I was in for more than three hours and felt good, but in terms of the longer version of the game it proved to be something of a false dawn. Derbyshire had signed a South African batsman called Adrian Kuiper, whom Kim had spotted when he played there on the 1990 rebel tour for England in the unofficial Tests. He was instrumental in our Sunday League success but struggled in the Championship. Our top three batsmen – Kim, Pete Bowler and John Morris, who would get his chance for England after scoring 1,353 runs at 61.50 the following winter – all dipped their bread and scored over 1,000 runs as did Bruce Roberts, our

Rhodesian-born batsman, but it was a tough summer for the bowlers and, trying to redress the balance to provide a fairer contest, the club found itself in trouble.

We played Middlesex, who were to become champions, at Derby in August and thrashed them by 171 runs – their first defeat of the season – after bowling them out for 99 in their second innings. But the pitch was reported by the umpires as being unsatisfactory and we were docked 25 points, dropping from eighth to 12th in the final table as a result – the first time a county had been punished in this way for a poor pitch. Fifteen of the wickets were taken by the spinners – John Emburey and Geoff Miller, who was in his final season with Derbyshire – but we scored 249 and 230 and didn't think it was that bad.

Back in May we had played Nottinghamshire, also at Derby, and although the umpires were satisfied with the pitch they also noted that it was too green and the Test and County Cricket Board (the forerunner of the ECB) took the unprecedented step of ordering our groundsman to shave our wickets. Kim enjoyed another fantastic season, passing 30 career hundreds and thus establishing a new Derbyshire record but, with hindsight, it may have been the time when he decided that our pitches needed to offer more help to our seam bowlers, which was still our strength despite the consistent performances of our core of experienced batsmen. We had Bishop, Malcolm, Mortensen and Alan Warner, who were all experienced bowlers, and emerging players like Martin Jean-Jacques and Dominic Cork, who made his Championship debut that season.

In addition, we'd signed Simon Base from Glamorgan in 1989. He wasn't quick but in the right conditions was a handful. He took 50 wickets in his first season, and played for England A, and another 35 in 1990. Batsmen like myself, Tim O'Gorman and Steve Goldsmith still hadn't nailed down a place in the side.

I got on well with Tim, who would come and play cricket midway through the season after he had finished term time at Durham University, where he was studying law. On his day he could take an attack apart and I enjoyed batting with him because he didn't take things too seriously. He packed up in 1996 and went on to become chairman of the Professional Cricketers' Association and proved to be a useful ally during the second half of my career. At that stage, though, we were both trying to bridge that gap from being promising youngsters to seasoned professionals.

Two things made 1990 a good year for me. We won the Sunday League and I was at the wicket when Steve Goldsmith hit the winning runs against Essex in Derby in front of a crowd of 8,000. I remember being carried off the pitch and slowly losing items of clothing while clinging desperately on to my bat which I definitely did not want to be parted with. Later than night I can recall serving pints in the bar above the dressing rooms wearing just a jockstrap as we celebrated the county's first trophy since 1981, and only the third in its history, long into the night. I had an excuse for my lack of modesty, most of my clothing having been pinched by jubilant supporters a few hours earlier.

Adrian Kuiper struggled in the Championship but he was a phenomenal performer in the one-day stuff. I remember batting together with him in one of our early games against Sussex at Hove. We needed 77 off the last ten overs which, back then, you had perhaps a one in five chance of achieving. He went ballistic, hitting the ball to all corners. It was the best display of clean hitting I had ever seen. Kuiper the Swiper we called him, which was a bit unfair because he rarely hit across the line. Kim invariably gave us good starts – he scored 699 runs that season – and Adrian, and sometimes I, provided us with some momentum towards the end of the 40 overs. The balance of the team was right as well. Simon Base was a good one-day bowler and Adrian picked up 19 wickets himself while Pete Bowler kept wicket and ended up with 22 catches.

I went out to bat at Taunton in one game to face the last ball with one run to win and Kuiper on strike. His instructions were fairly simple, 'As soon as the bowler bowls run as hard as you can. I'll try to get bat on ball.' The bowler was a Dutchman called Roland Lefebvre, who had a great yorker. As soon as he released the ball I set off like the clappers and had got halfway down the wicket when I looked up and saw Adrian staring in the direction of the churchyard at long off. I turned round just in time to see the ball settling in among the tombstones, the game having been won with an enormous six.

During my time at Derby we had never beaten Essex and went into the decisive game having just lost to them inside two days in the Championship. But it was our day, one made even more special by the presence of my uncle Richard and his son Robert being there. Richard and I had become quite close. He loved sport and played football and cricket to a decent level locally and we met up most weeks for a pint. He was only 45 when he died of a brain tumour a few years later, a loss that still cuts so deep with all of us, especially Mum.

A few days after our Sunday League triumph I ticked off another landmark, a maiden Championship hundred at Scarborough, the ground where I'd made my Derbyshire debut nearly three years earlier. Conditions for batting were perfect. The pitch was flat and Yorkshire's attack didn't scare anyone back then. The county were still not employing overseas players so, unlike most of their rivals, were unable to fight fire with fire and offer a really potent new-ball threat. I got established and John Morris was at the other end for most of my innings. He kept encouraging me, basically talking me through things when I got into the 90s. 'Think big, think big,' he kept repeating at the end of every over. I got there in the end – 101 – before top-edging a sweep off Phil Carrick. I was fuming but it taught me a valuable lesson. We had a drink in the bar afterwards and John gave me some useful advice, 'You score a hundred for yourself and 150 for the team.' In other words, it was a nice personal achievement but the team needed more. 'Fergie', as Carrick was nicknamed, wandered over, shook my hand and said he knew he would get me out, 'You were so overcome emotionally with getting your first hundred that I knew your discipline would go and I'd have my chance to get you out.' I wasn't the only batsman to enjoy those four days. Yorkshire conceded three centuries in the same innings for the first time since 1986 then Ashley Metcalfe and Phil Robinson both made 150 for them and they knocked off their target of 300 in 59 overs.

It was a memorable moment of course, but what happened to me at Old Trafford at the beginning of August probably rivalled it. England were taking on India in the second Test and with Derbyshire not playing Tim O'Gorman and I were summoned to Manchester to do 12th man duties. For a 20-year-old it was a fantastic experience although not all of it was particularly pleasurable. I remember getting a fearful bollocking from Eddie Hemmings, England's veteran off-spinner, for not having a hot bath ready for him when he came off and thinking what an arse he was, given that no one had instructed us to turn the taps on for him.

We decided that if a close-in fielder was needed it would be me, and if they needed someone in the deep it would be Tim. On the final morning India were left to score 408 in 88 overs to level the series, having gone 1-0 down at Lord's when England captain Graham Gooch made his record-breaking 333. I was fielding at short leg and Gooch pushed me a couple of yards deeper than I was used to for the second over which was bowled by Angus Fraser. He cramped the batsman, Navjot Sidhu, for room with his first ball and Sidhu got an inside edge, the ball looping into the air. I instinctively took off and caught the ball in the dirt inches from the ground. I looked up and saw the umpire raise his finger, before being mobbed by my new team-mates. A bit later I did it again to remove Sanjay Manjrekar, who had scored 50, off Hemmings who suddenly decided I was his friend for life!

Sadly, that day's play won't be remembered for two catches by the England substitute but for a phenomenal hundred by a young Indian batsman called Sachin Tendulkar. Earlier in the tour we had played the Indians at Chesterfield on a good pitch and he'd scored 105, which was 105 more than I had managed. We all remarked at the time how composed he was. When the Indian team manager told us he was only 17 we didn't believe him. He looked young but how could anyone of that age play with so much composure and authority? His century at Old Trafford came aged 17 years and 112 days and he played with astonishing maturity. It was the start of a brilliant career and although Richie Benaud mentioned England's sub fielder at the post-match presentations there was no doubt who was going to win the champagne moment, even if the recipient wasn't legally old enough to drink it.

# 5

# Gold Mercedes

AT the start of 1991 I felt I was getting somewhere. I had played pretty much the whole of the previous season, my captain and coach seemed to rate me and this was the year I decided I was really going to rip it up. I'd had another life experience during the winter of 1990/91 as well which I thought would improve my cricket.

Adrian Kuiper had arranged for Sam and I to go to Cape Town. It was the beginning of the end of apartheid and several English professionals headed there including three Warwickshire lads, Paul Smith, Graeme Welch and Dominic Ostler, and Nigel Felton of Northamptonshire, who sort of organised things. I was assigned to Primrose CC, a Muslim-only club, and my first coaching session was something of an eye-opener. I turned up and there must have been around 150 kids of all ages waiting, along with a few dads. Their equipment consisted of a bagful of old balls and a couple of sets of spring-back stumps. All I could do was arrange some coaching stations, run by one of the dads, which basically consisted of fielding drills while the older lads headed off to a concrete strip surrounded by waste ground to practise with a couple of bats I had with me. This was their preparation for some pretty competitive league cricket at the weekend. The kids seemed to enjoy it and they clearly had a lot of enthusiasm for the game but with no practice facilities as such it was hard for me to get myself attuned to play a Saturday league game when the English pro tended to be the prized scalp.

Primrose didn't even have a home ground, all our games were played away. But with no proper facilities to practice on you had to make the most of every innings because it would be another week before your next opportunity. For the first time since I became a professional I learned to really value my wicket. The cricket was comparable to a good English club standard, I scored a few runs and a real bonus was playing at some wonderful grounds, including Newlands and the University of Cape Town, where Duncan Fletcher was just embarking on his coaching career. For the rest of the time Sam and I enjoyed ourselves exploring the beaches of Cape Town and I worked hard on my fitness.

One adventure very early in the trip dissuaded us from ever going too far off the beaten track. We were invited to meet up with the other English lads on the waterfront one evening but after hailing a cab in the street Sam and I found ourselves sharing a minibus taxi with eight or nine guys who were on their way back from a day's graft somewhere. Straight away they started eyeing us suspiciously. Whether our instructions to be let off at the waterfront complex had been lost in translation or not, we ended up being dumped in an area of the city where I wouldn't have left my worst enemy. Thankfully another cab drove up and I pleaded with the driver to take us to the waterfront. It was only when I offered to give him the contents of my wallet that he agreed to take us. Apparently we'd stumbled across an area of Cape Town where some sort of turf war between local taxi firms was taking place and a week later I read in the paper of two fatal shootings on the same night we'd been stranded there, about 50 yards from where I'd managed to persuade this driver to give us a lift. After that, Sam insisted that we walked everywhere.

In 1991 we had a good year at Derbyshire. We finished third in the County Championship, our best position since 1954, and we went into the last few weeks with a genuine chance of claiming the title before a heavy defeat to Essex effectively ended our hopes. On a personal level, though, I didn't rip it up at all. I played in 12 Championship games, scored just one hundred in a modest aggregate of 436 runs, and halfway through the season was back in the second team, an environment I thought I had left behind for good.

I had only been on the professional staff for three years but I guess I thought I was already the complete player when the reality was somewhat different and I didn't really know who to turn to for some advice when I lost my way.

Much as we all loved Phil Russell, he was more of a team manager than a pure cricket coach. Phil's strength was spotting talent. Even if we were playing, he would leave our game on a Saturday and spend the afternoon driving around the local grounds in Derbyshire trying to find raw potential. He first encountered Devon Malcolm, for instance, in the Sheffield Thursday League. Kim's position was as entrenched as it had ever been. He ran the dressing room as he had done for years.

What cost us the chance of the title was probably the absence of a quality spinner. We had a good group of seamers, with Dominic Cork flourishing, and that year we played on some great wickets, ones that offered help to the bowlers but which also allowed our batsmen to play with a degree of freedom too. What we didn't have was a decent slow bowler and during the season, when you played on such a variety of surfaces, a good spinner can win a match or two for you.

In 1990 David had played virtually the whole of the season in the second XI trying desperately to get a contract. His left-arm spin was really developing and it had seemed likely that he would be taken on. But just before the decision was made a left-arm spinner called Richard Sladdin arrived on trial from Yorkshire and bowled Kim out twice in an old, much-used net that was turning square. That made Kim's mind up. Sladdin was taken on and it was curtains for David.

I was fortunate to play alongside some wonderful batsmen during my career but few made more of an impact on me than Mohammad Azharuddin, the India captain who was our overseas player in 1991. If anyone ripped it up that year it was Azhar, who scored more than 2,000 runs and played on a different level to everyone else, including players like Kim, John Morris and Pete Bowler whom I aspired to become. I'd never seen anyone manipulate the ball into the outfield like he could. He wasn't physically strong but his touch was just wonderful. His wrists were like ball bearings and on some days you got the impression he was almost taking the piss out of the opposition bowlers, such was his ability to manoeuvre the ball pretty much where ever he wanted to put it.

We'd heard stories before he arrived that he could be quite aloof. Didn't he once conduct a press conference while clipping his toenails? But he was extremely likeable and took me under his wing to a certain extent. He was the first player who showed me what a difference having a good bat could make. I remember picking up one of his for the first time and couldn't believe how light or how thin the handle was. I actually changed my grip slightly as a result, basically copying Azhar. Nowadays you can shape the blade and handle of any bat to your own specification but back then you got what you were given and if it came from a sponsor it was always gratefully received. At best you got through three bats in a season but a lot of players only had one.

Making as fundamental a change to your set-up might seem a strange thing to do halfway through the season, especially when you are struggling for form as I was, but I was in awe of Azhar a little bit. I remember one afternoon after training following him to the house he rented in Derby. Lying on one of the beds were about 15 different bats. 'Go on, choose one. Help yourself,' he told me. I ended up using the bat I picked out for the next couple of years.

The one thing Azhar had stipulated in his contract was the use of a Mercedes for the summer. Perhaps the club baulked at the idea because they were already paying him well and money, as always seemed to be the case at Derbyshire then, was tight. Anyway, John Morris, who worked for a BMW dealership during the winter, arranged for a brand new 5 Series to be in the car park when Azhar arrived. I pulled up alongside it in my sponsored Montego and was very jealous. I thought that if this was one of the perks of being a great player I wanted to get to the top.

Azhar, though, was not impressed. 'I'm not driving that,' were his only words when he saw it so I ended up being his chauffeur. A few weeks later, he got his Mercedes. We were playing in London and after play he invited me to go with him for a curry where he was meeting a business acquaintance of his. Azhar was feted wherever he went and his friend was soon fawning all over him while we ate our food. I couldn't help but notice the gold-coloured Mercedes parked across the road from the restaurant and, at the end of the evening, Azhar's friend tossed him the keys. Azhar didn't seem in the least bit surprised. 'If you drive me home the car is yours for the rest of the season,' said his friend. 'And at the end of the season I will have it shipped over to India and it will be yours to keep.'

I thought of that night when, nine years later, Azhar got a lifetime ban for match fixing. It did seem an extraordinary gesture on behalf of his friend although Azhar was afforded god-like status wherever he went in England. We certainly didn't have to pay for a curry any time we went out with him.

Azhar gave me some advice but by mid-July I found myself in the seconds. It worked a treat. There was much less pressure of course and Bernie Maher, who had taken over from Bud Hill as second-team coach, regarded me like a senior player, even though I was still only 21. I only made two fifties in my first eight innings in the Second XI Championship but I knew I was playing well and I then scored an unbeaten 139 against Nottinghamshire and 121 against Leicestershire. It proved one thing. I was too good for second-team cricket and that I could dominate at that level.

As a side, we didn't have the squad depth that counties like Middlesex and Essex had to compete in the different formats and while we had a great season in the Championship our one-day performances were average. We won our first two games in defence of the Sunday League title then lost the next eight and our NatWest Trophy hopes were ended by Hertfordshire. The game was played at Bishop's Stortford but after it rained for two days we all trooped outside for Derbyshire's first ever bowl-out. Having had no experience of this Kim rightly opted to employ his usual bowlers and I remember Ole Mortensen bowling two absolute beauties that pitched on middle and leg and missed the off stump by a couple of inches. If a batsman had been standing 22 yards away it would have been the perfect delivery but it was no good for an unguarded set of stumps. I seem to recall Frankie Griffith bowled a bouncer! Anyway, we only hit the target twice while Hertfordshire employed their batsmen to come in off one pace, a much more effective approach, and they knocked us out.

By then I had given up on the off spin. I was spending more time fielding the ball in the nets than bowling and in match situations I was getting bludgeoned. So I switched to medium pace and although I didn't bowl much that year I was quite pleased with my progress. I think I had a bowler's instinct for what a batsman wanted to do, particularly in one-day cricket, although it wasn't until I moved to Sussex that it started to pay dividends.

I got back in the team towards the end of the season and scored 112 – my only hundred – in the victory over Yorkshire at Chesterfield where we clinched third place. I was dropped three times but I ended the season feeling very positive and when I came back the following April, having not been abroad during the winter, I felt refreshed and revitalised.

So what clicked in 1992? I scored 1,000 first-class runs for the first time and broke two Derbyshire batting records which, incredibly, still stand today. Technically I didn't do anything different but I remember having several lengthy conversations with John Morris about the process of batting. What did I think about when I went out to bat? Not a lot was my initial response. I was still largely playing on instinct. There was little structure to my innings. I tried to play myself in and once I felt I had I would go after the bowling. I enjoyed the challenge of playing fast bowling and I wasn't scared of it. It was pitched-up, in or out swingers, which were the dangerous deliveries for me and it wasn't until Les Stillman arrived as Derbyshire coach in 1996 that I feel I got the specific coaching that helped to correct the flaws in my technique.

I started the season well with a century against Worcestershire in our second game and kicked on from there. The two records – for the highest List A score and the quickest first-class century – were made within a few weeks of each other. I scored 141 in a Sunday League game against Kent and remember feeling empowered, that nothing or no one was going to stop me that day. The pitch at Chesterfield was true and I was seeing the ball so well. They had a decent attack but I was coming down the wicket to Martin McCague and Dean Headley, making everything into a half-volley and smashing the ball back over their heads. When they dropped short I'd belt it over square leg or go deep in the crease and hit it over cow corner. There were very few days, certainly not a number in double figures, when everything came off but that was one of them. I remember one of my sixes heading towards the pavilion and Devon Malcolm leaning over the balcony and catching it! When that happened I knew it was my day.

I'd been given a regular slot at number four and felt settled there. It suited my game because there was less scoreboard pressure. Okay, there were days when I might come in at 20/2 with the ball doing all sorts but more often Kim and John had established a base and I could try and build an innings, putting into practice what John was trying to drill into me.

I can't deny that I have faced tougher attacks than that against which I made a hundred in 57 minutes, breaking a record that had been held by Stan Worthington since 1933. Kim and his opposite number Tom Moody couldn't agree on a last-day target for them to chase so Tom brought the field in and got Tim Curtis and Damian D'Oliveira to throw a few up. It was the perfect scenario for me and I was soon clobbering sixes towards Worcester Cathedral. With no sign of a declaration Tom had enough and brought back Neal Radford and Phil Newport, his best bowlers, but by then I was into my stride and got to a hundred. It was the journalist Neil Hallam, who watched a lot of my innings back then, who told me I'd broken a record. It was a good year for our batsmen. Peter Bowler and Azharuddin both scored more than 2,000 runs and Kim equalled the county record by passing 1,000 runs for the tenth successive season.

On 22 July 1992 I received my county cap along with Tim O'Gorman. A special moment for sure until I realised that I was actually worse off financially. As a capped player you received less meal and travel allowance and a smaller win bonus and it wasn't until the end of the season that I got a nice pay rise.

By the end of the season I finally felt I was established and for the first time I was starting to be talked about in the cricket pages as a potential England player, although the selectors were rarely spotted at our games. In the dressing room I was no longer regarded merely as a youngster with unfulfilled talent.

I had definite ambitions for the future. I wanted to play for my country but, like everyone else in that squad, I longed to be part of a Derbyshire team that won trophies on a regular basis. The Sunday League success in 1990 had given us a taste for it. I'm sure those ambitions were shared in the committee room but the club was still run fairly unprofessionally, which was a source of great frustration to the players at times. At the end of the season Steve Goldsmith found out on local radio that he and Andrew Brown, a solid but unspectacular opening batsman, were being released. What made it worse was that Andy heard the news as he drove to the ground in a sponsored car he'd only picked up the day before! Derbyshire, like most counties, was still run by an old-style committee and none of the players had any great faith in their decisions or the processes by which they were taken. Nearly everything they decided was leaked to the press as well, as Steve and Andy discovered.

But we still had a good squad, with a core of experienced pros and players like myself who were starting to come through. And in 1993 we delivered one of the greatest days in Derbyshire's history.

# 6

# A Row Over Lunch

LOOKING back now, more than 20 years later, 1993 was the year things started to unravel for me at Derbyshire although at the time it didn't feel like that. For only the fourth time in its history the county won a major trophy, very much against the odds when we beat Lancashire at Lord's in the final of the Benson & Hedges Cup. Not even a now infamous row in the dining room I was involved in could overshadow our triumph.

Off the field, though, Derbyshire was in a bit of a mess. The club had reached its bank overdraft of £400,000 and halfway through the season three of the major decision-makers, including the chief executive Bob Lark, were made redundant and Bud Hill ended up spending three months as acting secretary along with his coaching duties. Meanwhile, in the dressing room, there were the first inklings that Kim Barnett's formidable power base was not built on as strong a foundation as we all imagined.

Kim was in his 11th season as captain and that summer he set a new county record for the number of games in charge. As I know from my own experience at Sussex, you almost have to be superhuman to keep yourself motivated to do the captain's job as long as that, and to keep enjoying leadership, while, of course, making sure your own game is in good order. In that regard Kim had no worries. He struggled with back problems but he was still fitter than a lot of younger players in our squad and still churning out runs for us on a consistent basis. In 1990 he had addressed the squad in pre-season, which was unusual for him, and announced that John Morris was going to be vice-captain. John was well respected by the rest of us and about to have a brief but eventful taste of life as an England cricketer, although after the infamous incident on his only tour to Australia, when he buzzed a ground in a Tiger Moth plane with captain David Gower in 1991, the chance to play Test cricket for his country never came again. That was a shame because I'm convinced he would have flourished at international level. He was a very fine player and had the mental strength to play long, match-winning innings.

At the time I thought that John would eventually succeed Kim as captain but three years on nothing had changed, it was still very much Kim's ship and he showed little inclination to step down as captain. During the season Phil Russell announced his decision to leave at the end of 1993 to take over as groundsman at Kingsmead in Durban. I felt then that Kim's succession plan was that he would replace Phil as coach with Dominic Cork, whom Kim had great faith in both as a cricketer and a person, taking over as skipper. John and Pete Bowler, who were both considered potential future captains of Derbyshire, were left frustrated. John departed in 1993 to join Durham and a year later Pete was on his way to Somerset. In their last year the relationship between Kim and John was strained, although they never had any out-and-out disagreements beyond the normal stuff that was part and parcel of dressing room life during a long season.

I could see why Kim had such faith in Dominic. He was being widely tipped for the England team (and duly made his debut in 1995) and in 1993 he took 92 wickets for Derbyshire. On the open market he would have had no shortage of counties keen to secure his services and the club had to do all it could to keep him. Dominic was already a big character in our dressing room, even though he was just 22, with occasionally outspoken views. But he thought about the game and a lot of people at the club shared Kim's view that he was a potential future captain a few years down the line.

John's departure left a big hole in our batting that would need filling. The club must have felt I was the person to step in because at the end of 1993 I was offered a five-year contract, something unheard of back then when the most you could expect was three years. I had some very positive discussions with Kim who assured me he would do all he could to help me fulfil my ambitions to play for England. For me that meant playing on pitches that were not as bowler-friendly. That year we'd been without an overseas player for much of the summer after Ian Bishop broke down with a stress fracture of his back. It was obviously a big blow but guys like Dominic Cork, Ole Mortensen and Simon Base were good bowlers in English conditions and on a typically green Derby-seamer, a handful for any opposition. The best word to describe the pitches we played on at Derby that summer would be challenging.

But I signed the contract. Although the length of the deal would cause me problems a few years down the line, when I decided to leave, I was always going to sign it. I was only 23 and it offered me a good pay rise and fantastic career security. That, and the assurances I got from Kim that he would try and make sure our pitches would help our batsmen as much as our seamers, were all the reasons I needed to commit myself to the club.

In the County Championship we dropped from fifth to 15th place but our one-day form was better and I had my best season so far in limited-overs cricket. I scored 652 runs in the Sunday League, passed 50 eleven times in one-day matches and got out in the 90s three times. The innings I remember the most was the unbeaten 53 that helped get us to the Lord's final. I'd made 58 against Middlesex earlier in the competition and then played my part with the ball in the quarter-final at Taunton which turned into a farce. Rain had washed out two days and Kim and Chris Tavare couldn't agree on whether conditions were fit for a ten or 20 over slog. Because of this impasse the matter was left to the TCCB to sort out but they refused to reschedule the game. There was no alternative, we were facing another bowl-out.

Kim's experience of what happened at Bishop's Stortford in 1991 stood him in good stead. Dominic, Steve Goldsmith, Kim and myself were chosen and I hit the stumps twice bowling off one pace. We won 6-3 to set up a home semi-final against Northamptonshire. That day we bowled well to leave ourselves with a target of 211 and I had never felt more focussed in my career when I went out to join

John Morris with just under 100 runs needed and Curtly Ambrose back into the attack. He was bowling superbly as always so looked a little surprised when straight away I took three or four steps forward and hit him for a one-bounce four over midwicket. Curtly was a man of few words but, sure enough, I was on the end of one of his infamous stares as he stalked back to his mark. Did I get under his skin? I like to think so but just doing that to a bowler of his quality filled me with confidence. I was the aggressor in our partnership as we put on 95 in 12 overs to seal victory and I hit the winning runs with 21 balls to spare.

The wicket we used was on the far side of the square and all I remember after hugging John in the middle was turning to see the other lads charging towards us followed by hundreds of Derbyshire supporters. Once again, as had been the case when we clinched the Sunday League title in 1990, our jubilant followers carried me off the field. I will never forget those celebrations. In my 20-year playing career it was one of the major highlights, as special as all the success I would enjoy at Sussex.

A couple of weeks before we were due to face Lancashire in the final the sides met in the Championship at Derby. The wicket was pancake-flat and Dominic was banned from bowling after running on the pitch during the first innings, such was his frustration at the lack of assistance in the wicket. We replied to their 477 with 426, of which I contributed 74, and their declaration on 327/8 left us needing 379 to win on the final day. We were cruising on 216/1. An hour later, after a phenomenal spell of bowling by Wasim Akram, we had been hustled out for 267.

Back then we'd had very little, if any, experience of reverse swing, especially at Derby where the square tended to be very verdant so the ball rarely lost its shine. All of a sudden that day Wasim got the ball to go all over the shop. In seven overs he took 6-11 and while I was at the crease we lost five batsmen for scores of a duck, three, two more noughts and one. As a succession of team-mates departed they were glancing ruefully at Wasim rather than the pitch, which until then had been perfect for batting. A new law had been introduced giving the umpires the power to inspect the ball at any stage of the match. I wasn't sure whether this applied to batsmen as well but as wickets clattered at the other end I asked Vanburn Holder if I could take a look after Wasim had castled another of our batsmen. He threw me the ball, I gave it nothing more than a cursory glance and tossed it back to him.

Wasim and his Pakistan compatriot Waqar Younis were both extremely skilful bowlers who had the ability to swing the ball late and at high speed. But there normally needed to be some assistance, either in the atmospheric conditions or from a hard, abrasive square that would rough up one side of the ball, to get it to reverse. That day I had never seen a ball do so much. We'd heard stories on the circuit about players putting their finger or thumbnail down the seam and making a slight flap under the leather to create natural resistance. At the end of the over it was easy just to smooth the leather back down and no one would be any the wiser, least of all the umpires who knew as little as the players about this process.

When I got back to the dressing room Kim, who'd seen me looking at the ball, confronted me. 'What sort of condition was it in?' he asked. I had to be honest. If there was something wrong with it I hadn't noticed it and I didn't really know what I was looking for anyway. Kim headed off to the umpires' room and returned a few minutes later with the ball, which looked as if a dog had been chewing it. The ball was despatched to Lord's for further inspection but the TCCB threw out our complaint.

The press picked up the story and Kim told them that I had asked to see the ball, which was perfectly true. It wasn't mentioned, of course, that I had not accused Wasim or any of the Lancashire players of altering its condition but, not surprisingly I guess, in Lancashire's eyes I was accusing them of cheating.

The build-up to the final was a wonderful experience. The club paid for wives and girlfriends to join us in the hotel the day before and I remember BBC Radio Derby broadcasting live from the breakfast room as we got stuck into bacon and eggs. I had been a first-year pro back in 1989 when we lost the Benson & Hedges Cup Final to Hampshire, sitting in the crowd and leaving before the finish to get an earlier train home with Hampshire cruising to victory.

We were huge underdogs but we were dangerous opponents because we had players like Dominic and John Morris who were potential match-winners if it was their day. I hadn't given the Championship match a second thought during preparations for the final but as Tim O'Gorman and I walked back from the Nursery Ground after a pre-match net Wasim completely blanked me when I said hello to him and Gehan Mendis, as they walked past us heading towards the nets.

When Wasim bowled that beamer at me I didn't feel any pain at all. It was the first ball I'd faced and I guess my initial reaction, like everyone else, was complete surprise. It struck me flush on the left shoulder as I tried to weave out of the way. I went down on my haunches and our physio, Ann Brentnall, came out to give me some treatment. There were boos in the crowd and Wasim waved his hand at me. Was he trying to apologise? It didn't feel like it at the time. The umpire, Barry Meyer, gave him a warning and the game carried on. These days he would have been banned from the attack but Meyer must have thought Wasim's hand-waving gesture *was* an apology.

I was certainly a lot angrier when I got out for 11 and we had lurched to 66/4. Back then there was a lunch break during the final and when I returned to the dressing room they were replaying the incident on the TV in the corner. Jack Bannister, who was commentating for the BBC, called it a disgrace and the more it was shown the more frustrated I was becoming. Eventually, Pete Bowler put his arm around my shoulder and took me off to get something to eat.

The players' dining room at Lord's isn't the biggest space and when we got there we had to squeeze past a table where Wasim was sitting with a friend. Just as I approached him he burst out laughing, presumably at something his pal had said. I lost it. Leaning over as he looked up I whispered, 'Do that again and I will knock your fucking head off.' Wasim stood up and towered over me but I wasn't going to back down. This time I jabbed him in the chest and repeated my threat. In a book Wasim later claimed that I'd threatened him with a butter knife but that was categorically not the case. By now a few more players were in the dining room and after a few moments of silence I heard the unmistakable voice of David Lloyd, the Lancashire coach, in the corner. 'Now then young man. Sit down. Calm down. And have your lunch.' So I did. I think the only other words spoken in the dining room for the next 40 minutes were, 'Do you want custard with that?'

The incident certainly affected me better than Wasim and as a team we were transformed when we resumed our innings. The sun had come out, conditions had eased and Dominic hit a sensational 92 not out. Tim O'Gorman made 49 and Karl Krikken added 37 not out to get us to 252/6 from our 55 overs while Wasim's 11 overs went for 65 and he was their most expensive bowler. By no means was it a match-winning total but it represented a great recovery from 66/4.

Early in their reply I took a superb slip catch, low to my left and one-handed, to get rid of Steve Titchard and that lifted the team and I hugely. Before the game Kim had stressed that we should try and keep Mike Atherton out there as long as we could. He wasn't exactly instructing us to deliberately drop the ball if he gave us a catch but we knew that if he stayed in for any length of time it would chew up a lot of balls.

Atherton scored 54 and although Lancashire still had eight wickets left, after an hour's break because of rain, they needed 112 from 17 overs which, back then, took some getting. Neil Fairbrother looked as if he might play a match-winning innings but we bowled and fielded superbly before Frankie Griffith conceded just four runs from the final over, which he bowled in semi-darkness, and we had won by six runs. I'm sure Kim had planned for Alan Warner, who finished with 3-31, to bowl the last over but Frankie sent down six yorkers and a few moments later I was charging off the pitch, stump in hand, with hundreds of jubilant Derbyshire supporters in pursuit.

At the presentation on the balcony we each shook hands with every Lancashire player, including Wasim, but there was still no apology. An hour or so later though, as we were sitting in the dressing room celebrating, Wasim asked to see me and he did apologise. He said he was trying to bowl a yorker and that it wasn't intentional. Apology accepted, although it was a lot easier to take having just won the trophy.

I'm happy to say that since that day I have never had a problem with Wasim, in fact when we have played together in charity games we've always had a laugh. One of his last matches in England came a decade later when he was playing for Hampshire and I was at Sussex. He was desperate to lead them to a Lord's final in his last year before retirement but I managed to take 21 off him in the penultimate over of a NatWest Trophy tie at the Rose Bowl and we got home by four wickets. Wasim, competitive to the last, was totally crestfallen that he had lost Hampshire the game.

Our celebrations at Lord's continued long into the night. Derbyshire had now won four trophies in their history and I had been involved in two of them. My abiding memory of the hours that followed our victory is of our supporters drinking champagne out of the trophy when we passed it around in the Tavern pub next to the ground.

It was a wonderful moment for the players and the club but there was never much chance of us building on it. Although there was a change at the top in 1994, with Alan Hill replacing Phil Russell as coach, Kim led the side for the 12th successive season. The departure of John Morris was filled by the signing of Phil DeFreitas from Lancashire and Colin Wells, who came up from Sussex.

Two more players with big characters and plenty to say to add to the mix but the environment around the team did not encourage a great deal of open discussion. Instead, we started to question some of Kim's decisions behind his back so the atmosphere steadily got worse.

Finances prevented Derbyshire from bringing in a coach with a higher profile than Bud, who will admit himself that he was over-promoted and found it tough to deal with a dressing room full of big egos, including mine. I didn't have a bad summer. In the Championship I scored 926 runs, more than anyone else, but I did not feel there was an improvement in our wickets. Early in the season we played Durham at Chesterfield and the game produced 1,570 runs. Kim insisted that we had to play on pitches with more grass and Ken Roe, who was the chairman of our grounds committee, resigned in protest. I had most of my 926 runs by the beginning of June, including my only hundred at The Oval, but after that, as we started playing on more seamer-friendly pitches, I struggled to adapt again. I wasn't the only one. Mohammad Azharuddin had returned but after scoring 205 in that Durham run-feast he hardly scored a run and at various times we lost Kim, Pete Bowler and Frankie Griffith to injury. Kim dropped down to number five so Adrian Rollins, a powerfully-built opening batsman, got his opportunity. We lost both knockout quarter-finals at home on pitches prepared so we could fight fire with fire in the mistaken belief that our seam attack would prove to be better than our opponents'. That didn't help the mood around the club much.

Halfway through the season Brian Bolus, one of the England selectors, spoke to me after a day's play during which I had made a few runs. He told me that I was pencilled in for an A tour that winter if I maintained the form I had shown in the first half of the season. I was absolutely elated but the possibility of finally representing my country seemed to inhibit rather than inspire me. I finished the season with 926 Championship runs although I would have got to 1,000 had five of our last six days not been lost to rain. For the first time since 1927 no Derbyshire player reached the 1,000-run landmark and as the season wore on I got more and more frustrated. I wasn't very good at dealing with situations I couldn't control, such as the state of our wickets, and didn't react very well. The meeting with Bolus should have given me all the incentive I needed to try and forget all the other distractions in an increasingly discordant dressing room and kick on, but I didn't. This was the first year of my new five-year contract but by the end of that summer of 1994 I had started to regret making such a long-term commitment. For me, Derbyshire had gone a bit stale.

Kim might have sensed the same for at the beginning of 1995 he announced that it would be his last year as captain. We had a new chairman in Mike Horton by then, a driven, dynamic individual determined to drag the club in a new direction. We got on well. He sorted out the club's finances, which had been in a mess, and because he was a Derby lad and a visible presence at our home games the supporters liked and identified with him.

On the playing side it wasn't a great year unless you were a bowler. Between them, Devon Malcolm, Alan Warner, Phil DeFreitas and Dominic Cork, who made his England Test debut at Lord's that summer, took 290 Championship wickets. But their consistency was not matched by our batsmen. I scored 1,084 runs but we finished 14th in the Championship and made no progress in the one-day competitions.

To help shore up the batting we'd signed Daryl Cullinan, the experienced South African. His arrival pushed me up the order to three which I wasn't pleased about having, I felt, produced my best performances at four. But, as with Mohammad Azharuddin before him, I wanted to learn from Daryl and was happy to have the peg next to his in the changing room, although as the summer unfolded he gave very little away. Even Daryl will admit he took his cricket perhaps a little too seriously back then. He'd barely been introduced to the other lads on the day he arrived when he decided to get something off his chest. 'Look guys, I'm a serious bloke and I'm very serious about my cricket,' he told us. 'I don't like practical jokes and I don't like banter. By all means you enjoy that but do not involve me.'

So of course when we played at Lord's a few weeks later Dominic Cork borrowed his car keys while Daryl was out batting and drove his Mercedes right round to the Nursery End and parked it in a spot tucked away by the groundsman's sheds that probably only the groundsman himself knew existed. We were staying at a hotel across the road from Lord's and would walk back there after play so it wasn't until the final day that Dominic faced his dilemma. Did he have the bottle to leave Daryl's car hidden away? Some of the other lads egged him on but in the end he drove the car back round. Daryl never mentioned it but he certainly didn't forget it or the merciless stick he would take from guys like Colin Wells about the South African rugby team during that World Cup year.

On the penultimate day of the season the lads decided to throw a party in the changing room after play. We were on our way to beating Lancashire and only had to take a couple of wickets in the morning to complete our victory. A load of beers were brought in and we had a great night until a few of the lads noticed that Daryl, who hadn't come along and who would be flying home immediately after the game, had already immaculately packed his coffin, probably to ensure he didn't have to stay in Derby a minute longer than was necessary. It was an easy target for a few of his more boisterous team-mates who filled the coffin with a mixture of Guinness, blackcurrant juice and lager. And I mean filled. When the lid came down just enough seeped out of the top and trickled down its sides.

When I got to the ground the following day six or seven of the players were already on the pitch loosening up, which was unusual because the time for our formal pre-match warm-up was still 20 minutes away. Daryl walked in, exchanged a terse good morning greeting with me, opened the lid of his coffin, which had his Derbyshire sweater, now a very dark blue with purple stains on the badge breast pocket, lying on top and closed it again before walking out in silence. Having not witnessed what had happened the previous night I rushed out to warn the others. After we'd completed our victory and Kim had said a few words Daryl, who hadn't even been on the field for the last rites of the match, walked in, picked up his wallet and car keys and left again. A moment later, just as we were starting to relax, he burst through the door and pointed to Dominic Cork, Colin Wells, Phil DeFreitas and Karl Krikken one by one. 'If any of you fuckers ever come to South Africa watch your backs.' Dominic's face went white. With England due to tour there that winter he took the threat very seriously. Poor old Karl Krikken was in a right flap too, which was understandable as he hadn't even been at the party the night before!

The highlight of that year for me was my maiden double hundred, although its aftermath led to me asking to be released from my Derbyshire contract for the first but not the last time.

We were playing Kent at Maidstone and the wicket was flat. Aravinda de Silva scored a brilliant 255 for them and what impressed me the most about his innings was how he rarely hit the ball in the air. I learned from that and it was only when I got past 150, and fatigue started to creep in, that I began to take a few risks. Until then I had played as well as at any time in my career. It had been a hot day and when I got back to the hotel I was all for an early night, but Phil felt this landmark in a player's career should be celebrated and ordered a bottle of champagne from the bar which three or four of us duly shared.

In an attempt to exert his authority Bud Hill had instigated a midnight curfew and, amazingly, it hadn't been breached up until then but that night I think I got back to the room I was sharing with Dominic at a minute or two past midnight. I was too tired to contemplate breaking the curfew properly and sampling Maidstone's nightlife and as soon as my head hit the pillow I was out like a light.

The following day we played Kent in the Sunday League and I scored 79 but, unusually for me, had a bad day in the field and dropped four catches, three of them on the boundary. There were certainly no recriminations afterwards from either Bud or Kim but the following day, after we'd returned to Derby, Reg Taylor, the club secretary, called me into his office.

He congratulated me on the double hundred and then told me that I'd broken the midnight curfew and was going to be fined. I told him that yes, I hadn't been back in the room bang on midnight but had only been a minute or two later than that and asked for a little leeway, bearing in mind I'd scored 216 a few hours earlier. I knew for a fact that others had broken the curfew but I didn't want to exacerbate the situation. But my pleas cut no ice with the secretary so I told him that I wasn't going to pay the fine and I wasn't going to play either. If that's how Derbyshire wanted to treat me then I was effectively going on strike.

Reg reported this to Mike Horton and after a brief stand-off the fine was rescinded and I was given a verbal warning instead. My strike was off but I was still fuming about my treatment and a few days later I wrote to the club asking to be released. It was nothing more than a warning shot because I knew legally I had no chance of getting out of the contract, which still had three more years to run. I felt it was in my best interests to get a fresh start somewhere where batsmen would be valued a bit more than I thought they were at Derbyshire. I desperately wanted to play for my country but I was no nearer even an A tour than I'd been a year earlier after my conversation with Brian Bolus. Back then my ritual when the winter tour squads were announced was to get in the car and drive into the countryside and listen to the announcement on the radio. Once they'd got to Butcher I knew I'd be spending another winter at home.

A couple of days after the season ended I took a surprise phonecall from Dean Jones, the Australian batsman and a player I greatly admired. He had just been appointed Kim's successor as captain, which was a complete shock to me, and said that he would be bringing Les Stillman, the successful coach of Victoria, with him. 'Look Grizz, it's a fresh start,' Dean said. 'I want you to bat at number three and I promise to give you my proper backing. I've seen enough of you to know that you can have a very good career. See you next April.'

Having been so despondent a few days earlier, as I contemplated a long winter trying to extricate myself from my Derbyshire contract, I felt elated. Finally, things appeared to be changing at the club and when I withdrew my request to leave Mike Horton wasn't in the least bit surprised. 'I think Les and Dean will get the best out of you,' Mike said. He had no evidence to back up that statement but he was spot on.

## 7

# Oval And Out

THE Oval has played a big part in my life in cricket. I made my first first-class appearance there and a decade or so later made my England debut. It is also the ground where, thanks to the Australian coach Les Stillman, I rebooted my career. I always used to enjoy The Oval. The wickets were usually bouncy and quick which, I felt, suited my game, but when I turned up there in early June 1997 I was in a bit of a mess.

A few weeks earlier Les and our new captain Dean Jones swept into the club and I knew straight away that things were never going to be the same again at Derbyshire. They certainly made a favourable first impression. Instead of slogging around the old racecourse in pre-season we were taken to Ampleforth College for three days. It was a traditional old-style fitness boot camp but also a chance to get to know our new coach. Dean arrived a few days later but he had clearly had a big input into how we would prepare for the new season.

Les told a story about his own career which I use myself today when I am coaching youngsters. He'd been a modest cricketer who'd played a few first-class games for South Australia and Victoria in the 1970s. He then worked in commerce and became a middle-ranking manager, coaching the game in his spare time. He was asked by his boss one day to tell a guy who was due to retire that week that if he hung on for another three months the company would throw him a lavish leaving party and present him with a gold carriage clock. Les relayed the information to his colleague who told him, 'I've done 40 years with the company and I cannot do another day.' So he left that afternoon and Les followed him out of the door.

He didn't want to end up like that guy, full of regrets that he didn't follow the path he wanted. So he quit and concentrated on coaching.

He came with Dean after a bust-up at Victoria, where they had enjoyed some success, and were a real double act. Dean's approach was typically Australian. He was forthright in the extreme and no words were left unsaid when he was on one. Les was a bit calmer but he was good at building relationships with the players and was quick to identify each of our strengths and weaknesses.

What really helped create a positive environment was that Dean and Les had no agenda. Everyone on the staff was considered a first-team player and they weren't afraid to follow a hunch and back unproven guys. That had a good effect on the team in two ways. Players who thought they were an automatic selection suddenly weren't sure and the youngsters who felt a long summer of second team cricket lay ahead suddenly had every incentive to impress Dean and Les.

And of course Dean was still a fantastic player. In our second Championship game at Sheffield against Yorkshire, on an admittedly easy-paced pitch, he scored a superb 214. More importantly though, from the perspective of the team, a lad called John Owen, who they had called up for his debut, scored a century.

The atmosphere around the dressing room and the club was the best I'd experienced in my time at Derbyshire. For me, Dean's approach was just what I needed. I wanted to play hard, aggressive cricket but I also wanted my leaders to challenge me, be hard on me and help me achieve my own ambition, which I'd spoken to Les about in pre-season, and that was to play for England.

But while everyone else seemed invigorated by the new regime and were scoring runs or taking wickets in those early weeks, I was struggling. I got a half-century against Essex in late May, a game I remember more because Devon Malcolm bowled Graham Gooch in both innings with two of the quickest deliveries I'd ever seen. Gooch had just joined the England selection panel and it was Devon's way of getting back at the chairman of selectors, Ray Illingworth, who had criticised Devon in a book that had just been published.

When we turned up to play Surrey I felt under pressure for my place. In the first innings I got to 24 before Chris Lewis had me caught in the covers. It had been a terrible knock, full of frantic slashes over the slips and much playing and missing. I trudged off feeling very sorry for myself. I realised I had problems and that opposition bowlers had worked me out. They knew I liked width outside off stump and that I was prepared to risk taking on the short ball. Some days it came off but increasingly it didn't.

I was never one for throwing bats and kit around when I got out so when Les popped his head around the dressing room door a bit later I must have given the impression of being surprisingly calm, even though inside I was totally fed up. So the player who thought he was good enough to play for England asked his coach, 'What did you think?' Les gave me a look of utter contempt, as if it was an affront to him merely to offer a response. 'For someone who keeps telling me he should be playing for England it was one of the worst innings I have ever seen. You will never ever play for England playing the way you do and with the game you've got. In fact, you might not be playing for Derbyshire much longer.'

Talk about giving it to me straight. Now I was raging. Normally I would have puffed my chest out and told him I'd prove him wrong but this time I didn't have an answer. Amid the shock and anger I felt at Les's blunt assessment I knew he was right. An hour later, after I'd let the anger subside, I found him in the dining area behind the changing rooms. 'Les, you're right. If you are such a good coach help me get where I want to be.' So he did.

He asked me to go back to the hotel that night and think about the cricketer I wanted to be and that we'd meet at The Oval at 7.30 the next morning to start work, long before the other players arrived to practise. When I got to the ground at about 7am I still didn't know what sort of player I wanted to be, only that I wanted to be better. Back then the players used to park behind the stands at the Vauxhall End, climb the stairs into the ground and walk around to the pavilion. As I made my way up the stairs all I could hear was the sound of the ball hitting the bat. When I got to the top there in the nets, on their own, was

Graham Thorpe, who had made 185 earlier in the game, hitting balls back to his coach, Alan Butcher. I sat behind the net for a few minutes watching Thorpe hit throw-downs, one after another. That was my Eureka moment. That's who I wanted to be, or at least a right-handed version. Graham Thorpe, a player I'd first encountered at the Schools Festival in Oxford a decade or so earlier but now established as one of the best batsmen in the world.

I had always stayed left side of the ball, side on and trying to get on to the front foot so I could attack anything on or outside off stump. Les got me over to the off stump and aligned me to get me looking straight back down the pitch so, at the moment the bowler released the ball, I could hit it straight back down that pathway. We scratched out lines in the net where he wanted my back and front foot to go to help me come into the ball straighter. It's a popular trigger movement these days but back then most players stayed side on and looked to get a big stride into the ball. It was a major reconstruction and I honestly believed that after that initial session, which lasted no more than 45 minutes, that I would be fixed. When Les told me this was just the beginning I felt a bit despondent, although I was determined to stick with it. I was committed to change, all I needed once I had got used to the new trigger movements was to get my timing right. Back and across, back and across, back and across…

In the second innings I was keen to implement my new technique and scored 42. I felt awful and really scratched around. When I got out I felt worse than I had in the first innings and told Les it must have looked bad. His reply surprised me, 'It was the best innings I have seen you play. It was an innings that matched your desire to play at the highest level. All that was missing was timing, and that will come with practice.' What Les could not comprehend was that I had started work on a fundamental technical adjustment in the morning and implemented it in a game situation the same day. 'I admire your courage,' he added. I left feeling absolutely elated.

It was a major turning point in my career. I was committing my game to Les but neither of us could have foreseen how quickly it would pay dividends. Three days after the Surrey game ended we played Hampshire at Southampton and I batted for 407 minutes – more than a day – and scored a career-best 239, hitting 27 fours and five sixes. Afterwards, Les told me a story about Dean, who would often struggle to back up a good score. He was right. Since the double hundred at Sheffield he hadn't passed 50 in the Championship, although his one-day form was superb and he went on to score 1,151 runs in the limited-overs game that summer, a new county record. 'Don't make it a one-off, back it up, back it up,' was the message he drummed home all the way back to Derby.

I got out to Anil Kumble for one when we beat India for the first time since 1932 in our next game but in the following Championship match against Middlesex at Derby I scored 125 and 136 not out, the first time a Derbyshire player had made hundreds in the same game since 1990. By then my movements and timing were in synch. Even against such experienced operators as Angus Fraser, who would always bowl that nagging length that you weren't sure whether to come forward or play back to I just felt I had so much time to play the ball. Anything short I would punch through the leg side and anything full I was drilling back down the ground. The only downside was I'd lost the ability to play the cut, but that was always a risky shot for me and because I was scoring in other areas it didn't matter. I scored six hundreds and finished with an aggregate of 1,590 runs that season.

All around me team-mates were feeling the benefits of the new regime. Kim dropped down to number five and scored 1,436 and passed the Derbyshire record for the most first-class runs. Phil DeFreitas (62 wickets) and Devon Malcolm (70) had great seasons with the ball and Andrew 'A.J.' Harris took 48 in his first full season. We started to win games consistently and Mike Horton and the committee rightly gave themselves a pat on the back for choosing Dean and Les. In August we won four matches in a row and suddenly had a chance of winning the Championship. We went down to Taunton and had Somerset eight wickets down chasing 383. Dean was criticised for a cautious declaration afterwards but the thing that really did for us was when Jason Kerr was bowled by Daffy first ball and the umpire, Tony Clarkson, ruled that Kerr hadn't been ready to face the delivery. He went on to score an unbeaten 68 and save the game.

Dean had made another wildcard selection for that game, a slow left-armer called Glenn Roberts who came in for his debut, but he struggled while in the next game, at home to Warwickshire, Dominic Cork suffered a broken shoulder when he was hit by Dougie Brown and was unable to bowl. We then lost by four wickets. Leicestershire, a relatively small county like ourselves, ended up champions but if I'm honest I never felt we could win the title. We didn't have a decent spinner, which had been an issue at Derbyshire for a number of years, and we lacked the experience and nous to negotiate those tense last few weeks of the season.

Dean's philosophy throughout the summer remained the same, in fact it was the creed by which he lived his life. Play hard, leave nothing on the pitch and be brutally honest, both with yourself and your team-mates. He was constantly challenging individuals in the team. 'Did you do your best?' I liked that you could go hard at him as well, challenge what he said and the assumptions he made about how you felt. As soon as we left the dressing room Dean was happy to share a beer or two with you and forget what had just been said. It was open and honest but towards the end of the season I sensed that not everyone shared my views on Dean and Les, and in particular some of the senior players led by Kim. I didn't agree but I could understand their view. Did they really want another season of being challenged and shouted at one minute by someone who a few minutes later would try to be everyone's best mate?

I liked Dean's approach and Les had been a fantastic help, but as the season came to an end I knew it was a minority view.

Despite having had my best first-class season there was no reward in the form of England recognition, even on the A tour. I was absolutely devastated. It was one of the lowest points of my career and for a few days I was inconsolable. I had enjoyed working with Dean and Les but deep down I knew I had to leave. I was convinced the 'Derbyshire factor' was stopping me fulfilling my ambitions to play for my country. I was prepared to give it one more year there but I also vowed that it would be my last.

It was well known around the circuit that I had itchy feet and a few weeks after the season finished I took a call from

Alan Wells, captain of Sussex. They wanted me and were prepared to pay what it took. I was flattered but a couple of weeks later Alan was sacked and his departure sparked a major exodus from the club with five more established names leaving Hove. There was talk of interest from Yorkshire, with whom I had a strong affinity because Dad was born there, and Nottinghamshire. I'd got a few mates in the dressing room at Edgbaston and I consoled myself with the thought that if I did leave I would have plenty of options. At 26 I might not have still been the player I wanted to be but I was at the peak of my earning powers.

Dad was chief executive of Southend United and through working with players on transfers he got to know the agent Jonathan Barnett, who had sorted out Dean Jones's Derbyshire deal. That winter we had lots of discussions as to how I would get out of my contract, which still had two more years to run. In football players moved all the time even though they were under contract. A player would be tapped up and offered more money elsewhere, the club would dig their heels in and eventually after a stand-off they invariably sold him to cut their losses and get an unhappy player off their hands. Nothing like that existed in cricket; it was very rare that anyone was released by a county when they were still under contract. Jonathan's idea was to get the club who wanted me to pay Derbyshire the final year of my contract, a kind of transfer fee if you liked. 'Any county that wants you enough will pay it,' he told me. At the time I was earning around £38k a year, which was about average for a capped player of my experience.

We broached the subject that winter with Derbyshire but not surprisingly they dug their heels in. I remember reading all sorts of nonsense at the time that we were going to take our case to the courts but if those discussions took place they lasted no more than a few seconds. We knew we would have to sit tight.

When I reported back at the start of the 1997 season part of me still hoped that the anti-Jones and Stillman faction had weakened during the winter but within a few days it was obvious this was not the case. Andy Hayhurst had come in to coach the second XI which meant another person was bringing ideas to the mix. Dean seemed distracted when he arrived. His wife was on crutches and struggling to get around, having broken her ankle, so with two young children to look after he had more responsibilities at home. Meanwhile, Les was increasingly aligning himself away from Dean as battle lines were drawn and another Derbyshire row came slowly to the boil.

Les was quite political and while he wasn't in the same camp as the guys who wanted Dean out, he had backed Dean at Victoria and lost his job and he could sense history was about to repeat itself.

The atmosphere wasn't nasty but it seemed we were going through the motions again, the energy we'd had a year previously wasn't there. The anti-Jones faction knew he would in all likelihood be leaving at the end of the season so there wasn't the need to impress him anymore. Predictably, we started the season slowly. In fact it wasn't until August that we won our first Championship game and by then Dean was back in Australia and Les had been completely ostracised by the players.

Dean resigned after he'd cocked up a declaration and we lost to Hampshire at Chesterfield, but the incident that made his mind up to leave took place not on a cricket field but the golf course at Breadsall Priory, not far from the County Ground. We had a few serious golfers in the squad while Dean loved the game too and one afternoon after nets he asked if anyone wanted to join him for 18 holes. No one was keen so I said I'd accompany him and off we went. We were putting out on the first green when I heard some familiar voices a few yards away walking down another fairway. We looked over and there were Kim, Phil DeFreitas, Karl Krikken and Dominic Cork. Dean didn't say anything but his expression told me he was absolutely devastated. Of course he understood players were free to do their own thing but he couldn't figure out why they wanted to play without him or another team-mate. We hardly spoke for the rest of the round but that was the moment Dean knew he had lost the dressing room. He probably started packing his bags that night.

He was crucified for the declaration which left Hampshire needing 310 in 59 overs, a target they reached easily. Even I thought it was ridiculously generous but his argument was he had been prepared to gamble to get us a precious win. By now the local press were being briefed about an increasingly toxic dressing room atmosphere and the day after the game Dean walked into the office of the chairman of cricket, Ian Buxton, and resigned. He was on the plane home that day but if the club thought that things would settle down they were mistaken. Before he left Dean issued a statement, which had been sanctioned by the club, pouring rubbish on Derbyshire and hammering some of the players for a perceived lack of commitment towards him, for struggling to come to terms with what was needed to be a successful player and being unable to take personal criticism. Les had warned the club management weeks before that if they didn't back Dean he would walk and Dean was never one to glad-hand with committee members anyway. He would be left scratching his head when they criticised players in front of him. 'Why don't they pull for their team? I can't understand it,' he told me after one committee meeting.

Dean's departure left Les completely out on a limb. While Andy Hayhurst got more involved with the first team Les ended up with the seconds but within a few weeks he wasn't involved at all with the playing side. But because his house in Victoria had been rented out and his kids were settled in school he spent quite a bit of that summer taking them around the tourist attractions of England once they had broken up, so at least they benefitted out of another Derbyshire implosion!

Phil DeFreitas was appointed captain but Kim was still very much in charge of the dressing room and once the dust had settled he called the players together. He wanted to issue a statement answering some of the criticisms made of them by Dean. The club warned him against doing so and I told him I would not be one of the signatories. My stance wasn't unexpected of course, but I felt sorry for some of the younger lads in the squad who were coerced into signing because of peer pressure from the senior players.

Kim went on local radio during our next match against Warwickshire at Edgbaston, when Ian Blackwell made his Derbyshire debut, to expand on the statement. The club fined Kim £1,500 and it was suggested that the players chip in to help him pay. As soon as that was mentioned I told them I would not be getting my chequebook out. At our next match at home to Sussex, Kim spent part of the game off the field drafting a press release in response to the committee's decision to censure him and outlining that nine of the ten players had offered to chip in to pay the fine. It didn't take the press long to work out who the odd man out was.

By then I'd had a meeting with Phil and made my own position clear. I told him I was finished with Derbyshire and would be leaving at the end of the season, come what may. I added that I was happy to continue playing but I reiterated that when I did so it would not be for this team but for the club, its supporters and myself. I was done with that group of players. Phil picked me for the next few weeks which I was grateful for because it would have been easy to dump me in the seconds and let me rot for the rest of the season. Fortunately, Ian Buxton was quite sensible throughout all of this. He recognised mistakes on both sides and when we met he promised that I could leave at the end of the season, providing I remained 100 per cent committed to Derbyshire between now and then which I was happy to do. I repeated what I said to Phil, which Ian accepted, before he offered me the captaincy for the rest of the season which came as a total surprise. I politely declined his offer. If the others weren't going to listen to Dean Jones what chance did I have?

In any case, I was desperately trying to keep a low profile after an incident just before Dean departed which drew me into conflict for the first and not the last time with the TCCB's disciplinary panel and a certain Shane Warne.

We played Australia at the start of their tour and the game was live on Sky Sports. Before going out to bat I asked Dean how to play Warne, whom I'd never faced before. He told me to treat him like an off-spinner and hit against the spin. I had got to seven when he bowled me his slider, the ball that goes straight on. I got deep in the crease and managed to deflect it fine for four runs. Shane was already appealing when the ball pitched because he thought it was going to skid on. I turned to see where it had gone, looked up and saw Shane running past me to celebrate with Ian Healy. I told the umpire, Vanburn Holder, that I'd hit it for four. I can still remember his reply now, 'I know you hit it, but I've given you out.' Vanburn had made a mistake and if he'd admitted as much then I would have just had to accept it. This exchange between Vanburn and I and was repeated a couple of times before I dragged myself off. On my way past Healy he tried to be sympathetic, 'Tough luck mate.' I turned and replied, 'You're surely not going to claim that are you?' Which was the worst thing I could have done because within seconds the entire Australian team, including the lads who had brought on drinks, were giving me a load of abuse to which I responded with a few choice words of my own, pointing the bat at them as I got back to the pavilion. For the first and only time in my career I threw my bat across the dressing room, damaging it badly on the corner of my coffin, which only made things worse.

Not long after that I was summoned to the chairman's office. The whole incident had been replayed several times on Sky and the TCCB had already been in touch with Derbyshire. The upshot was a £750 fine and some bad publicity in the next day's papers. I partly redeemed myself in the second innings by scoring 91 from 76 balls to set up a one-wicket victory, Derbyshire's first over Australia since 1919. I attracted a lot of positive reviews for that knock but the damage had already been done.

I only made one Championship hundred that season and finished with around 900 fewer runs than I'd made in 1996, but my one-day form was excellent. I scored 445 runs in 11 Sunday League games and in the quarter-final of the

NatWest Trophy made an unbeaten 129 against Sussex. It remains one of the favourite innings of my career because of the circumstances in which it was made.

I spent most of the night before the game vomiting down the toilet. Not only was the dressing room atmosphere at the club pretty toxic, it appeared the water system was contaminated as well because when I got Sam to phone Ann Brentnall on the morning of the game to tell her I was too ill to play it emerged she'd had the same conversation with about eight or nine other players. I was asked to report to the ground anyway and remember sitting in the dressing room as one ashen-faced team-mate after another walked through the door. Thankfully Kim won the toss and we batted because if we'd been in the field I'm not sure we'd have been able to bowl. We did no warm-up as such and I had to change my whites twice before going out to bat because of a toilet emergency!

It was a warm day but the pitch was flat and Sussex's attack was fairly modest. I hardly scored a run for the first ten overs but the adrenalin slowly kicked in and I started to feel a bit better. Suddenly I was playing as well as I had all season and celebrating a hundred. I finished on 129 and our total was a new record for 60-over matches. Even after that, though, the response to my efforts was pretty lukewarm. One of the lads told me afterwards that the consensus was I should have sacrificed my wicket at the end so we could get a few more runs. A new competition record clearly wasn't enough.

Those extra three hours or so batting enabled a few of our bowlers to rest and we were confident of defending our score, only for Rajesh Rao to take the game away from us with a brilliant 158 not out as Sussex chased 328 to win with four wickets and four balls in hand. Talk about every dog having its day. Raj played brilliantly but we didn't bowl or field well. Phil, by his own admission, wasn't the greatest tactician but his bowlers let him down and our last chance of salvaging something from the season had gone.

I played in a couple more Championship games but just before a Sunday League match against Leicestershire at Grace Road in late August I was approached by Andy Hayhurst who told me they were going to give a few youngsters a go and that I was being left out. My only motivation by then was to try and beat Kim's record for the most one-day runs in a season of 1,123 by a non-overseas batsman. I was on 988 and with four league games left I thought I had a good chance but it wasn't to be. I packed up my kit for the last time. My Derbyshire career was over.

I'm frequently asked what my relationship is like with those former team-mates now, nearly two decades later, and I'm happy to report that by and large we have no problems when we bump into each other at Derbyshire reunions or PCA golf days. A few years ago I played against Kim for the Glenn McGrath Foundation against an Old Derbyshire XI at Chesterfield and we had a good chat. I think we both accept that we said and did things at the time that we now regret. Kim also moved on at the end of 1997 to join Gloucestershire and I think moving to a new county helped revive his career. I still see the likes of Pete Bowler, Tim O'Gorman, John Morris and Karl Krikken and have a good relationship with all of them. I have no axe to grind with Dominic Cork either. Corky was, shall we say, the most interesting character at Derbyshire back then.

In September 1997 all I could do was look to the future. It was time for pastures new.

## 8

# Sussex By The Sea

ONE of the biggest fallacies about my career was the amount I was paid when I joined Sussex in 1998. I remember reading that not only was I to become the highest-paid player in county cricket but that my salary was in excess of £100,000 a year. The truth is that if money had been my prime motivation when I left Derbyshire I would have joined Nottinghamshire. Moving to Trent Bridge made sense in other ways as well. I would not have to move house and uproot our young family and Nottinghamshire, based at a Test match venue, were regarded as a big county and certainly one with a higher profile than Sussex.

I wanted a fresh start after years of turmoil at Derbyshire but, just as importantly, Sam and I wanted to put some distance between the county and us. We were ready to fly, although we knew it would be tough because our families were still in Derbyshire and leaving them would be a wrench.

In all these things timing is crucial so the fact that I scored that 129 against Sussex in the NatWest Trophy in 1997 a couple of days after I'd met their chief executive Tony Pigott for the first time certainly made them even more convinced that they wanted me. Their win that day was a rare highlight in a dispiriting summer. The loss of captain Alan Wells the previous winter, as well as five more capped players, may have forced the off-field revolution that paved the way for the success we were to enjoy in the next decade but it had left Sussex bereft on the pitch. They were one of only two sides to finish below us in the Championship in 1997, which said a lot.

So when I met Tony at a service station on the M1 for the first time I did not walk away convinced I was going to sign for Sussex. He sold the club really well and explained that Don Trangmar, a main board member for Marks & Spencer and a cricket nut, was going to replace Robin Marlar as chairman. Tony outlined their ambitious plans to improve the squad and revive the club, which had stood still for years, as a whole.

Apart from my innings a couple of days later, the one thing I remembered from that game was how well organised Sussex had been in their warm-ups. Although Des Haynes was coach – he was sacked ten days later – it was obvious that the captain, Pete Moores, was running the show. They were very well drilled and despite not having great resources to call upon I was impressed with the work ethic and team spirit Pete seemed to have engendered.

When news of my release from Derbyshire was made public, my agent Jonathan Barnett had phonecalls from nine counties. When he started talking figures six dropped out straight away including Yorkshire, which disappointed me, leaving Sussex, Nottinghamshire and Kent in the frame. Sam and I embarked on a road trip around the shires to weigh up what they each had to offer.

As we made our way down to Sussex I'd decided that everything about their proposal had to be right. We wanted to put some distance between Derbyshire and ourselves but I'd forgotten just how far away Brighton was. We were in danger of being late for our meeting with Tony and had to pull over in Preston Park as we drove into the city, nip behind a bush and change into smarter clothes! It was a beautiful autumn day and as we drove along the seafront before turning right towards the ground Sussex's appeal began to grow on us. We got to the ground and Tony was there to greet us and he made a special fuss of Sam, which impressed her.

We had a very positive discussion and Tony told us that they wanted to sign Shane Warne as overseas player and captain and that he had earmarked me for the vice-captaincy. If nothing else, it showed Sussex's ambition. Sam and I left Tony to discuss the finances with Jonathan and we headed up to the old squash club in the corner of the ground, which was by that point a restaurant called Willows, for a spot of lunch. We'd barely started perusing the menus when Tony and Jonathan appeared with a bottle of champagne. 'All sorted,' said my agent.

Well, not quite. I had promised myself and Sam that we would only make our mind up after we'd seen Kent and Nottinghamshire but all the time I was getting more excited with what Sussex could offer. The champagne had to stay on ice, for a few days at least.

The club had put us up in the Grand Hotel on Brighton seafront for the night and that afternoon we spent a wonderful few hours driving around the villages in the South Downs, looking at potential places to live. We fell in love with the place. We both felt we could put down some roots here and that it would be a good area to bring up our family. The contract on offer was £75,000 a season for three years with a car and rented accommodation for the first year on top.

The following day we drove to Canterbury where we met the coach John Wright, who I knew from my early days at Derbyshire. I liked John and they had a decent squad already but the meeting with the chief executive, Paul Millman, was a strange affair. The basic salary wasn't much more than I'd been earning at Derbyshire but it would be topped up with various sponsorships. We ruled out Kent straight away and headed to Trent Bridge.

There, coach Alan Ormrod, and chief executive Mark Arthur met us. Finances were not an issue. Nottinghamshire would match any offer I had received elsewhere and I had been earmarked as vice-captain to Jason Gallian, who had been recruited from Lancashire as the new skipper. Mark and I headed off to lunch and we'd barely sat down when he asked me if I was going to sign. 'If you do, you can have this as well.' He reached for his top pocket and pulled out a cheque for £50,000, a signing-on fee if you like. I was staggered. The amount was the value of the house Sam and I had moved into in Whitwell when we had got married and would have given us real financial security. Tempted though I was, I told Mark that I needed 48 hours to speak to Sam and Jonathan before making my decision.

We knew it would be tough to move away but it didn't take long for us to reach the same conclusion. The prospect of starting a new life in Sussex held massive appeal and I was impressed with the way Tony and Don had handled the negotiations. And if it didn't work out, I still had plenty of good years left in my career, which I could continue elsewhere. I phoned John Wright and Mark Arthur to tell them I was headed for Hove. A few days later Pete, who had been appointed coach by then, and Keith Greenfield, the second XI coach, met me in a pub not far from Whitwell and just off the M1 and I signed a three-year contract.

I was due to travel back down to Hove a fortnight later for my official unveiling. I'd had a conversation with Tony in the meantime who said there might be a couple of changes, which intrigued rather than worried me.

I will never forget driving through the Tate Gates to be greeted by a dozen or so photographers and a TV crew filming our arrival. Paparazzi at Hove! I'd never experienced that at Derby. Just before the press conference Tony told me that they hadn't been able to persuade Shane Warne to sign and that they had instead recruited another Australian, Michael Bevan, as their overseas player. Sussex now wanted me to be captain and had extended the contract from three to five years. I agreed to both straight away and then met the media.

Afterwards Pete and I had a chat, our first as coach and captain. We clicked within a few minutes, our thinking on so many aspects of how a team should be run and the culture we wanted to develop within the squad almost completely aligned. We were talking so much that we were late for the scheduled meeting where I was to meet the committee for the first time. Don Trangmar was in charge in Robin Marlar's absence. 'Well, that's not a very good start – you're five minutes late!' he boomed, with all the seriousness he could muster before he burst out laughing.

That evening Pete and his wife Karen joined us at Tony's house and we talked long into the night about what sort of cricket club we wanted to be part of. Within a few weeks we had sold our house in Whitwell and the following spring headed down to Sussex to start our new life.

Not only was it a fresh start for me it was the beginning of a new era for Sussex. They had been through a period of blood-letting, culminating in the 'revolution' at the start of 1997 and the stormy AGM at the Grand Hotel which made the internecine warfare at Derbyshire look like a tea party in the vicarage. I realised as soon as I arrived for pre-season at the start of 1998 that I would have a higher profile than the one I'd enjoyed at Derbyshire but that there was massive expectation to deliver not just in terms of my captaincy but also my own personal performances. I was being paid well and expected to perform.

During our opening Championship game against Lancashire Sam and my Mum were sitting in front of the old squash club and when I got out in the first innings for five the first rumblings from the members about me started. There was a decent crowd in and a couple of rows in front of Sam someone muttered, 'Oh dear, the best thing since sliced bread has just failed.' If I wasn't already aware just what was expected of me it only took one failure with the bat to bring the reality of the pressure I was under into focus.

I always enjoyed pre-season. Even those early days at Derby when we'd run around the old racecourse were special because you were catching up with your mates again after not seeing a lot of them for six months and the hard graft you were putting in physically, which I always enjoyed, was setting you up for the long summer ahead.

When I spoke to the Sussex players for the first time I made no bones about what I wanted from the team. I hadn't come to Sussex for a jolly or the money. I wanted the team to win because I knew that would help my own personal ambitions to play for England, something I was almost fixated upon at that stage of my career. Within a few weeks of the 1998 season starting I got my opportunity and although two one-day internationals hardly constituted an international career it just served to make me even more determined to make sure further opportunities came my way. Looking back now, I was probably at my peak as a batsman at that time. I'd had two good final years at Derbyshire and felt if I could maintain that form in a new environment at Hove then I would get more chances to play for my country.

On the first day of pre-season Pete and I decided to test the commitment of the squad. We walked from the ground to the seafront at Hove dressed just in our swimming shorts, lined up on the beach and then walked slowly and without saying anything into the icy cold of the English Channel in late March. We didn't realise but after a few steps there was a sudden drop and within seconds we were all submerged under the water for a few seconds! The players loved it though, especially that we had invited the local TV station to witness this unusual start to the new era at Sussex.

Before I arrived I had written down a list of all the good things I had learned from the two captains I had played under, Kim Barnett and Dean Jones. I admired Kim's positive attitude, the space he gave to the players to perform so they could find their game and that he didn't over-complicate. Like Dean, I also wanted to embrace an open environment among the group where anything could be said without fear of recrimination afterwards. I didn't want the guys to turn up shooting from the hip, rather I asked them to think about what they wanted to contribute beforehand and make constructive points. Pete was in total agreement and although we had the odd difference of opinion as a squad I felt the environment we created very early on was crucial in ensuring that we went on to enjoy, by recent Sussex standards, a very successful season.

Pete's world was about challenging the players to keep trying to improve. I was totally in tune with that but for a new captain, trying to balance personal needs with those of the team, it was a pretty draining experience initially, until I learned how to manage my time better and prioritise. Pete and I had spoken to the groundsman, Peter Eaton, and asked him to try and prepare good batting wickets but to also leave some grass on that gave the bowlers good carry, if not necessarily sideways movement. Peter was delighted. For the previous few years his instruction was to prepare flat pitches that lasted four days, something that did not really challenge his skills and utilise his vast experience.

I quickly developed a good instinct for negotiating too, something I still have these days. Against Lancashire in our opener, in a game heavily rain affected, I managed to persuade their captain John Crawley to let us chase 260 in 78 overs. I got the impression that Lancashire thought it would be easy to roll us over but already we had become a pretty tight unit and we won with two balls to spare thanks to a gutsy half-century from a Durham University student called Robin Martin-Jenkins, who was at home on his holidays before going back to complete his degree course.

As well as myself, Sussex had signed Wasim Khan, the opening batsman from Warwickshire, but there was still a fair bit of inexperience in our side. Neil Taylor, who gave Sussex a couple of good years after a great career with Kent, offered a lot of nous in the middle order with Pete, but there were a lot of players in our team for my first game who had played very few first-class matches, guys like Toby Peirce, Rajesh Rao, Keith Newell and James Kirtley. Michael Bevan had not arrived by then and it was obvious that our strength lay in our seam bowling attack. The 'awesome foursome' – as they became known – all played against Lancashire: Kirtley, Jason Lewry, RMJ and Mark Robinson.

I rated Jason and James as among the best new-ball pairs in the country. I had encountered James before at Derbyshire and remembered him as someone who ran in hard all day although initially I wasn't entirely convinced about him. He was left out of the side a few times in those early weeks of the Adams era.

We had the experienced Paul Jarvis as another option and where possible I tried to play a slow bowler. A cheerful leg-spinner called Amer Khan was on the staff and Bev could also bowl his chinamen.

I must also admit that when I came to Sussex I didn't see much of a future for Mark Robinson. He'd been on the circuit for a while but wasn't a bowler who had ever troubled me. He wasn't particularly quick but I have played with few cricketers with more determination than Robbo and he soon changed my mind about him. In the first winter after he'd come to Sussex he had worked with Pete on how to make him more of a threat. Pete told him he would stand up to him and initially, like all bowlers of similar pace, Robbo considered this a personal affront. But once he got over the shock he became an integral part of the team. Batsmen couldn't step out of their crease anymore and Pete got him to bowl stump to stump. Because of this accuracy and the seam movement he got he offered great control. He could also bowl long spells, sometimes up to 12 overs, and didn't mind operating up the slope at Hove and into the wind. All of a sudden the opposition found themselves going nowhere and they would take liberties. Between them, our seam quartet took 180 wickets in 1998 and Robin only took part in eight games. They played a big part in ensuring we achieved our main goal which was to finish in the top eight and qualify for the Benson & Hedges Super Cup in 1999.

While I still had reservations about James, I knew straight away what a key bowler Jason Lewry would be for me. Back then Jason was a bit of a one-trick pony. With the new ball he could get even great players out but it was often more difficult for him during his second and third spells when the ball was doing less. In those early years Jason would often pick up a couple of early wickets then come back with the second new ball and wipe out the tail. It wasn't until 2003, when Mushtaq Ahmed and then Rana Naved taught him the art of reverse swing, that Jason became an outstanding bowler. He never had much confidence in his own ability and, by his own admission, he didn't enjoy his one experience with England on an A tour to Zimbabwe during that winter of 1998/99. Jason hated leaving Sussex, never mind the country and was really homesick. He should have got another chance to play for his country though. When you think of some of the players who did play Test cricket during his time it's amazing that someone who ended up with more than 600 first-class wickets did not get a chance.

It also helped in my first year that we had a batsman as good as Michael Bevan in our team. I rate Bev as one of the top five players I have played alongside. A lot was made during his career of his struggles against the short ball at Test level and it probably cost him a longer international career with Australia. But he was a wonderful technician and a remorseless accumulator; almost robotic at times in the way he built an innings. He kept thing simple and trusted in his technique and I admired him a great deal.

If he let himself down in any way it was his reluctance to accept that other people had a different way of approaching the game; he was a very intense individual who invariably would be the first person to speak at team meetings after Pete and I had asked for feedback from the team. The message was always the same, 'Look, you guys have got to understand this is the way it should be.' Bev's way, the Australian way. I remember specifically asking him before one gathering to hold fire and let the others open up. But as soon as I stopped speaking Bev was on his feet. I collared him afterwards. 'Why did you butt in?' 'Well, you said we were all part of the same team and that includes me so I thought I'd give my opinion.' It was that black and white for Bev.

He hated the excuse culture which was prevalent in county cricket back then and still is I guess. He didn't suffer fools and was very taciturn in his dealings with the press, which didn't paint Sussex in a good light. Journalists would often complain to me that any interview with Bev had to be conducted on the hoof, while he walked back to his car to go home after a day's play as the reporters thrust a tape recorder in his direction and tried to keep up. Not all his team-mates were enamoured with his forthright opinions but the senior boys, especially Mark Robinson who was in charge of the fines committee, took great delight in bringing him down a peg or two if they felt it necessary and Bev generally took it in the spirit in which it was intended.

Batting with him could be quite intimidating but he was so good at managing situations, particularly batting with the tail. I remember one game when he was joined by Jason Lewry, who wasn't the bravest if the bowling was above 70mph, and Jason proceeded to play a few frantic swipes outside off stump. At the end of the over Bev marched down with instructions. 'Look, this is what you've got to do. Watch the ball, stand still and hit it as hard as you can along the ground.' That was it. No chit-chat. Jason did exactly as he was told and drilled the next one to deep extra for a single, enabling Bev to get back down to the danger end so he could manipulate the strike, something he was very good at. They put on 30 or 40 runs and Jason came back feeling ten feet tall. We had our moments but I got on well with Bev. We travelled to away games and our wives became close friends. Sam still keeps in touch with Tracy Bevan these days and when we've been to Australia we have always hooked up with them for a couple of days.

My own form that first season was good. I topped the Sussex first-class averages with 1,174 runs at 41.92 and at Chelmsford in early season I became only the third player, along with C.B. Fry and Alan Butcher, to score two hundreds in the same game for different counties. I also remember making 54 in a Benson & Hedges Cup game at Lord's when I smashed Angus Fraser flat and hard back past him and the ball hit the brickwork next to the doors leading into the Long Room. The indentation is still there to this day. I know because every time I go to Lord's I check!

We won six Championship games and finished seventh. Objective achieved. We had also set our stall out from day one to make gains on our rivals in terms of our attitude and work ethic. We would always be at the ground and warming up before the opposition and when we did so we looked like a team. There was a professionalism and structure to everything we did and we had identified young players who bought into our ethos and gave them a chance, even if they weren't as talented as some of the more experienced players. A great example of that was Jamie Carpenter, someone who wasn't too hung up about his game and who just gave it his best.

We had quickly become a team greater than the sum of its individual parts which I soon became aware from Pete and others at the club was in stark contrast to previous Sussex teams who had more individual talent but lacked unity. Back then, for Sussex to be successful a four-day game was a real physical effort for all of us. It wasn't until Mushtaq Ahmed came and used his individual brilliance to help us claim victories in three and sometimes two days that winning wasn't always a long grind. By then the work ethic and team culture had become so ingrained at Sussex, allowing Mushy to flourish.

After my brief taste of international cricket at the end of May I came back and had a good one-day season, scoring 600 runs although our 16th place finish in the Sunday League, while two places better than 1997, was disappointing.

I also got my first hat-trick, even though it was several months before I discovered the fact. We played Middlesex under lights and among my victims were the two Fraser brothers, Angus and Alastair. Alastair was my third wicket but then there was a lengthy rain delay and when we came back out I didn't initially bring myself back on. But later I got Richard Johnson and Gus out to finish with 5-16. Not bad for someone who'd taken three wickets in ten years in the one-day league before then, but reward for the fact that I worked hard on my bowling that year and discovered that with the white Reader ball, which tended to get very soft quite quickly, at my military medium pace my in-swingers were quite hard to hit. It was only when a Sussex member wrote to me during the winter that I realised I'd taken a hat-trick.

The game was played under lights, one of several day-night matches we staged at Hove that year which proved popular with the Sussex supporters and another innovation Tony Pigott brought to the club. Others, like starting certain Championship matches later so that people could see a session after work, were less well received but Sussex were getting a reputation for forward-thinking leadership on and off the field. Dave Gilbert had arrived from Surrey as Tony's assistant and director of cricket to provide some experience on the cricket side behind the scenes. At the time I thought it was an odd appointment because at The Oval Tony had worked under Dave when he coached Surrey's second team. Pete and I were largely left to get on with running the team and we welcomed the lack of interference. In my first season I can only remember one meaningful conversation with Dave which came during a rain-affected game against Leicestershire at Grace Road.

On the third day I had begun tentative negotiations with Chris Lewis, their captain, about setting up a game on the final day. Pete's view was that we had to try and be positive but I was concerned that we could risk too much and end up losing. Dave was at Hove but had rung Pete and then called me, concerned that Pete's inexperience as a coach would end up costing us the game. Up until then Pete and I had agreed on everything in terms of team selection and game management and for the first time I would have to overrule him. Bev felt the same as Pete and that we should try and set something up but the equation Leicestershire were offering wasn't enough of an incentive and we ended up batting through the final day in front of a handful of spectators with Bev getting 149 not out. Afterwards I told Pete about the conversation I'd had with Dave. His reaction did not surprise me. Why was the director of cricket intervening in a matter that should have been decided by the coach and captain?

It was the start of an unhealthy relationship between Pete and Dave, who by now increasingly had the ear of our chairman, Don Trangmar. I don't think Dave necessarily coveted Pete's job – he'd done that at Surrey – but he wanted to manoeuvre himself into a position whereby he had a measure of control over Pete and myself. Pete was still finding his way as a coach and in the first couple of months he combined the role with that of a player before concentrating on coaching. Like Bev, Dave was very sure of his own beliefs with regard to coaching and struggled with the notion that someone else might have a different view. For my part I didn't manage the situation very well. It brought home to me that there was more to captaincy than merely making decisions about the team. Dave had also identified areas where he felt Tony was underperforming and when some of Tony's hunches didn't come off Dave wasn't slow in coming forward and undermining him. He had coveted Tony's job virtually from the moment he arrived and he didn't care who knew. He even told Tony, who by the start of 1999 was increasingly focussed on external matters relating to the club.

One of Tony's last appointments was a business manager called Adam Tarrant who persuaded him and the committee to invest £40,000 in a TV marketing campaign designed to increase membership. It was unheard of among county clubs to market themselves in this way but appealed to Tony's entrepreneurial spirit. Our one-day team had been rebranded the Sussex Sharks and the theme of the campaign was a shark swimming around whose face eventually morphed into yours truly. When we saw the final cut it was like something from a kids' TV programme. If you'd seen it on *Rainbow* you'd have laughed, it was that bad. It had no discernible effect on membership and in fact it probably dissuaded a few people from signing up. When Tony left Sussex in the winter of 1999 the club had just announced a loss of £200,000, which was a shock to the committee, who had been used to announcing small profits. It all counted against him when it came down to whether he or Dave would depart. I was in South Africa with England when Pete rang to tell me Tony had become the victim of a power struggle. I was very disappointed. No one had done more than him to get me to Sussex and I felt I had lost one of my main allies.

By the start of 1999 Dave was making the big cricket decisions, one of which was to award me a new six-year contract just a year into the five-year deal I had signed when I came to the club. At the end of it I was to get a benefit in recognition of the years I'd had at Derbyshire before heading to Hove. This was an example of Dave's forward thinking, although the length of the contract again raised questions among my critics about how much I was being paid. In fact I didn't receive a pay rise at all but I was still happy to sign. The family was settled and we had just brought our first house in Bolney, having lived in a rented place for a while.

Another of Dave's good decisions was to bring Michael Di Venuto in as replacement for Bev, who was unavailable because of Australia commitments. Although he had played a few one-day internationals Diva (not dee-va, he was far from being that!) was an unknown quantity but he quickly settled in and had a terrific season. He and Glamorgan's experienced campaigner Tony Cottey, who had also joined us along with Richard Montgomerie, the former Northamptonshire opener, gave the batting a much more solid look. Early in the season Diva and Cotts both scored hundreds as we chased down 455 to beat Gloucestershire at Hove and establish a new record for Sussex's highest total in the fourth innings. Square of the wicket, Diva was prolific and he was a wonderful team man. By the end of the season a few of the lads were privately hoping that he rather than Bev would return in 2000.

It was the year the Championship would be split into two with the top nine forming the new First Division. Getting into the top flight and improving our one-day form were the targets we set at the start of the season and we achieved one and came desperately close to the other.

My one-day form that season got me back into the England team. My first-class record in 1999 of 956 runs with only one century was modest but I scored 1,011 runs in limited-overs cricket including 798 runs as we won 13 of our 16 games to clinch promotion to the First Division of the new National League. Diva had formed a pretty effective opening partnership with Richard Montgomerie and I would often come in at number three with a good base having already been established. There are so many highlights. My love affair with the Castle Ground at Arundel began that summer when I scored 163 off 107 balls against Middlesex, a Sussex record that still stands. By then every time I went to the crease in a one-day game I knew I would score runs. Everything was coming off. That day I was on 97 and drilled a ball from Ben Hutton back towards him with such ferocity that I was staggered when he stuck out a hand and managed to parry it. It must have hurt because in his frustration he hurled the ball back at the wicketkeeper, David Nash, and missed the stumps by two feet and the ball sped to the boundary to bring up my century.

In the Benson & Hedges Super Cup I made 73 in a quarter-final win over Lancashire at Old Trafford a couple of days after I scored 51 in a NatWest Trophy tie against Cumberland in Kendal when one of my sixes was caught one-handed by Don Trangmar in front of the pavilion. Winning at Old Trafford gave us such confidence and we ought to have gone all the way to Lord's for a final. Chasing 242 to beat Gloucestershire at Bristol in the semi we were well placed at 176/3 but when I was last out for 88 we had collapsed and been bowled out for 217.

In the Championship we won six games, one more than two of the sides who finished in the top nine. We headed to Edgbaston for our final game knowing that victory or a good draw would probably be enough to get us the right side of the line but they had prepared a green top for their battery of seamers and we were rolled over for 99 in the first innings and lost inside two days. I was furious and when I spoke to the press I didn't hold back, calling Warwickshire's approach 'blatant cheating' and demanding an enquiry by the ECB. Nothing happened of course and instead we headed over to Derby to prepare for the final game of the National League season knowing that victory would secure the title.

I was fretting a bit during the two spare days we had between the games. The day after the season finished I was due to meet up with the England lads ahead of the South Africa tour for fitness testing so when I took a phonecall from David Graveney to warn me that my criticism of Warwickshire was likely to get me into trouble I spent the next couple of hours fretting about the consequences of my outburst.

Don was there and I spoke to him and Pete at length before deciding I would offer an apology to the ECB secretary Tim Lamb. As I was about to call him Pete grabbed the phone and persuaded me it might not be a good idea. A few seconds later, as the other lads tried to control their giggles, I realised I had been the victim of a hoax call, the perpetrator Wasim Khan who, to his day, is convinced the reason we released him at the end of 2000 was because of his surprisingly plausible impersonation of the chairman of selectors!

We went into the game at Derby with promotion secure but we were desperate to win the trophy. With Somerset just two points behind we knew only victory would do but with rain pouring down and Somerset on their way to beating Northamptonshire things looked bleak. But mercifully there was a break in the weather and with Sky

Sports covering the game live and anxious to show any sort of match we eventually started a 10-over game with second team coach Keith Greenfield, who had come up to support the lads, drafted into the team as an extra batsman wearing my spare blue uniform. Keith was there at the end too to hit the winning runs in a seven-wicket victory with five balls to spare. With England training the next day I left the lads to their celebrations at a sensible hour but I did establish a tradition that I maintained throughout the rest of my career by sleeping with the trophy next to me.

\* \* \* \* \*

A year after we'd enjoyed the champagne-soaked reverie at Derby, Pete and I met with the Sussex committee to fight for our jobs. If 1999 had been one of my most enjoyable years as captain then 2000 was by far the worst. I was playing angry and doing neither my team-mates, the club nor myself any good at all. If I had lost the captaincy I couldn't have blamed Sussex. It had been that bad.

South Africa had been a dispiriting experience and given the way my England career finished there hadn't really been any closure for me. When I reported back at Hove two months after coming back early from the tour I hadn't heard from David Graveney or Nasser Hussain, the captain, about whether I had any sort of future as an England player. I still felt I was good enough but the reality was I was in denial. I'd had my opportunity, squandered it, and I knew deep down that I wasn't good enough to get another chance. If I had been told that by a member of the England management I would have been able to put it to bed and concentrated on trying to improve on what we'd achieved at Sussex the previous year. I was not in a good place, either as a person or as captain and two incidents early in the season brought this sharply into focus.

We played Essex at Chelmsford needing to win to reach the knockout stages of the Benson & Hedges Cup, which had reverted back to its traditional format of group matches followed by quarter-finals. Nasser was Essex's captain and I was more fired up to perform than I think I'd ever been. We were stuck in on a typically damp early-season pitch and were 28/2 when Michael Bevan walked out to join me. I warned him that Ronnie Irani and Mark Ilott were hooping it around corners but Bev hit his first two balls from Irani to the boundary and I took the lead from that. Bev finished with 157 not out and I scored 122 as we added a record 271 for the fourth wicket. Every time I found the boundary or cleared the rope I had a little look to gauge Nasser's reaction but he was as inscrutable as always.

Essex lost wickets regularly chasing 317 and when Danny Law, a former Sussex player of course, came in it was a pretty hopeless cause. He smashed a few boundaries before James Kirtley bowled him a full toss that he swung into the deep. As he was running towards the umpire, Vanburn Holder, Danny kept shouting 'No ball!' as he questioned the legitimacy of the delivery. Vanburn upheld his decision and Danny was already halfway back to the pavilion when he looked up to see the rest of his team-mates urging him to turn around and have another go at trying to get Vanburn to change his decision, or at least consult with Tony Clarkson, who was standing at square leg. We had converged as a group to celebrate and when we saw Danny I told him he was out of order and with one hand gave him a push back towards the pavilion. The atmosphere afterwards wasn't great. Words were exchanged on the balcony as we walked past their dressing room to get to ours but we thought that was the end of it.

A few days later Dave Gilbert called me into his office and handed me a three-page handwritten letter from Nasser that had been copied and sent to the ECB alleging that I had forcibly struck Danny and also accused me of using foul and abusive language. Essex were demanding an investigation and that became inevitable now the England captain was involved. David hired a lawyer and six weeks later we all trooped off to Lord's for the hearing. On our side was a journalist whose impartial description of what happened backed up my own assertion that there was no malice intended in my action. In hindsight it was something that should have been sorted out afterwards with an apology and a handshake but having scored a hundred in front of the England captain I was in no mood in the immediate aftermath to back down. There was contact though, and I was fined £500 although I was cleared of swearing at Danny. In the corridor at Lord's after the verdict was announced I saw Danny and we shook hands. He agreed with me that it was a heat of the moment reaction and that no malice was intended. I certainly got the impression that he never intended to take it this far. The whole thing had been a costly waste of time but I was glad it was over and the following day I scored 90 against Glamorgan to help us win our first Championship match of the season.

Between the incident at Chelmsford and the hearing was another incident when my conduct, if anything, deserved a bigger punishment. We were playing Warwickshire at Hove and shortly before tea on the third day, as we battled to stave off an innings defeat, the umpire David Constant gave me out leg before to Ashley Giles to a ball

*Babe in arms. Mum, dad and David shortly after I came into the world at the cottage in Whitwell.*

*Ride 'em cowboy. On a camping trip to France.*

*Aged six, having just gone to school for the first time.*

*In the back garden at Whitwell with David, who thought he was the right-handed David Gower!*

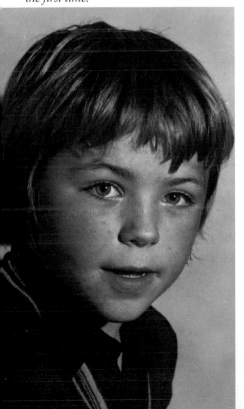

*National Cricket Association Young Cricketers, 1987. Among my team-mates was Joe Root's dad, Matthew, sitting on the right-hand end of the front row.*

*In Northern Ireland in 1987, with the NCA North squad.*

*Derbyshire days. Sam used to style my hair then.*

*Dickie Bird told me to stick to batting!*

*Sachin Tendulkar walks off to the applause of myself and the England team after scoring his first Test century at Old Trafford in 1990.*

*The first of my two catches as an England sub fielder against India in 1990.*

*The Derbyshire squad with our Sunday League title, 1990.*

*Making my Test debut at Johannesburg in 1999. We were 2 for 4 when I walked out to bat!*

*Batting during the one-day series in South Africa in 2000. I had to fly home early when Sophie was taken ill – and was told I could not rejoin the tour.*

*At Headingley in 1998 after making my England debut in the one-day series.*

*England at Cape Town, 2000.*

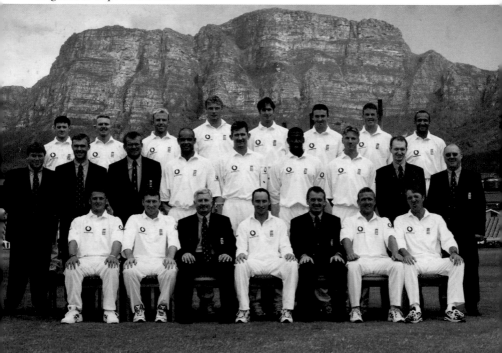

My first day at Hove with chief executive Tony Pigott, who did so much to persuade me to move to Sussex.

Joining Sussex in 1997.

Celebrations on the balcony at Hove. Sussex's long wait for the County Championship was finally over.

All mine. The first title was extra special as I'd struggled for form until the last few weeks of the season.

*Gotcha! A slip catch safely held during my first season with Sussex.*

*Forward pass? Touch rugby with the Sussex boys.*

*Good times with Umer Rashid.*

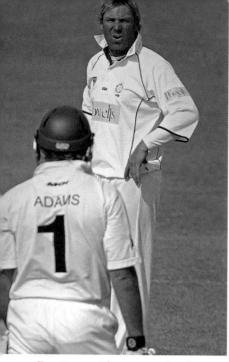

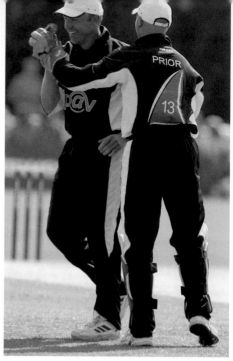

Fronting up. There was no love lost between Shane Warne and I, although I loved going up against him when he was Hampshire captain.

I loved batting with Matt Prior, in whom I saw a lot of my characteristics. Not so sure about that kit though!

Celebrating Sussex's first Championship with Peter Moores. We enjoyed some great moments as coach and captain.

*Mark Robinson was a different coach to Peter Moores, but I had a very successful relationship with Robbo.*

*Winning Sussex's first Lord's final for 20 years was one of the many highlights of a fabulous year.*

*On the front foot against Durham at Horsham in 2007 when I scored a hundred.*

*With Mushy after our 2007 Championship triumph. We waited all afternoon before we could start celebrating.*

*Legends. Murray Goodwin's runs and Mushtaq Ahmed's wickets were crucial to our three Championships.*

*Last but by no means least. With my final trophy as captain after that memorable one-day game at Trent Bridge in 2008.*

*Surrey man. My first press conference at The Oval.*

*Celebrating at Lord's in 2011 with Rory Hamilton-Brown after we won the Pro40 title. A year later he had left Surrey and my days were numbered.*

*Doing what I love most. Coaching session at The Oval in 2012.*

*Tom Maynard.*

*My girls.*

*Georgia coaching in the South African townships with the England Academy.*

*Sophie, Mollie and Georgia.*

*Team-building with the Netherlands in South Africa, January 2015.*

which I thought was going well down the leg side. There had been quite a bit of sympathy from the Warwickshire players when I'd been dismissed by Connie, lbw to Alan Richardson, in the first innings, not least from their wicketkeeper Keith Piper who'd only joined in the appeal on both occasions after the bowler, a tell-tale sign that he didn't think I was out. The second dismissal happened in the last over before tea and when I came off I threw my bat on to my kit and marched around to the umpires' room which back then was at the far end of the pavilion at Hove, under the committee room, still wearing my pads. I barged straight in without even knocking and just unloaded on poor Connie, an umpire I'd known for many years and someone I greatly respected. 'What the fuck have I done to you? Here I am battling to score runs to get back into the England team and you have sawn me off not once but twice. Have you got something against me?'

Connie was shocked and started crying. As soon as I saw the tears the realisation of what I had done dawned on me. I knew I had made a massive mistake and spent the next couple of minutes apologising profusely to Connie and George Sharp, the other umpire. They were both pretty good about the situation and Connie didn't even mention it in his match report but the damage had been done. The press box at Hove overlooked the umpires' room and a couple of reporters had seen me barging in. When I came out they were waiting to find out what had been said – whether it was my version of events or Connie's they didn't really care. Chris Adams was fighting the authorities again and that was always going to make good copy.

Connie came out to resume umpiring duties and was surrounded by the Warwickshire players anxious to deny that they had questioned his decision-making and making me out to be some sort of ogre. How I got away without censure from the ECB for that little fracas I will never know.

England had a twin series against Zimbabwe and West Indies that year and when I wasn't named in the squads it helped me concentrate a bit more on the day job. Michael Bevan had come back and almost single-handedly got us into a position where we could push for promotion in the Championship. He scored four hundreds in five innings in July to take us to the top of the Second Division but at the beginning of August was called back to Australia to play in a one-day tournament, having scored 2,183 runs in all competitions.

We had a team meeting where I stressed that I felt we had the resources to finish the job even without our talisman but the truth was we'd become heavily reliant on him. Of our batsmen I was the only other player to score more than 750 runs and James Kirtley and Jason Lewry had bowled more than 1,000 overs and taken 114 wickets between them with negligible support.

We lost back-to-back games to Northamptonshire before heading to Colwyn Bay to play Glamorgan for a game that has gone down in Sussex history for all the wrong reasons. Our preparations were not ideal. When we got to the team hotel in Llandudno we discovered there weren't enough rooms so Jason and I, who had brought our wives up with us, had to decamp to a bed and breakfast down the road. And any hopes of rallying the lads at a team meeting on the evening before the game were scuppered when Billy Taylor and Umer Rashid rang to say they had got to Cardiff and asked how far they were from Colwyn Bay. About 200 miles was the answer.

It had been a gruelling season for all our seamers and Billy had travelled because we were going to rest one of the established quartet, but when we got to the ground the next morning we saw a pitch with a good covering of grass and all of a sudden they were desperate to play in anticipation of rich pickings, especially when I won the toss and stuck Glamorgan in. Back then counties had the choice of whether they used Reader or Dukes balls. Our bowlers preferred Dukes because they swung more but James Kirtley had to choose from a box of Readers, which tended to stop swinging quite quickly. All of a sudden they all wanted to rest again but by then Billy had been given the bad news and was on his way back to Sussex, via a more direct route.

Sure enough Jason's first ball went around corners but his second, which was just outside off stump, was launched on to the bank at one end for six by Matthew Elliott. By lunch Glamorgan were 150-odd without loss and when they finally declared on the second afternoon we'd taken three wickets in 162 overs and Steve James was 309 not out in a total of 718. I scored 156, my only Championship hundred of the season, and Umer Rashid made his maiden century as we managed to drag it out until the fourth day before losing by an innings. But mentally and physically we looked like a team running on empty and that manifested itself in some poor shot selection. Robin Martin-Jenkins struggled against the short ball at that stage of his career and when he was caught at deep midwicket the delivery after the bowler, Steve Watkin, had put a fielder there and then dug one in short I couldn't hold back. I described the shot as 'brainless', which made for a great one-word headline on the back page of the next day's *Brighton Evening*

*Argus*. Dave Gilbert faxed a copy of the page to the team hotel, his way of asking what the hell was going on. Not only was Dave furious, so was Robin's father Christopher, the eminent cricket writer and broadcaster who had the ear of quite a few of our committee members.

Dave pulled me in when we got back to Hove and I apologised to Robin who, to his credit, told me he should have been the one apologising for playing such a poor shot. The whole incident was indicative of the state we were in at the time. A day before the Glamorgan game the club chose to announce the departures of five players, Toby Peirce, Wasim Khan, Shaun Humphries, Andy Patterson and Justin Bates, which, in hindsight, was pretty bad timing. There were still three games to go and all might still have had a part to play.

We lost four of our last five in the Championship and when Gloucestershire beat us in two days at Hove in the final game of the season we had gone from top to bottom in the space of six weeks. We had also finished bottom of the National League First Division and were relegated after one season. When we went out to start our second innings against Gloucestershire, Don Trangmar had gone off to the dentist. An hour and a half later he returned to discover we'd been bowled out for 71 in 25 overs. The club had decided to present the end of season awards after the match, regardless of the result. Amazingly, quite a few people stayed on to watch but they were in a restless mood. Sussex supporters were losing faith with the Moores– Adams regime and we sensed they weren't alone.

A few days later we had to face the committee and before the meeting I was convinced one of us, more likely Peter I felt, would lose their job. If it was me, I could at least console myself with a return to the ranks under a new captain. Pete had a lot more to lose. Dave Gilbert had clearly primed each committee member to ask a difficult question but Pete fronted up. He accepted mistakes had been made and pleaded for a chance to go away and work out how to improve. It was like a closing statement in a court case before the jury goes away to consider its verdict.

It was then that Don Trangmar came to our rescue and, in hindsight, made one of the boldest decisions in the history of Sussex cricket. 'There has been too much blood-letting at this club in recent years and the committee need to take responsibility,' he said. 'Having appointed Peter and Chris two years ago we now need to back them. We need to be patient.' Don finished by warning us not to waste any time in ensuring that 2000 was merely a setback after the progress we'd made in the previous two years and which probably helped earn us a reprieve. There was to be no vote. Don shut his notebook and ended the meeting. We had survived. Just.

It was the players' end of season party and when we got to the pub a few minutes later there was a big cheer. At least, we thought, the lads still believed in us. We'd had a reprieve but we knew that if things did not improve in 2001 we'd be gone.

# 9

# England

I HAVE absolutely no doubt that moving from Derbyshire to Sussex enhanced my chances of finally representing my country. Of course, there is an argument that if I'd continued to score as heavily for Derbyshire as I did in 1996 that eventually I would get an opportunity but I'm not sure. Where England were concerned, Derbyshire traditionally provided seam bowlers like the great Les Jackson and Cliff Gladwin. There was the odd batsman – Kim Barnett – the occasional spinner like Geoff Miller and, of course, the brilliant Bob Taylor behind the stumps but I must admit I'm struggling to name any other England players from Derbyshire who weren't seamers. Denis Smith, who scored more than 20,000 runs for the county in the pre-war era, for instance, was never called up.

The wickets Derbyshire played on suited fast or medium-fast bowlers who hit the seam and could swing the ball. To a certain extent, it's still the same now.

My move to Hove certainly made the headlines, not least the speculation over what I was earning for my labours. I didn't turn down any interview requests during that winter and spring of 1997/98. I would play a straight bat to questions about my wages easily enough. I just wanted to remind people of my record for Derbyshire and why I felt I deserved an opportunity to play for my country. I didn't see anything wrong in that.

Towards the end of 1997, shortly before I decided to join Sussex, I spoke to David Graveney, the chairman of selectors. He told me that I was still in their thoughts but warned me, in the nicest possible way, to ease back on the interviews and juicy soundbites. I took it with a pinch of salt. A lot of knowledgeable cricket writers were openly questioning in their columns why I kept being ignored, even for A tours. If it made the selectors feel a bit uncomfortable then so be it.

Back then, A tours were still relatively new. For about three years from around 1993 I listened to every single England squad announcement on the radio, even when I knew I had no realistic chance of being involved. As the names were announced alphabetically as soon as they got to Mark Butcher, for instance, I'd turn it off.

I was out-scoring my supposed rivals but still nothing. In 1996 only Glamorgan opener Steve James and the prolific Graham Gooch scored more first-class runs than my tally of 1,742 for Derbyshire but I was ignored for the A tour to Australia in favour of guys like Jason Gallian, Anthony McGrath, Owais Shah and Michael Vaughan. All fine players and most a few years younger than me but having scored so heavily that year, and not even had a phonecall to say I was close, was desperately frustrating.

The nearest I'd been to the international set-up was when the selectors picked 12 players to train as part of the Whittingdale Programme, a coaching scheme funded by an investment banker called Patrick Whittingdale which started in 1993. He pumped in £2m over the next three years to try and help develop the next generation of England cricketers, which was some financial commitment especially at a time when the fortunes of the England Test team were at a pretty low ebb. The chosen players would spend a few a few weeks netting at Lilleshall before heading out to Portugal for warm-weather training prior to Christmas.

In 1992 Peter Bowler and I had good seasons for Derbyshire. Peter scored more than 2,000 runs in the Championship and although I didn't get anywhere near that, I did score the fastest hundred in the county's history. My one-day form was decent and I seemed to fit the criteria as a young and emerging player who could benefit from spending time on the programme and a winter working on honing my technique.

When that winter's intake of 12 was named I wasn't in it. Guys like Nick Knight, Ben Smith and Ronnie Irani were but my record compared favourably to a lot of the six batsmen (together with six bowlers) who were chosen so I asked our coach at the time, Phil Russell, to ring Micky Stewart, who was coming to the end of his time as England team manager. Phil asked why I hadn't been invited. 'Hasn't he?' came the reply. 'Oh, there must have been a mistake. Send him down anyway and we'll have a look at him.' Have a look at him? I felt like some youngster who'd turned up on the off chance of a trial.

So off I went to Lilleshall, slightly chastened that I was an afterthought but looking forward to pushing my claims nonetheless. When I showed up the other lads were a bit surprised that their ranks had been swelled to 13. The two coaches, Clive Radley and Bob Cottam, split the group into batsmen and bowlers. Micky told Bob to take me under his wing. 'But Grizz is a batsman Micky, he's not a bowler,' said Bob. Stewart looked a little puzzled. 'Is he? Well, there isn't really room for him with Clive.' Which is why I ended up bowling medium-pace shite all morning at the six batsmen before being sent back to Derbyshire. As a first experience of cricket at the 'top' level, it was pretty underwhelming.

Sussex may have been struggling for a few years when I joined them in 1997 but they were a county who had much more of a profile than Derbyshire. It helped, for instance, that Christopher Martin-Jenkins, the foremost voice in cricket both in print and on the radio at the time, was a Sussex man and that his son played for the county. Selectors would turn up at Hove on a regular basis. For starters, it was a lot easier to get to from London than Derby or Chesterfield. That might sound daft but it's true. And if I knew a selector was at the ground it definitely gave me more of an edge when I went out to bat. I was quite happy to be put under scrutiny.

Sussex started 1998 well. We beat Lancashire at Hove in a rain-affected opening Championship game with two balls to spare. I didn't make many runs – eight and 39 – but beating one of the big counties infused the team with confidence as well as their captain. The club were delighted. After what had gone on in 1996 it was just what we needed to launch the new era.

Our next Championship game was at Chelmsford. Despite modest scores against Lancashire I felt good at the crease. The pitch was pretty slow and I cashed in, becoming the third player to score hundreds in both innings (135 and 105) for two different counties. It was an odd trio: C.J. Adams, C.B. Fry (Hampshire and Sussex) and Alan Butcher (Surrey and Glamorgan). In fact, I did it twice for Derbyshire back in 1995 and then again the following year. Nasser Hussain ended up in charge of Essex after Paul Pritchard went off with shin splints during the game and I could see straight away that he wasn't dissimilar to me in the way he led his team. He was hard-bitten, had a shrewd tactical brain and totally immersed himself in the job. I must admit I was impressed.

Two hundreds in the same game was quite a story, even if the game fizzled out to a draw because of rain. A couple of days later the first England squad of the season was due to be announced for three one-dayers against South Africa and most of the papers speculated that I would be included. Christopher Martin-Jenkins got the squad spot-on in his preview and when I saw C.J. Adams among the 14 names he had chosen I was thrilled. I knew that newspaper correspondents got tipped off as to who was going to be involved ahead of squad unveilings.

On the day before the Sunday squad announcement Sam and I travelled north for the first time since the move to Sussex. We had a National League game against Nottinghamshire at Trent Bridge and the hotel where we stayed, which was halfway between Nottingham and Derby, was also being used by Warwickshire, who were playing Derbyshire the following day. Nick Knight, of Warwickshire, was there and Graveney called him on the Saturday evening with the good news. He was in the squad but when I went to bed that night there had been no phonecall.

A few days earlier I'd done an interview with Peter Hayter of the *Mail on Sunday*. He'd asked me if leaving Derbyshire with a year left on my contract had felt like playing a 'get out of jail free card'. I couldn't disagree. His piece was pretty fair, but the headline 'Leaving Derbyshire felt like playing my get out of jail free card' did not do me many favours. When I read that on Sunday morning I felt pretty depressed. There was still no phonecall from Graveney and now I thought I'd been stitched up a bit by the paper.

I was getting my gear ready to head over to Trent Bridge when Graveney called. His tone was serious, I felt like the headmaster back at Repton was addressing me. He told me the article had been unhelpful and warned me for the second time in a few months that it might be wise to tone down my utterances in the public prints. Then, after the telling-off, he matter-of-factly added, 'I am about to give you the news you've been waiting for.' No congratulations, just instructions on where to meet the rest of the squad the next day in London and who to report to! It wasn't quite how I expected to hear the best news of my career but when I put the phone down I was absolutely thrilled. Sam was in tears and the rest of the Sussex boys were delighted for me. When I went out to bat later that day I was on top of the world. I scored a hundred, including three successive sixes off Paul Strang, and we won the game. The memories of that day are still crystal-clear. I will never forget it.

A couple of days later we met up at The Oval. My abiding memory of walking into the home dressing room for the first time were the pictures of great English statesmen on the walls. This was our coach David Lloyd's way of trying to find the inner patriot in us. There were images of Winston Churchill and Lord Kitchener among others with Churchill's famous wartime speeches playing quietly in the background. It does sound daft now, but back then it was considered quite an innovative way of bonding the boys together. I'm a proud Englishman so once I'd got used to seeing a picture of Churchill staring at me from above Adam Hollioake's peg in the dressing room I quite liked it. Did it inspire me? Probably not, but I admired Bumble for trying something different.

On TV commentary Bumble comes across as this gregarious, fun-loving person but I didn't see much evidence of it in the brief time I worked with him. He was quite quiet actually. There were no big speeches; no bursts of Churchillian oratory as we prepared to face the foe, in this case South Africa. Bumble has a deep-rooted competitive nature, which I guess was forged during his playing days when he took on Dennis Lillee and Jeff Thomson in their pomp without much protection or, on one famous occasion at Perth, none at all! He was capable of the odd spontaneous eruption of emotion. Occasionally he struggled to contain those emotions but he was good to work with. Honest, hard-working and not afraid to try things.

Another of his ideas was a 15-minute video that we watched of all the players in the squad doing great things. There was Alec Stewart crunching the ball through the covers, Matthew Fleming hoisting a six over long on, Mark Ealham knocking back off stump with an in-swinger. If you were one of the players featured it must have been quite inspiring. Unfortunately for me and Darren Maddy, who had also been called up, there was just a head and shoulders picture of us right at the end of the clip to get our competitive juices flowing.

Since moving to Sussex I'd been working once or twice a month on a one-to-one basis with Graham Gooch, who was on the selection panel. When I went into nets at The Oval for the first time Graham was standing next to the net with the other selector, Mike Gatting. If that felt quite intimidating it was nothing compared to when Darren Gough and Chris Lewis started charging in. I still regard it as the quickest net session I have ever faced. Lewis really took the bus off his back that day. He had a reputation for occasionally slipping himself and bowling fast when he needed to and he clearly regarded this as his pre-series audition. As preparation for facing Allan Donald and co. it couldn't have been any better. It was quite terrifying and a massive step up from what I had previously experienced at county level. But Gooch nodded his approval as I came out of the net and I felt good.

Bumble told me the night before that I would be playing. Nasser Hussain had been called into the squad at short notice because of an injury to Graham Thorpe and he would bat at number four, the place earmarked for me, and I had to move up to three. I was a bit disappointed not to be in the position I felt best suited me, especially as I felt I was a better one-day player than Hussain, but I would have quite happily batted at number 11. I slept well that night and when I arrived at The Oval on the Thursday morning of 21 May 1998 I could not have been in a better frame of mind. As I feared, Kim Barnett had exercised the right of reply offered to him by a journalist in the *Daily Mail* following my 'get out of jail free card' headline of a few days earlier, calling me a spoilsport and a crybaby. Regrettable, of course, but I didn't really give it much thought.

So this is what it is all about. International cricket. The buzz. The adrenalin rush. A big crowd in one of the most famous grounds in the world, but one I knew well and had enjoyed some success at in the past. The Oval is the closest ground in England to places like the MCG and the Wanderers in Johannesburg. A coliseum if you like, if on a slightly smaller scale. The attendance that overcast Thursday was 16,000, which meant it wasn't full but it looked pretty packed to me.

Alec Stewart and Nick Knight gave us a decent start with 58 for the first wicket against Shaun Pollock and Lance Klusener but then Allan Donald came on first change and bowled Stewart for 27. It was my turn.

As I made my way down the steps the noise from the stands was simply deafening, increasing in volume when the announcer read out my name. Sam was in the crowd, along with my Mum and Dad and David. It definitely felt like the supporters wanted me to do well.

Looking back, at that stage of my career I was probably technically as good as I have ever been. Thanks to the work I had done on the same ground with Les Stillman two years earlier I was playing side-on, my trigger movements were cohesive and when I went into the ball I felt confident enough to be able to hit it all around the wicket but especially through the off side between cover and mid-off. During those first few weeks of the 1998 season I was batting as well as I ever did. It was only later on that I became a bit more chest-on so I could open up scoring opportunities on the leg side again.

Donald and Hansie Cronje were bowling and, as I expected, it was hard work. There wasn't a lot of loose stuff but I felt I handled Donald's extra pace pretty well. I didn't feel nervous or overawed but I never felt properly settled either. I got to 25 when I pushed at a ball from Jacques Kallis, which just did enough off the seam, and I got a nick. At that stage of his career, South African wicketkeeper Mark Boucher had plenty of rough edges but he held on to the ball. It was an okay delivery but I wouldn't have got out to that sort of shot playing for Sussex. I was just a little tentative. I got a nice ovation coming off but I knew I'd missed out. It was a feeling I would experience all too often in my brief England career.

Knight made 64 before Jonty Rhodes brilliantly ran him out and thereafter the innings subsided a bit. It was quite a slow pitch but 223/9 from our 50 overs felt 20 to 30 runs short and although our two spinners, Robert Croft and Ashley Giles, took five wickets between them South Africa won by three wickets with eight balls to spare, Kallis making a classy 62 before Cronje (40) and Rhodes (39 not out) saw them over the line.

Prior to the second game at Old Trafford there had clearly been a discussion about the batting order involving coach, captain and senior players. There had been some speculation after The Oval that Matthew Fleming might play as a pinch-hitter but in the end Ali Brown was brought in at three, Hussain stayed where he was (he'd made 27 at The Oval) and I was bunted down to five. No explanation. Take it or leave it. Of course if I'd had 20 appearances to my name I would have sought out Lloyd as to why I'd gone from three to five and been ignored in the position where I'd scored the runs that had got me noticed in the first place. But I kept my own counsel. I sensed Adam Hollioake was having his own problems convincing Bumble and the selectors after a run of defeats that he was the right choice as captain so I didn't feel I could burden him either. He had enough on his plate.

Being demoted down the order shouldn't have got to me but it did. I didn't feel as energised as I had at The Oval and even though there were more people in the ground (19,000) the atmosphere was a bit flat. We kept them to 226/9, a total inflated by a half-century from Klusener, and with someone of Chris Lewis's mercurial talent coming in at number nine we fancied our chances of success with a strong batting line-up. Alec Stewart looked good until he was run out by Rhodes for 52 and when I came in I hardly got going before I was out, sawn off by my old pal Ray Julian the umpire.

Ray had a reputation as an 'outer'. He used to tell journalists that he 'liked to keep the game moving'. One reporter told me that if Ray was in charge of the match he was covering he'd only book in for two nights instead of three in anticipation of an early finish! He was a good umpire and a very likeable character but more often than not bowlers got the benefit of the doubt. I was on three and Pat Symcox, their burly off-spinner, was bowling. He got one to turn a little, it hit my pad and up went Ray's finger without a hint of deliberation. I went goggle-eyed watching the replay on TV when I got back to the dressing room. I must have seen it about 25 times and each time the ball pitched outside off stump by six or eight inches. We lost the game by 32 runs and with it the series.

I'd made a conscious effort since moving to Sussex to monitor, as captain, how players reacted to being dropped and how a negative response would impact on the atmosphere among the group. I'd banned the word 'sorry' and had short shrift for players who'd go into a massive sulk if they were left out. Now it was my turn to practise what I preached.

The third and final match in the series was at Headingley two days later, on a Bank Holiday Monday. We were 2-0 down in the rubber so I expected there to be changes to the team. Sure enough, Maddy came in and I was omitted with Fleming at first drop. I'd been told the day before I wouldn't be playing but rather than go into my shell I made sure my attitude was positive as it could be. I netted well and although I never got any feedback on how I'd done Adam did put his arm around my shoulder as we walked off after nets and thanked me. Graham Gooch was also positive.

He said it looked as if I could make the step up and the only thing now was to score heavily in county cricket to keep my name in the frame. We would go on working together for a while yet. Brown justified his inclusion with a 31-ball half-century as England won by seven wickets with 15 overs to spare but you could tell, with the series won, that South Africa lacked the intensity they had shown in the first two matches.

As I drove back home from Headingley I certainly didn't think my international career was over before it had really started. I looked at my peers in the team and felt, with one or two technical tweaks which Gooch and Peter Moores, the Sussex coach, could help me with, that I could do more than merely survive at that level. It had been a massive step up, far bigger looking back now than I had anticipated.

At the end of 1998 I was again left out of the touring squads. I had, by then, got used to it of course but having made my debut earlier that year and done well in my first season at Sussex I thought I might get a look-in. I spoke to Graveney who reiterated that there was still strong competition for places and that I had been considered. As a consolation prize, I was offered the captaincy of the Super 8s team who would take part in a new limited-overs competition in Australia. In its previous incarnation the tournament had been known as the Hong Kong Sixes. It wasn't quite what I wanted but it was still representing your country in an environment I'd not experienced before. Unfortunately, a few weeks later, the tournament was canned and I was left seeking alternative winter employment.

My agent at the time, Jonathan Barnett, came up with a couple of proposals: playing for Boland in the South African domestic competition or Canberra Comets in the Australian one-day competition. Sam was due to give birth to our second child, Sophie, at the time and I was undecided about whether to go away or stay at home. But Graveney suggested if I went to Australia and did well, and someone dropped out of the touring party that was contesting the one-day series after the Ashes, I'd be in pole position. Financially, it wasn't as good an offer as the one from Boland but, with Sam's blessing, I headed out to Canberra.

When the one-day squad was named I wasn't in it and after a few days in Canberra I was already beginning to regret my decision. I was distracted. Sam had a rough time when Sophie was born and ended up in hospital for a few days. I played three 50-over games for the Comets and didn't pull up any trees and with no prospect of linking up with England I decided to head home.

The only enjoyable experience of the trip was sharing a flat with the great Australian fast bowler Merv Hughes. Jeez, what a character. I remember after nets one night Merv decided we'd have a boys night in. He got some beer organised and I went off in search of a video, stopping off at the Chinese restaurant on the way home to pick up the takeaway he'd ordered by phone. When I got there it took about two minutes for the guy to bring our order to the counter. Merv had ordered the set meal for four! I just about finished off my quarter and left the rest to Merv. What a trencherman. He scoffed the lot then settled down to watch the video, patting his stomach contentedly like a pregnant mum.

As 1999 began I could at least reflect that I was now an England cricketer. I certainly believed my career was still on the rise. I was 28, in my peak years and convinced I would play for my country again. The only surprise for me was it took another 18 months for it to happen.

# 10

# Testing Times

WHEN he took over as England coach, Duncan Fletcher had stressed that he wanted to give any new players brought in an extended opportunity to see if they could crack it at international level. So while I was disappointed with my scores in the first Test of the South Africa series in Johannesburg I felt confident I would get another chance in the second match in Port Elizabeth.

Giving players time to settle in at the highest level was an approach practised by Australia and South Africa, the top two teams in the world at the time, as a matter of course. Jacques Kallis, for instance, only averaged 8.3 after his first five Tests. South Africa trusted in his talent and he repaid them for another 15 years.

If I'd been told I would definitely be playing the first three Tests it could, in hindsight, have helped me settle down a bit. I still hadn't had much feedback on what I needed to work on after Johannesburg so the pressure to get a score and keep my place was enormous. It was the same for Michael Vaughan, who had found the transition just as difficult.

Before the Test we played a four-day game in Durban against Kwazulu-Natal, whose team included a 16-year-old debutant from the local high school called Hashim Amla and an off-spinning all-rounder hidden down the order at number nine called Kevin Pietersen. Most of the first Test team played, which gave me confidence that we'd all get another chance. Alan Mullally and Chris Silverwood were injured and Chris Read got a game behind the stumps so Alec Stewart could have a rest.

It's a good job I went into the game pretty secure in the knowledge that I'd get another chance. I was out on the third day of a rain-affected game, bowled by Pietersen – who'd earlier scored 61 not out – for a duck! KP actually picked up four wickets, including Atherton, Vaughan and Hussain – who made 103, the first first-class hundred by an England batsman that year. He also bowled 55 overs on one of the flattest pitches I've ever played on. The game was drawn but a tranquil few days did allow the squad to regroup before we moved on to PE.

I let myself down in the second Test but as a side we were also let down by some shocking decisions by South African umpire Rudi Koertzen, who ended up trying to apologise to me through the media after he gave me out lbw in the second innings on the final day as the game was drifting towards a draw. The major incident took place in the second innings. Phil Tufnell was bowling beautifully and when Jacques Kallis pushed forward the ball turned to hit bat and pad and I managed to grab the ball with my hand underneath it at silly point. I knew I had caught it cleanly but Kallis stood his ground. I guess in similar circumstances I would probably have done the same. He was on 12 at the time and had been playing quite skittishly. The umpires, Koertzen and Steve Bucknor, referred it to the third umpire Dave Orchard, who only had access to replays from the South African TV coverage, which were not conclusive. On Sky, meanwhile, replays showed what I knew already – that it was a clean catch. Ironically, the South African board had made Sky's pictures available at Johannesburg but didn't use them in this Test.

Once he'd been reprieved Kallis started on me, 'You're a cheating fuck.' So I gave him some back. At the end of the over Nasser came over and told me to keep sledging him. To be honest, I was never the best sledger. I have heard some very amusing sledges during my career and I could certainly hold my own in a verbal confrontation but premeditated sledging? I couldn't do that to order and after a few minutes it calmed down and we got on with the game.

I felt bad. Kallis was within his rights to stay if he felt there was some doubt over the validity of the catch. It wasn't his fault that the umpires couldn't do their job properly. At the end of the session, as we were walking off, I apologised to him. He was very gracious at the time but I soon discovered that, as far as their players were concerned, I had become their main target.

We had them 146/5 when they batted first but then Lance Klusener came in and smashed a brilliant 174, his career best and the biggest score made at St George's Park. It was a pretty flat deck and we made a reasonable fist of replying to their 450 with 373, of which Atherton made 108 and I contributed 25. The positive I took from that innings was that I felt comfortable defending the ball against a pace attack which now included Nantie Hayward, who was quicker than both Allan Donald and Shaun Pollock but lacked, at that stage of his career, the control to go with it.

The problem I was discovering was that I never felt relaxed enough so that I could play my natural game, which was to attack the bowling. I felt a bit better than I had at the Wanderers but most of those 25 runs were deflections off an angled bat. What I was struggling to adjust to was the extra bounce Donald and Pollock in particular could get. I was used to English conditions where the ball tended to skid through.

In South Africa the ball got a different elevation, forcing you to play later and with a horizontal bat. When he got me out Pollock bowled slightly wide, short of a length and when I moved back to try and punch it through the off side I ended up getting a thick edge and Kallis took the catch, to his obvious delight of course, at third slip.

South Africa's second innings was a real go-slow affair. There didn't seem to be much urgency even after Kallis was reprieved and went on to make an undefeated 85. It meant their declaration was delayed until 30 minutes into the final day when we were left to chase 302, or defend 79 overs. We lost Atherton and Mark Butcher quickly and it needed Nasser to steady the ship with an unbeaten 70. He was waiting for me when I went out to bat with 20 overs left and the draw still far from secure.

Koertzen had angered us with four questionable decisions already: Mark Boucher and Gary Kirsten reprieved in the first and second innings respectively and Butcher and Vaughan given out in our second dig. Now it was my turn. Hansie Cronje had brought himself on to bowl and I was just looking to defend and bat out time.

He brought the field in, bowled me an in-swinger that struck the inside of my bat and deflected on to my pad before ballooning into the off side. Cronje half-heartedly appealed and, after what seemed like an age, Koertzen slowly raised his index finger. I had to go of course but I was fuming. Not only had I hit it, but the ball was probably missing the stumps by six inches. Out for one and no nearer establishing myself as a Test batsman. It was left to Nasser and Andy Caddick to bat out time for the draw. It seemed every time I batted with the captain there was some sort of incident. During one of the warm-up games prior to the first Test I found myself standing side by side with him after facing just two deliveries. I had called for a run, Nasser refused and I was left stranded as the bails were taken off at the other end. I walked off because he was going well even though the umpires weren't sure. At least Koertzen wasn't involved on that occasion.

A couple of days after the Port Elizabeth Test Koertzen was tracked down by a few of the English journalists and admitted he'd had a shocker. He even offered to meet with the team before the fifth Test at Centurion, when he was due to stand again, to placate us. The meeting never took place of course. What would it have achieved anyway? It was the latest in a succession of umpiring mistakes at the top level that had blighted the international game for years and eventually led to the appointment of two neutral umpires in Test matches.

At 122 days including the four one-dayers at the end, the tour was the longest England had undertaken since 1990. We prepared for the back-to-back Tests in Durban and Cape Town with a one-day game against a combined Border & Eastern Province team and four days in East

London against the same opposition. After getting a first-baller in the one-day match, one of four victims for the slow left-armer Robin Peterson, I batted with a lot more freedom in the four-day game, which was severely rain affected. Darren Maddy had scored 133 when we won the one-day fixture convincingly and he got another opportunity in the next match, opening with Mark Butcher with me coming in at three.

Darren made 14 but I played fluently, hitting 11 boundaries in my 59 not out before it rained at tea on the second day and we never got back out. If the selectors were thinking of changes, their minds were made up for them really when Michael Vaughan badly bruised his index finger and was ruled out of the third Test. Maddy was going to play his first overseas Test batting at number four.

The Test was due to start on Boxing Day and a few days before Christmas the families flew in to watch it and the following match. It was great to see Sam, Georgia and Sophie, who took her first steps while they were there, but precious time with loved ones was pretty scarce. For the fortnight they were there ten days were scheduled playing time and on the other four we trained, including Christmas Day. It was the last time England toured so extensively. I remember on that trip some of the senior players openly complaining that there were too many games. Eventually tours were shortened with only a couple of warm-up matches before the main event. I was enjoying the experience immensely but even I was starting to feel a bit jaded, having played in every game bar one up to that point.

We should have won the third Test in Durban and would have done but for a fabulous knock by Gary Kirsten who batted for nearly 11 hours in the second innings to score 275 and help save the game. At the time only one batsman, Pakistan's Hanif Mohammed, had batted for longer in a Test.

It was an even more impressive display of concentration given the fierce heat throughout the five days. It was so oppressive that we would do our warm-up before the start of each day's play in the hotel pool rather than the ground, change into our tracksuits and head straight on to the coach to Kingsmead. If anyone then wanted a net they could have one but most of us preferred to prepare in an air-conditioned changing room.

The ball swung on the first couple of days but my problems this time weren't with Donald or Pollock but their left-arm chinaman bowler Paul Adams, whom few of us had encountered before although we'd seen that idiosyncratic action of his enough on TV. There were so few chinaman bowlers in England and because of his unusual run-up – famously likened to a frog in a blender – I ended up watching him more than what he was doing with the ball. He didn't turn it much but, as a wrist spinner, he didn't need to do that much with it off the straight to cause problems. He also got the ball to drop, often quite late, though I could offer no excuse for the shot I got out to when I'd made 19, having put on 42 with Nasser who was on his way to a magnificent unbeaten hundred.

It was a full toss that I went to smash out of the ground but at the last minute it dipped a fraction and bowled me. I was mortified. It must have looked awful – an international cricketer bowled by a loopy full toss. As I trudged off I shook my head at my own ineptitude, while the photographers' cameras snapped away. The picture in the papers the next day didn't look good, especially with the captain at the other end. To make things worse, I spent far too long afterwards trying to process what had happened. I must have sat in the dressing room for nearly an hour with my pads on while the other lads tiptoed around me and left me with my thoughts. Just as I'd done in Port Elizabeth I'd got a start and not kicked on. This felt worse because we were going well. I started questioning my luck. Out to a full toss, a dodgy lbw decision. When you start doing that you've got problems. I was struggling.

We made 366 and then Andy Caddick produced a masterful display in helpful conditions, taking seven wickets including three in five balls as we bowled South Africa out for 156. Bearing in mind the fourth Test was due to start three days later we perhaps should have batted again, but having been under the pump throughout most of the series thus far I didn't disagree with Nasser's decision to stick them back in and try and wrest back some of the initiative.

It meant we spent the last two days leather-chasing and watching Kirsten build a really special innings as the pitch flattened out. Their top order basically batted around him and in the end we employed nine different bowlers, including Nasser himself, to try and winkle them out. It was to no avail. The pitch had got slower and slower with Kirsten rooted defiantly to the crease and relishing such a placid surface.

I did, at least, take my first (and only) Test wicket and it was a decent one too. I had Boucher caught behind – but only after he'd made 108. In those days I bowled quite regularly, especially in one-day cricket, with my medium-pace wobblers. I finished with 1-42 from 13 overs including three maidens. Not bad, but little consolation after my aberration against my namesake with the bat.

Three days later we were in Cape Town. This was always going to be one of the highlights of the tour, especially as there were thousands of England supporters there hoping to see us square the series. Back in 1990, I'd played cricket in Cape Town for a Muslim club in the suburbs called Primrose. I never went to Newlands then but after scoring runs there in the warm-up game earlier in the tour I was desperate to play.

Vaughan returned to the team and, fortunately for me, it was Maddy and not I who made way. It must have been a close call for Duncan and Nasser. I couldn't have complained if they'd dropped me but I was aware this was probably my final opportunity to impress. I was running out of chances.

The match started just three days after we'd finished a gruelling Test in Durban and fortunately we won the toss. The pitch was rock-hard and looked a belter. Atherton and Butcher took us past 100 but we were pegged back after lunch by Donald and Adams and a few of the top order batsmen got out to rash shots, including Atherton and Stewart caught in the deep by men placed deliberately for the hook shot when Donald dropped short.

Towards the end of the day Nasser told me that if a wicket fell anytime during the last five overs he would be sending in Caddick ahead of me as night-watchman. There were six overs left when we lost a wicket and I marched down the steps ready to bat. I was only two or three paces from setting foot on to the outfield when I heard Nasser screaming over the dressing-room balcony for me to come back. I passed a disgusted Caddick on the steps muttering under his breath! Sure enough, Caddy was out for a duck and I had to go out and negotiate the last few overs.

I liked Caddy. He could rub people up the wrong way because he was quite opinionated, and if you didn't agree with his point of view he would argue strongly until you ended up concurring just to shut him up! But when the mood took him and conditions were right he was a superb bowler. The bounce he generated from his tall frame caused their batsmen lots of problems. Chris Silverwood, and not Darren Gough, was probably our quickest bowler on that tour but it was Caddick the South Africans respected the most.

The second day – a Saturday – was sold out, and just to add to the sense of occasion the authorities had left clackers on every seat. Donald began the bowling and as he steamed in the noise from the crowd and those bloody clackers was absolutely deafening. He then hit me under the armpit – a real stinger and probably the most painful blow I'd ever experienced on a cricket pitch.

If that wasn't enough I knew I needed a score. It was my most important innings of the tour. Atherton came up to me before I went out, put his arm around my shoulder and said, 'It's your day today.' It was a simple gesture but it meant a lot. But if I was going to be accepted by Nasser and the senior players I had to get some runs. For a while I felt okay. I got to ten without too many problems and saw off Donald and Pollock. Kallis came on and perhaps I subconsciously relaxed. He was bowling wicket-to-wicket and giving me little opportunity to score. Then he threw one a bit wider and I took the bait. You can probably guess the rest by now.

There was an elderly England supporter sitting by the gate at the bottom of the steps. As I approached him

I clocked the look of utter disgust on his face. As I walked past he shook his head and muttered, 'Not again.' If it was any consolation to him, I felt an awful lot worse. My brief Test career was unravelling and the deafening silence which greeted my return to the dressing room suggested my team- mates probably felt the same.

Having been 213/3 we were bowled out for 258 after lunch on the second day. After his exertions in Durban Caddick was really struggling and Daryl Cullinan and Kallis both made centuries, though from 246/2 we fought hard to keep them to 421. I bowled seven overs for 17 runs. Perhaps my future lay as an all-rounder. Trailing by 163 we didn't put up much of a fight in the second innings. Atherton made 35 and I was second-top scorer with 31, my Test best as it was to turn out. It was the first time I'd gone out to bat not feeling any pressure. The game – and the series – were gone and, as wickets tumbled, I decided to play a few shots. I felt liberated, probably because I accepted that it was going to be my last innings of the Test series. With Andrew Flintoff injured and unable to bat we were beaten by an innings and 37 runs before tea on the fourth day. It was South Africa's biggest winning margin against England.

We had one more game before the final Test and the management drafted in four of the players who had arrived for the limited-overs series. I was rested but used the time in Port Elizabeth productively to start thinking about my approach to the one-day games that would start two days after the Test series finished. What happened in Cape Town confirmed to me that if I was to have any sort of England career it would probably be in white ball cricket so that's what I focussed on.

I was stunned when Duncan told me I was playing in the fifth Test. I had mentally prepared myself to be left out and was thinking about how I could best utilise the time in terms of preparing for the one-dayers. It was a nice surprise but the absence of Andrew Flintoff through injury probably forced their hand. I was to take part in one of the most infamous Tests in the history of the game.

Conditions were markedly different to Cape Town. Instead of dry heat the atmosphere at Centurion was damp and cool. There had been rain in the lead-up to the game and the start was delayed until after lunch on the first day. South Africa finished the first day on 155/6 but having won the toss we should have bowled them out cheaply because conditions were ideal.

That night it started to rain and pretty much didn't stop for the next three days. We were staying in Johannesburg about an hour away and by the time it got to the fourth day we seriously contemplated staying in the hotel rather than wasting time driving to Centurion. The outfield was damp and the run-ups sodden and there were no outdoor practice facilities for us to use either.

We were starting to get a little stir crazy. Duncan noticed our restlessness and ordered the physio, Dean Conway, to take us for a weights session. No one was particularly looking forward to it except Darren Gough, who immediately ripped off his t-shirt and began flexing his muscles. 'Does tha' know what they call me at Yorkshire?' he asked. 'No Darren, what?' 'They call me "Rhino" – because I'm as strong as an ox!' Good old Goughy. That little vignette certainly helped lighten the mood.

When we arrived on the final day the mood was different. It had stopped raining and the outfield was a hive of activity. Even the South African Cricket Board president Ali Bacher was out there, supervising the mopping-up operations. It looked as if we were going to play which, in normal circumstances, would have been great news. The problem for one or two of the team was that they had overdone it in the hotel bar the previous evening. There was a big golf tournament on near Johannesburg and all the European Tour players were staying at our hotel. My clearest memory of that evening – and I stress I was in bed at the normal time along with the majority of the team – was Ian Botham, who was commentating for Sky, and Ian Woosnam having a putting competition in the hotel bar while I watched bemused from the 14th floor balcony. Darren Gough was particularly worse for wear the next morning although he did manage to get on the bus on time. Fletcher was a stickler for timekeeping. If you weren't there at the allotted time the transport left without you. One or two players had only made it with seconds to spare and as we left that morning there was the unmistakable figure of Phil Tufnell haring down the road trying to attract the driver's attention. Tuffers eventually gave up as the bus pulled out with the rest of us trying to contain our mirth but he still got to Centurion before us, having hailed a cab. When we got to the ground he was doing laps of the outfield! Duncan just shook his head.

The senior players went to check conditions and came back confident we wouldn't get out there. A few minutes later, though, the umpires Darrell Hair and our old friend Rudi Koertzen told us we were going to get started. I have played in far worse conditions to be fair and we wanted to be positive, not least for the local organisers who hadn't insured the game against rain and had lost nearly two million rand.

By then Hansie Cronje and Nasser had already had one conversation about setting something up. Nasser wanted to see how bad – or good – conditions were before entering further negotiations. When he saw that the ball wasn't doing a great deal off the straight and that the overheads were pretty good Nasser nipped off and asked Cronje if the offer was still open. It was and, even better for us, Donald wasn't playing because of gout and Cronje had adjusted his original target of 255 runs in 73 overs to 249 in 76.

No one suspected anything underhand. In fact, we applauded Cronje's gesture. He was obviously in a position of strength because the series was already won but I was seriously impressed. There wasn't actually a law then allowing for the forfeiture of a first innings, which was what Cronje was proposing, although a change to allow it was due to take effect later in the year. Our innings was officially declared at 0/0 even though we didn't actually take the field and shortly afterwards Butcher and Atherton set out to begin the run chase.

We lost wickets regularly and when I came out to bat with Michael Vaughan I think we both sensed this was a pivotal moment for us in terms of our England careers. Michael had played some resolute innings during the series without pushing on to make a really big score while I had frittered away some reasonable starts. But because we were chasing a target it felt like a one-day game, which was perfect for me.

Well, one of us seized the moment. When I got to the crease, Mark Boucher had wandered right up to the stumps. His words were the first he'd spoken to me in English during the series, 'Mr Adams, I'd just like to welcome you to the final day of your Test career.' I must admit even I found it amusing and tried hard to suppress a smile. And he was right. Three balls later I gloved one from Nantie Hayward and was out for a single.

Vaughan batted magnificently. Paul Adams had broken a finger in the field when he crashed into a boundary board which helped and when Vaughan fell for 69 we needed nine off 13 balls. Somehow Gough and Silverwood scrambled the runs, Gough hitting Hayward for a boundary off the first ball of the last over to seal a two-wicket triumph. It also ended South Africa's winning run of 14 Tests.

A few months later, when it emerged that Cronje had accepted 53,000 rand (around £5,000) and a leather jacket from a bookmaker to initiate a positive result, I was absolutely staggered. Subsequently, a few players who took part in the match have said they had suspected something wasn't quite right in Cronje's gesture. That's nonsense. At the time we all thought what Cronje was doing was entirely for the good of cricket; to my knowledge no one had any reason to believe that a Test match was being 'fixed' for the first time. When we went back to the hotel and unwound with a few beers to celebrate the victory it was never a topic for discussion. As always, it's helpful to be wise after the event.

As a cricketer there was a lot to admire in Cronje. He was a fierce competitor who got the best out of some very talented players. Sussex were playing Kent at Tunbridge Wells in June 2002 when I came off at lunch to be told he'd been killed in a plane crash earlier that day. I just felt acute sadness at how desperate he must have been to sell himself to the fixers for such a piffling amount.

# 11

# Stay At Home

AS we celebrated our Test win at Centurion my over-riding feeling was one of relief. There was some elation, of course, that we'd won a match even if our victory was to be tarnished somewhat later on. I had found the step up to Test cricket, without the benefit of a great deal of previous international experience, too much. But I didn't think I had played my last Test. I still felt, if I could score consistently for Sussex, that I would get another opportunity and, having experienced it already, that I could prosper, especially in a home series. I could now concentrate on the one-day series and doing myself justice.

Having had a taste of it in 1998, against the same opponents, and with three months of experience of southern African conditions under my belt, I felt very positive. My mood improved even further when Duncan Fletcher asked Graeme Hick and I to join the management committee for the series, which involved four matches in

Zimbabwe to follow the tri-series, also involving South Africa.

Just two days after we finished the Test series we played a warm-up game in Potchefstroom against Northerns. Hick looked in good order and made 77 and I scored 47 as we won comfortably. The management group picked the team for our first game against South Africa in Bloemfontein and I stuck myself down at number four, only to be outvoted by the others who wanted Vikram Solanki, Hick's Worcestershire team-mate, to bat there on his debut. In the event neither of us were needed as we strolled to a morale-boosting nine-wicket win after Darren Gough had taken four wickets and then Nasser Hussain and Nick Knight had put on 165 for the first wicket as we chased 185.

I was a little perturbed that I still wasn't batting in what I considered my best position as we moved to Cape Town for a day-nighter against South Africa. Having won so convincingly I knew the batting order wouldn't change. I made 42 but should have won us the game. Had I done so I'm convinced my career in international cricket would have gone on a lot longer than it did.

We were chasing 205 on a slow pitch under the lights and although I was batting well the run rate was climbing to seven an over and it was proving hard to force the pace with a soft ball and damp outfield. I came down the wicket trying to hit Lance Klusener over the top and ended up giving a catch to extra cover.

My critics in the press box had a field day. One minute Adams was insisting the days when he gave his wicket away were history and the next he was playing a poor shot like that in a pressure situation. They had a point and I knew it.

We lost the game by one run and in the next match two days later, also at Newlands but this time against Zimbabwe, we ran into Henry Olonga in inspired form. When he got it right Olonga was a pretty useful seamer and that day things ran for him. He finished up with 6/19, including me for a single, and as a team we underperformed badly. Nasser was fuming afterwards. Having beaten South Africa and then lost to them by the narrowest of margins we went into the game a bit complacent.

And that was the end of my international career.

We flew up to Kimberley to play Zimbabwe again. It was a nice ground with decent facilities and the weather was red-hot. I was preparing to play on the outfield when Nasser wandered over and said, 'Sorry mate, we've decided to give [Darren] Maddy a go in this one.' That was it. Mind you, there isn't a lot more a captain can say when he's dropped you. It took a while to sink in and as the other lads heard the news they came over and offered their sympathies. Gough was fuming. He couldn't believe I'd been left out and I had to stop him from seeking out Duncan to find out why I'd been dropped.

I asked Duncan to come to the nets with me once the game had started, the main purpose of which was to try and find out why I had been left out. As usual, Duncan didn't give much away. He just told me to speak to Nasser. I was depressed but, as I'd been at Headingley back in 1998, I was determined to remain the model pro. I told Duncan that if I wasn't in the side I wanted to perform 12th man duties when we were in the field and when I had to come on a couple of times I threw myself around like a man possessed, or at least a man with a point to prove. The trouble was the time for proving a point had probably gone.

Finally, four days later in East London, I literally followed Nasser to his hotel room to seek an explanation. That's all I wanted. I wasn't looking for any sort of confrontation. I just wanted to know where I stood. He told me that the word from back home was that it was time to look at Darren Maddy. By 'back home' I assumed he meant David Graveney, the chairman of selectors, who had gone back to England at the end of the Test series. He said the way I'd got out in Cape Town had no bearing on their decision and he promised I would get another opportunity later in the series or when we went to Zimbabwe.

That chance never came. Instead, a few days later I was heading home wondering if I'd ever see little Sophie alive again.

We qualified for the final and headed to Johannesburg for the final. A couple of days before the game I got a phonecall from Sam's mum Sandra to say that Sam had found Sophie, who was just over a year old, face down in the hallway at home foaming at the mouth. She had suffered some sort of fit. Apparently Sam was calmness personified. I was in bits. The first thing I wanted to know was whether I should come home. After a worrying few hours I spoke to Sam. The doctors had stabilised Sophie and she'd been allowed to go home.

The next morning I was on the bus waiting to go to training and phoned Sam. I could hear Sophie in the background playing. We were chatting away when exactly the same thing happened – poor Sophie started foaming at the mouth and once again went into some sort of convulsion. Sam rang off and I got hold of Phil Neale, our tour manager, and explained what happened and that I needed to be near a phone and couldn't go to the ground to practise. Sophie was rushed to hospital and this time the doctors decided to keep her in for observation. I eventually got through to Sam and she was in floods of tears. Then I spoke to the doctor who urged me to get home as soon as possible. He said that the worst-case scenario was that Sophie might not pull through.

I got hold of Phil and he did brilliantly to get me on the next flight from Johannesburg. I didn't even have time to say goodbye to the others. I flung my stuff into a suitcase in about 15 minutes and the following morning I was heading from Heathrow back to Brighton in a taxi having hardly slept and fearing the worst.

Sam was shattered, as I expected, and Sophie was still in a lot of distress. But slowly she got better. She had a horribly pained expression on her face the first time I saw her but a couple of days later she was back to her old self. The doctors had run exhaustive tests and couldn't detect anything wrong. To be honest, it felt good to be at home again spending time with the girls but after a couple of days I wanted to re-join the tour. We'd lost the tri-series final to South Africa by 38 runs but there was still the Zimbabwe leg to come. I phoned Graveney and stressed that I felt it was important for me to return and finish the tour. He sounded sympathetic and I was quite hopeful but a few hours later he rung me back. Nasser and Duncan felt I was better off staying at home but they would call me up if any of the batsmen picked up an injury.

They had made their mind up about me – for the time being at least. I wasn't entirely surprised. I couldn't accuse them of not giving me an opportunity. In fact, they could argue that they stuck with me longer than I deserved. I watched the Zimbabwe matches on TV but didn't really feel part of it at all. My international career was over but I endured some painful experiences in domestic cricket that summer of 2000 before I finally accepted it.

# 12

# Champions

HAVING come out of my England experience so badly and then had my angry summer, the winter of 2000/01 was a much more pleasant experience. Ian Salisbury, the former Sussex and England leg-spinner with whom I was to work at Surrey a decade later, offered me the chance to play grade cricket for his club in Sydney and I made a spur-of-the-moment decision to accept. It was one of the best decisions of my career. We loved the climate and lifestyle and my game definitely benefitted. The cricket was tough and competitive but the wickets suited me and I won a Sydney Grade batting award, which was pretty rare for a Pom.

Another player who relished Australian conditions was Murray Goodwin and when I took a phonecall from Pete Moores to tell me that we'd signed him as our overseas player for 2001 I was intrigued. Michael Bevan had been under contract that season but was touring with Australia and we both felt Murray was a good signing. What we didn't realise at the time of course was just how good he would turn out to be. Murray had a decent Test career with Zimbabwe and I had come across him a couple of times with England in the one-day series in South Africa. Dave Gilbert had sorted it out without consulting either Peter or I. That was disappointing although, in truth, after what had happened in 2000 we were hardly in the position to argue. A year later Dave returned to Australia to work for the New South Wales Cricket Association. His relationship with Pete in particular was never warm but every Sussex supporter should be grateful that he signed Murray.

Murray made his debut in a Championship game at New Road against Worcestershire, when he was pressed into service as an opener and scored an impressive 94. After what had happened the previous year there was a lot of pressure on us all at the start of the season and the team meeting we had beforehand was a tense affair, the mood only lightened when Muz stuck his hand up and asked to say a few words, 'Hey guys, just enjoy the game and remember this. You could be cleaning condoms in Kenya!'

Murray loved life off the field and early in his Sussex career he challenged the team's ethos more than once by enjoying himself too much. Everyone wanted to be treated as an equal but I fought to cut him some slack because it quickly became clear how good a player he was. He was a reluctant opener but was happy to do a job for the team and that season he scored 2,465 runs in all competitions, including eight centuries. His opening partner, Richard Montgomerie, seemed to feed off Murray and made 1,461 Championship runs himself. I also passed 1,000 runs for the second time for Sussex and that gave us a solid base.

A year after finishing bottom we beat Gloucestershire in the final game of the season to clinch the Second Division title, having won nine of our 16 games. James Kirtley finished with 75 wickets and Mark Robinson and Jason Lewry both got more than 50. Robin Martin-Jenkins also made important contributions as he began to emerge as a genuine all-rounder. When he scored his maiden century in the final game we came off to the sound of champagne corks popping in the press box as his dad Christopher celebrated his son's landmark in style.

We also bedded in two outstanding young players in Matt Prior and Tim Ambrose. Since I'd come to Sussex we'd struggled to identify a wicketkeeper who could also score runs. Now we had two and at times it was so hard to choose between them that they both ended up playing. Tim was the better wicketkeeper back then while Matt was very raw, but a more attacking batsman in whom I saw a bit of myself. He always looked to take a step forward and could advance an innings rapidly. Matt wasn't as committed to his wicketkeeping, though, and would regularly question whether he should give up the gloves and concentrate on his batting. Pete made sure he persevered. He knew he had latent talent and as a focal point for our inner ring field he was ideal. In the second half of 2003, after we'd gone with Tim behind the stumps, Matt became a very good bat-pad catcher on the off side. With Tim behind the stumps and Montgomerie at short leg not many chances went down off our spinners.

Michael was due to come back for the last year of his contract in 2002, but we felt Murray was a better option. We had to settle up with Bev and that didn't leave a lot left in the pot to sign Murray. The club found the money but eventually we enlisted the help of the growing number of sponsors at Sussex to help finance player recruitment.

One Sunday after the 2003 season had ended I was having a pint in what was now Pete's local, the Royal Oak in Wineham, when Mike Borrisow, the boss of the club's main sponsors, wandered over. He was a great cricket enthusiast and we got talking about what would give us the best chance of making sure that first title was not to be the last. From that meeting the Players Club was formed. Mike lobbed in half of the £60,000 needed to put Murray on a new two-year contract and fend off interest from Nottinghamshire. Pete and I secured the rest after meetings with various other club sponsors. It's a source of personal pride that the Players Club is still going strong more than a decade later and has helped Sussex remain competitive in the marketplace compared to clubs with much greater resources.

If 2001 was enjoyable, 2002 was a grind, but we stayed up despite only winning three Championship games, our motivation made stronger by the tragic death of our team-mate Umer Rashid before we had even bowled a ball. It bound us together that year and for many more to follow. Umer was probably the most natural cricketer on the staff. Even now, I remember the fluent maiden hundred he got during the debacle at Colwyn Bay and the contribution he made the following year to the win over Durham which took us to the top of the Second Division when he scored a hundred and then took 4-9 in the second innings with his left-arm spin. He was developing into a good one-day player too and to see him cut off in his prime in such horrible circumstances is something I still find hard to come to terms with.

For the second year running the club had agreed that we could prepare for the new season in Grenada. The facilities were excellent and more and more English counties were going to the Caribbean to guarantee good weather. As usual, Pete had prepared a very detailed training and playing plan for the 11 days we were there and 1 April 2002 was our only scheduled day off. We were ready for a break and just after breakfast most of the squad were sitting around the pool, soaking up the sun and enjoying some well-deserved down time.

Umer had gone to the airport to collect his younger brother Burhan, who had arrived for a holiday with his girlfriend Caprice. When he got back to the hotel he invited all of his team-mates to come with them as they explored the island during the afternoon. Their destination was the Concord Falls on the other side of the capital, St George's. I often wonder, as I'm sure everyone who was there that day, if tragedy could have been averted had a couple of us decided to tag along.

A few hours later there was a call at the hotel bar, which Richard Montgomerie answered. Caprice had made the call and was hysterical. 'Something's happened! They're gone! They've disappeared!' she told Richard before the line went dead. Pete got through to Nigel Felton, the former Northamptonshire player who had organised the trip with Allan Lamb, the ex-England batsman. Nigel promised to find out what he could while the rest of us sat in stunned silence around the pool, praying for good news but privately fearing the worst.

An hour or so later Nigel rang back. The British Embassy had confirmed that divers had found two bodies in Concord Falls. Umer and Burhan had gone for a swim and Burhan got into difficulties. Umer tried to rescue him but had been pulled under by his brother. Pete, fearful that their family would hear the awful news through the media first, decided to call their father Mirza. Pete felt it was his duty but I will never forget the haunted look on his face when he came out of his room having spoken to Mr Rashid. The following day we all made the pilgrimage to Concord Falls to lay a wreath and pay silent tribute.

As cricketers, it was not a situation any of us were trained to deal with and some of the boys took it particularly hard, especially Tony Cottey, who was sharing a room with Umer, and his best friend in the squad, our Dutch batsman Bas Zuiderent. I don't think Bas ever got over what happened; in fact it probably finished his career.

By unhappy coincidence, our first Championship game was against Surrey, a club reeling from a tragedy of their own after Ben Hollioake had been killed in a car accident a few weeks before Umer had died. We presented the Rashid family with Umer's county cap, retired his shirt and a permanent memorial was erected on the main scoreboard at Hove.

Somehow we had to focus on cricket again but in those first few weeks of the 2002 season it was extremely tough. We only won three Championship games but developed into a resilient outfit that became hard to beat. I made a double hundred against Lancashire at Old Trafford but picked up a calf strain which kept me out of six matches and only James Kirtley took 50 wickets.

James had made his England debut a few months earlier but during the one-day series in Zimbabwe his bowling action had been reported by the umpire. James was dogged throughout his career with questions about the purity of his action but I played with few more determined and honest cricketers than him. He had to remodel his action again during the winter of 2005/06 but by then he had achieved his dream of playing Test cricket for his country. I don't think Duncan Fletcher, who was England coach at the time, ever felt James's action was totally right, even though all the biomechanics specialists had proved it was perfectly legal. I certainly faced a lot of bowlers in my career with worse actions and I felt there was a certain justice when he pinned his ears back for one last time in 2006 and played a huge part in our victory over Lancashire in the Lord's final with five wickets. As my vice-captain for many years he was superb and the consummate professional.

Arguably the most important game in 2002 was one we didn't win. We played Yorkshire at Arundel and had to bring Mark Robinson out of retirement because James and Jason Lewry were both unfit. He took five wickets and bowled superbly but it was his contribution with the bat that helped us stave off defeat when he blocked out 11 balls at the end with only Matt Prior for company at the other end. Robbo finished with a career average of 4.01 and had no pretensions as a batsman but I often say to Robbo that this was his single biggest contribution to Sussex cricket because the handful of extra points we got for the draw were crucial to our survival with three of the nine counties getting relegated in those days.

We finished sixth, Sussex's highest position for 18 years, and although our one-day record was average we felt we were making progress. Pete was increasingly gaining a reputation as an innovative and energetic coach, always looking for ways to give us an advantage over the opposition even if they were marginal gains. Other counties began to covet his services although I only discovered he'd been approached by Warwickshire at the end of the season from his wife, Karen.

Pete had never worked with the security of a contract and could have been fired by the club at any time with no recompense so I spoke to David Green, who had taken over as chairman from Don Trangmar at the beginning of the year, expressing my concerns that one of Sussex's biggest assets could easily be headhunted by a county with more financial muscle. It's to David's great credit that within a couple of days Pete had signed a new contract and we could start planning for 2003.

There was no fitter or better-drilled squad than us but winning a four-day match was still a lot of hard work. We had a decent seam attack and a strong core of experienced batsmen but we lacked that 'x factor', a bowler who could ease the workload on our seamers and get the opposition's best player out. We knew the Sussex committee wouldn't countenance paying the going rate for the best overseas players, which was about £100,000, something we discovered when we approached first Stuart MacGill, the Australian leg-spinner, and then Harbhajan Singh, the Indian off-spinner.

One of our victories that season had been against the eventual champions Surrey, when we squeezed home by four wickets on the last day thanks largely to the partnership Murray and I put together during the morning session when Alex Tudor and Mushtaq Ahmed had bowled in tandem. Mushy had been signed as short-term cover for his Pakistan compatriot Saqlain Mushtaq and although he went wicketless in the game I came off and remarked to Pete that it was the most intense bowling I'd faced since

Donald and Pollock in South Africa. It was certainly no surprise to me that Mushy took eight wickets in his next match against Leicestershire.

I felt he was just what we needed and Pete agreed. Mushy was overweight and the other concern was whether, at 33, he still had the appetite for the grind of the county circuit, his first stint in England with Somerset having ended in acrimony. They were factors we felt we could overcome. Persuading the Sussex committee to part with £50,000 was likely to prove trickier.

Pete and I came up with a strategy. We knew the committee wouldn't want to spend double that on someone like MacGill so Mushtaq, the player we really wanted to sign, was our second option. And if they surprised us by agreeing to pay for MacGill we'd still go for Mushy and use the spare cash on a domestic signing to improve the batting. Most vociferous of the doubters was John Snow, who felt Mushy was a washed-up has-been and told us so in no uncertain terms. There were a few nods of agreement around the room and although David Green was prepared to back us it needed the intervention of John Barclay, the former Sussex captain, to sway the doubters. The club had recently been left millions in the will of its former president Spen Cama and John, in that erudite and humorous way of his, painted a picture of Spen looking down on the room urging the committee to gamble a little with his largesse. Only John Snow voted against in the end and a few weeks later Mushy was introduced as a Sussex player.

He joined up with us in April 2003 and had clearly worked hard on his physical condition during the winter. Immediately he became a hugely popular member of our squad. He would end virtually every sentence with the word 'Inshallah' – 'God willing' – and his presence helped keep things nice and simple in the team environment at times of stress. And believe me, despite the success we enjoyed that year, there were lots of days when we needed his calming influence. He had re-connected with his Muslim faith and had many conversations with the more cerebral and inquisitive members of our squad about the teachings of the Quran, which he read daily after prayers.

It didn't take me long to work out how to handle Mushy the bowler. During his Pakistan career he had become used to coming on after Wasim Akram and Waqar Younis had made inroads with the new ball and bowling to ultra-attacking fields. He was expected to take wickets, even if it meant he could sometimes be expensive. That tactic would not suit us. We needed him to bowl lots of overs so our seamers could rotate at the other end and attack in short, sharp bursts. Our pitches at Hove were slow so I would encourage him to bowl quicker and straighter. I told him he could have as many fielders on the boundary as he wanted as long as we always had a slip, usually me, and a bat-pad on the off and leg side.

There is this myth about Mushy that he took the bulk of his wickets for us with an exotic concoction of googlies and flippers. In fact, I reckon about 60 per cent of his Sussex wickets came from straight balls. Leg-spinners were rare in county cricket, particularly ones of his quality, and he just loved bowling. He quickly recognised that the only way to get miles in his legs and build up his stamina was to bowl lots of overs and I never had a problem persuading him to come on. In fact, trying to get him to rest was far more difficult. He would inevitably get tired and when I sensed that I'd wander over and ask him how he felt. 'One more over please, one more over.' Invariably, the next over would go fizzing through and more often than not he'd take a wicket and be rejuvenated.

During his six seasons with us I only saw two batsmen pick Mushy – Darren Lehmann of Yorkshire and Kevin Pietersen, when he was with Nottinghamshire. Owais Shah of Middlesex played him as well as anyone but Mushy invariably got him out.

Mushy was soon taking lots of wickets for us but initially I don't remember too many pundits or rival counties taking our challenge for the title seriously. There would sometimes be sniping from the opposition about the increasing influence he was having and I would occasionally be accused of one-dimensional captaincy, but the criticism only normally came when we were winning while I was only employing the same tactics every one of my rival captains would have done had they had a player of Mushy's quality at their disposal.

So captaining the side that summer was relatively straightforward but my own performances with the bat had become a major concern by the halfway stage of the season. For the first time in my career I had lost the feeling of batting. It's hard to explain, but every aspect of getting in and building an innings seemed alien to me and I was scratching around desperately for form and confidence. Pete tried to help and would spend hours watching footage of me when I was playing well. I remember being woken by him at 1am one night telling me that he thought he knew what was wrong. We met in the nets at eight the following morning and spent three hours basically deconstructing my technique. In the short term it made little difference but I accepted the only way I was going to get out of the rut was to hit as many balls as I could in the nets, so much so I ended up with blisters on my hands.

Eventually my form returned at an opportune time when we played one of our main rivals Surrey at Hove and I scored a century, although I remember that game more for the stick I got from some Sussex supporters when I came off because of bad light on the third day when we were trying to set up a declaration so we could get at Surrey on a wearing pitch on the final day.

A few minutes later I locked the dressing room door – even Pete wasn't allowed in – and addressed the team. 'Look, I'm happy to go back out there but we are very much in this title race now. We can't win it in this game but we could definitely lose it. What do you think?' Tony Cottey piped up. He'd experienced a similar situation when Glamorgan won the title a few years earlier. 'I'm 100 per cent behind Grizz,' he said. 'This is not the time for bravado.' The game fizzled out into a draw but interestingly Surrey captain Adam Hollioake told me afterwards that he felt their failure to beat us had ended their own chances.

The title came down to Lancashire, a team we were due to meet home and away before the season finished, and ourselves. In the home game, I was probably guilty of leaving our declaration at Hove on the last day too late but thanks to Mushy and a fine spell down the slope by Billy Taylor we beat them with 12 minutes to spare. I scored a century in both innings and by then was playing as well as I'd done at any stage of my Sussex career. There were several choruses of 'Sussex by the Sea' belted out from our dressing room that night but I will never forget the look on the face of Warren Hegg, the Lancashire captain, as he left. I knew they would come at us hard when we went to Old Trafford for the penultimate game and that is exactly what happened. In the meantime we easily beat Essex at Colchester and then Mark Davis and Matt Prior dug us out of a hole against Middlesex at Hove by both scoring hundreds to set up another victory. We headed to Manchester knowing that a good draw would be enough to clinch the title.

There were a lot of nerves that week. This was a new experience for nearly all of us and we didn't cope well, least of all myself. From the moment we arrived on the day before the Wednesday start I didn't sleep a wink for five days. My mind was in complete turmoil and when rain arrived and started to eat into the playing time we increasingly began to think about the possibility of a draw. We were into the third day when Lancashire declared their first innings on 450/5 so our first target was to get to 301 and avoid the follow-on. We reckoned that would take enough time out of the remainder of the game to enable us to get the points we needed. We were 122/1 with Murray Goodwin going well when it all started to unravel. We collapsed to 157/7, and although Muz carried his bat and scored a hundred, despite a horrific facial injury when he was hit by Peter Martin's bouncer, from Peter Martin hit him we were bowled out for 251 and asked to follow on. We lost two wickets before stumps and on the last day only Muz got past 50 and we were thrashed by an innings.

Not that the Sussex supporters who came up on the final day seemed to mind too much. They wanted to see history made at Hove and already relegated Leicestershire seemed to be the ideal opponents as we sought the six points which would make us champions for the first time in the county's 164-year history. I felt less stress before that game than at any stage of the season. I knew that if we could get on top early we would win the game.

I couldn't have scripted the three days any better. Although I lost the toss, we rolled Leicestershire over for 179. The first big moment of the game came on the stroke of lunch when Mushy's googly deceived Brad Hodge and he became the first bowler since 1998 to take 100 wickets in a season. We reached 137/1 at the close and everything was set up for the next day.

The ground was already starting to fill up when we came out to warm up. I noticed a prim-and-proper-looking lady in a tweed suit sitting behind the boundary boards where we were practising slip catches and went over to her. 'It's my first visit to the ground,' she said, explaining that both her father and grandfather were big Sussex supporters. 'I've come here for them.' There were a lot of people who made similar pilgrimages that day. The Sussex 'family' were out in force. When we went into a huddle Murray spoke. 'Look guys, I'm going to be the player who gets the run which gets us the sixth point.' Easily said of course, but during my career Muz was one of the few batsmen I came across who backed up words with deeds.

Yet I could have stolen his thunder. As we closed in on 300, which would get us to our target, I faced two balls from Vasbert Drakes with the score on 294. I hit a boundary off the first and decided I'd throw the kitchen sink at whatever he bowled next up. What I didn't anticipate was a high bumper that I couldn't even reach. Murray sauntered down the pitch at the end of the over with a grin that suggested he knew his – and our – big moment was imminent, 'It's gonna be a helluva night tonight!'

Sure enough, in the next over he pulled a ball from Phil DeFreitas to the boundary in front of the pavilion and the wait was over. We embraced and within seconds were joined on the outfield by the rest of the squad as the Leicestershire lads looked on with some bemusement. The players were followed by our president Jim Parks, who was carrying a silver tray with champagne and glasses and it wasn't long before we were embarking on a lap of honour as 'Good Old Sussex by the Sea' blared out over the PA and everyone in the crowd stood to applaud. When we reached the Players Club I remember Ian Cameron, one of our sponsors, grabbing me in a headlock while Clive Roberts poured champagne down my throat – a brief taste of the celebrations to come over the next few days. It was the most magical day of my career.

Eventually the game restarted. I reached my hundred and got out shortly afterwards trying to play a big shot but Murray wasn't finished. He ended up making 335 not out, the highest individual score in Sussex's history at the time, but a record he was to beat at Taunton six years later. Even in the midst of what we'd achieved as a team Murray still had that insatiable hunger for individual runs and records.

After play we all headed down to the Sussex Cricketer pub, which was absolutely rammed with celebrating supporters. To be honest, the rest of the night was a blur. I remember squeezing Phil Tufnell's nuts seconds before he was about to start his cricket show on BBC 5 Live so that when the broadcast began there was complete silence. Phil, to his eternal credit, recovered his composure once I'd let go like the true professional he is. I still don't know how I got home that night but I did although the next day I felt awful and I wasn't the only one. Only Mushy, whose tipple of choice was Diet Coke, wasn't horribly hung over and he was already packing up ready for the airport to head back to Pakistan, having been recalled to their Test team.

James Kirtley had missed much of the run-in because of England Test commitments but he was thrilled when I asked him to lead the team at the start of the third day. He'd been a brilliant vice-captain for me and deserved some of the glory after all he'd given Sussex during the dark days.

Leicestershire showed a lot more fighting spirit on the third day and it needed a special spell by Jason Lewry to win us the game and earn us a day off for more celebrations. I was still too hung over to field at slip so stationed myself at mid-on and offered to run around the outfield in just a helmet and jockstrap if Jason took a wicket in the same over. He duly did so I upped the ante and offered to do a lap naked if he took another wicket in the next over, which of course he did. After we'd won the game and enjoyed another marvellous moment when I lifted the trophy on the dressing room balcony in front of a massive throng of our supporters as well as friends and family we carried on the celebrations. A few hours later we made our way on to the outfield and sat on the square, drinking beers and reminiscing about the special moments during an unforgettable season. I thought Jason had forgotten about my earlier dare but no such luck. Will House had lapped the outfield starkers a few years earlier and one of the residents of the flats overlooking the ground reported him to the club. This time there was no comeback as the Sussex captain did a lap as curtains twitched in the twilight.

There was an open-top bus parade and a visit to Buckingham Palace later in the year. It wasn't until the new year dawned that the celebrations stopped and we could focus on trying to retain our trophy. Pete and I knew that good teams became serial trophy winners and built a dynasty. We realised the other counties would target us much more and that while we had been celebrating they were undoubtedly working on plans to negate our biggest threat, Mushy.

But we recruited Ian Ward, the prolific Surrey opening batsman, and Pakistan seam bowler Mohammad Akram, whom Mushy had recommended, from a position of strength and felt our chances of challenging again were good. I was also keen to improve our one-day form, particularly in the T20 Cup, which had started in 2003 and was clearly going to change the landscape of county cricket.

Instead, we experienced something of a soft landing.

# 13

# Winning Mentality

IT was tough in 2004. Arguably, we had a stronger squad than the one that had won the Championship with Ian Ward and Mo Akram now in our ranks. Wardy passed 1,000 first-class runs and Akram took 46 wickets but they struggled to fit in. Through no fault of their own they didn't have that Sussex DNA. It wasn't long before Wardy was starting to think about his broadcasting career after cricket and at the end of the year Mo asked to be released from his contract and headed to Surrey because he wanted to be based in London all the time.

Halfway through the season we had won one Championship game, had made an early exit in the T20 Cup and only had Scotland below us in the one-day league and Akram had been reported by the umpires, Peter Willey and Barrie Leadbeater, for allegedly tampering with the seam when we were trying to prise Ian Bell out at Horsham when he made a double hundred on an absolute road.

Even Mushy had been relatively subdued but as the wickets dried out in the second half of the summer he rediscovered his form. We won three out of four in the Championship from July onwards and five out of six in the one-day league and went into our game with leaders Warwickshire at Edgbaston in late August knowing that victory would really open up the title race. During my entire Sussex career I never won a Championship game in Birmingham. We tried everything to end the hoodoo, which had stretched back to 1982 – swapping our normal hotel and changing our pre-match routine – to no avail. Even a draw there was considered a decent result and on this occasion we had them seven down just before tea on the final day but could not bowl them out and complete what would have been the formality of a small run chase. We finished fifth which was about right but I chalked off another personal milestone when I made 200 against Northamptonshire at Hove to have made a century against all 18 first-class counties. My own personal target had become to finish my career with 50 first-class hundreds.

The following year was my eighth as captain but I was still enthusiastic about leading the side. We still had the bulk of the team which had won the title in 2003 and we were also starting to see the emergence of some younger players like Mike Yardy and Luke Wright, whom we'd signed from Leicestershire in 2004. The dynamic of the team was still good and we improved to third place although we should have won the Championship, having gone top in August after beating Middlesex in two days at Lord's. We suffered a couple of bad defeats against Hampshire and Warwickshire (surprise, surprise) and with some better weather we would have won three games against Glamorgan, Nottinghamshire and Gloucestershire that finished as draws. We had a stronger bowling attack after signing Rana Naved, a previously unheralded Pakistan seamer who was Pete's parting gift to Sussex before he left at the end of 2005 to replace Rod Marsh as the ECB's academy director at Loughborough, coming in as our overseas player because Murray was now a Kolpak registration. Pete had, as always, done his homework. He'd watched hours of video and live footage of Rana playing for Pakistan in Australia and South Africa and felt his skill with the new ball and the old one, which he could get to reverse swing almost at will it seemed, would benefit us, especially at Hove. Because of the respect he had for Mushy he was a dream to captain and the other guys loved him, especially Jason Lewry. Rana taught Jason about reverse swing and it gave Jason a new lease of life.

The news that Peter was leaving was announced early in the season and left us in a state of flux. We didn't fulfil our potential and his impending departure definitely unsettled us. After the news broke David Green asked whether he thought I could combine the role of coach and captain. I said I'd give it a crack but in the end the committee opted for continuity by promoting Mark Robinson from the second team. At least we were able to give Pete a good send-off by winning the Second Division of the one-day league with victory over Yorkshire at Hove on the final day of the season.

I wasn't sure how my relationship with Robbo was going to pan out at first. We hadn't worked together much and we didn't get off to the best of starts. Pete and I had always had total transparency with each other on every decision. I'd never laid any ground rules down with

Robbo and when he started to plan the pre-season for 2006 without consulting me we had a big argument. It was my fault as much as his of course for not communicating. He'd come in feeling he had to start making his mark straight away but at least it cleared the air and, looking back, my relationship with Robbo was probably stronger than the one I had with Pete. I enjoyed both eras, but I had a more productive relationship with Mark.

Pete had been more of a dominating presence in the changing room when we discussed tactics with the players. If someone had made a concession on something it would normally be me. When Robbo replaced him he was quite happy for me to become the principal decision-maker but he was very clear about goal-setting for the squad. For instance, he had identified that we had become notoriously poor starters to the season and was very clear about what he wanted from the squad at the beginning of 2006 to change that. Whereas Pete was, and still is, a brilliant coach in a one-to-one situation Robbo instigated a process whereby small groups of senior players, led by me and often including Mushy, Jason Lewry and James Kirtley, would get together to chew over a variety of issues. If individuals made powerful statements in those forums he challenged them to back them up where it mattered – on the field. I'm convinced it helped several senior players and others find a bit in terms of their own performances.

Our second Championship success in 2006 was never going to be as good as the first but we were definitely a better team that year. We should have won the treble in fact, disappointingly losing our final one-day league game at Trent Bridge after we had been bowled out cheaply.

Robbo's insistence that we started the season strongly was borne out and we got on a roll quickly, winning six of our first eight games.

Halfway through the season I couldn't see anyone stopping us. We also won three of the last four and although it would have been nice to have wrapped things up at Hove we still enjoyed the celebrations after Mushy had gone past 100 wickets for the second time in the title-clinching win at Trent Bridge which we achieved just before it started to rain. As usual Mushy took most of the headlines and rightly so but 11 members of our squad that season had come through Sussex's junior ranks. Rana and Yasir Arafat, who shared the second overseas player duties, dovetailed superbly while Mike Yardy's consistent performances in one-day cricket earned him England selection.

We also won a thrilling Lord's final against our old rivals Lancashire and, if I'm honest, that success probably gave me more satisfaction than the Championship. A lot of Sussex people were still scarred by the memories of their last appearance at Lord's in 1993 when they failed to defend a score of more than 300 against Warwickshire. The competition was based on a group format initially but we beat Shane Warne's Hampshire at Hove and booked our place with a game to spare.

That was a special victory, as most were back then when we came up against Warne and his team. I loved playing against him. He was a ferocious competitor who was always looking to push the boundaries in terms of what was acceptable on-the-field behaviour. His reputation definitely got him a few wickets but he was still a magnificent bowler and going up against him, whatever the format, was always an occasion I looked forward to.

He was probably past his prime but he could still bowl magnificent spells, although he used to get frustrated at Hove because the wickets tended to be too slow and he didn't have the stamina to bowl the number of overs that Mushy sent down. As a fellow-leg spinner he had enormous respect for Mushy, certainly more than he had for the rest of us!

In 2005, he started calling Matt Prior 'Watermelons' after taking offence at Matt's confident strut to the wicket when he went out to bat. Warne stopped the whole game as he mimicked Matt's walk to the wicket by striding up and down the pitch with his arms out as if he was carrying a watermelon under each arm. It undermined Matt's normal confidence and angered me. After the game I told the press that I'd lost respect for Shane, a heat of the moment comment which I regretted as soon as I'd said it, especially when I was woken in the early hours of the following morning by the former Australian fast bowler Rod Hogg asking me to go on his radio show to explain my comments!

After that, every time we played them there was an incident of some kind and umpires must have hated standing in those matches. Mike Yardy got so wound up by a comment Simon Katich made to Mushy that he followed him off the field for about 40 yards, giving him an earful of abuse, after Mushy had got him out. Hampshire made an official complaint about James Kirtley's bowling action during a game at the Rose Bowl in 2005 and as a consequence James had to remodel his action again.

The following year in the decisive C&G Trophy game at Hove, James waved to Jim May after bowling Warne and Warne started to walk off that way as well. Then Warne had a pop at me in the press because the number one I had on the back of my shirt was wider than those worn by the rest of the team. It got so bad that both counties were warned by the ECB to calm things down.

Before we were due to play them at Arundel in 2007 I was chatting to Pete Moores about the situation and he came up with a good suggestion, 'Look, he will be expecting you to be aggressive again so why not do exactly the opposite and kill him with kindness? Make him feel like he's the best person on the planet.'

I was willing to try anything to win this battle of wills so when I got to the ground the day before the Championship fixture I told our dressing room attendant Mervyn Stevens to make sure everything Shane wanted he got, no questions asked. I then asked Brian Smith, who used to open and close the gate on to the field at all our home games, to greet Shane like a long-lost cousin when their bus arrived the following morning. Brian was a lovely guy who would always offer a consoling hug or pat on the shoulder if you'd got out cheaply but on this occasion he surpassed himself. When Shane got off the coach I was sure Brian was going to French kiss him! Shane was speechless but I had one more plan to execute.

The walls at Arundel are thin so you can always hear what's going on in the opposition's dressing room. As soon as Shane started his team talk I barged in without knocking, apologised for interrupting and asked Shane to sign a couple of scorecards for my girls 'because you are their favourite cricketer'. As Shane signed and his team struggled to contain their giggles I knew our charm offensive had worked. Shane didn't leave the dressing room for the next four days unless he was going to bat or field and we won the game easily. Matches against Hampshire were never the same after that.

We were desperate to win the C&G Trophy but the problem was that it was nearly two months after we'd reached the final before we headed up to Lord's and I was concerned we had lost the momentum we had built up. James Kirtley hadn't been a regular in the side at the start of the season but he was still an outstanding one-day bowler and I knew he would relish the big occasion and the opportunity to stick a metaphorical two fingers up at his critics who had doubted that he had the mental strength to bounce back again having remodelled his action for the second time earlier that year.

A few weeks before the final we played Lancashire in a one-day game at Hove. We were anxious to put down a marker against them and successfully chased a target of 277. I got 132 not out from 101 balls and batted as well as I'd ever done in one-day cricket for Sussex. Mushy missed the game, which disappointed Lancashire because they were keen to get after him and unsettle him ahead of the final, and afterwards he was full of praise for my performance. He called for hush in the dressing room and said: 'Skipper, I've only got two words to say. We love you!' We were still laughing about that the day we got to Lord's.

It will go down as one of the best Lord's finals ever. The pitch wasn't the best and the occasion got to us early on, as a succession of our batsmen succumbed to nervous shots. Thanks to Yardy and Yasir Arafat, who both made 37, we cobbled together 172. Yards was never the most aesthetically pleasing of players but he was a fighter. Lancashire's players gave him some real abuse that day and when we regrouped at the break he was as fired up as I'd ever seen him. After a few words from me I left the team talk to Yards. His emotional and passionate address was all we needed.

James Kirtley bowled superbly with the new ball to leave Lancashire 27/3 and Mushy and the other bowlers kept things tight in the middle overs. We fielded superbly and every time Lancashire tried to lift the tempo they lost a wicket. I kept three overs back for James and he delivered two more wickets to become only the third bowler to take five in a one-day match all lbw. When his appeal against Murali Kartik was answered in the affirmative and we'd won the match I made a beeline for the stumps because I knew James would be buried under a sea of bodies. As we walked off the field I handed one to him. I knew how special those souvenirs were from my own Lord's experience with Derbyshire 13 years earlier. Mike Atherton was doing the post-match presentation and looked gutted that his old county had lost. When I walked on to the dais I gave him a big kiss on the cheek to cheer him up. I'm not sure it helped but it must have given the Sky Sports viewers a laugh.

When we won the Championship a few weeks later there were eight survivors from the team that won in 2003. By then we were just happy to crawl over the finishing line, or be dragged over it by our inspirational leg-spinner. We were knackered, mentally and physically. It had been a long season. Fortunately Mushy had one more big performance left in him at Trent Bridge and it was an unforgettable moment when he took his 100th wicket of the season, dropped to his knees and offered a silent prayer as the rest of us respectfully gave him some space before engulfing him. Thirty minutes later he had completed a career-best

9-48 and it was all over, so quickly in fact that the ECB officials had still not arrived with the trophy.

Winning the title in front of 1,500 at a big ground like Trent Bridge could not compare to a sunny September afternoon at Hove three years earlier, but most of the crowd had come up from Sussex and we made the most of it. We filled the trophy with champagne and went into the pavilion where most of our supporters were celebrating. We passed the cup around and everyone took a sip which was a nice moment and Pete Moores, who was there working for Sky Sports, joined us which was fitting considering all he'd done to make those moments possible. I was so tired I must have got drunk pretty quickly back at the team hotel, where a lot of supporters had joined us. I woke on Saturday morning with a stinking hangover, further proof that at my age your powers of recovery are not those of a 21-year-old. I suppose I must have tried keeping up with some of the youngsters in the squad and failed miserably.

A few days later we did another open-top bus ride around Brighton and Hove. It was a cloudy Monday afternoon and as we drove along Western Road there were more bemused shoppers than flag-waving supporters chanting Mushy's name. It looked like the people of Sussex had come to expect their cricket team to win at least one trophy a year.

The Professional Cricketers' Association dinner in London is always one of the best nights of the year, whether you have won a trophy or not. Everyone attends and it's a fantastic occasion to catch up and gossip with other players and do a bit of detective work on who is out of contract and available. It was where we first got wind that Tony Cottey was unhappy and interested in leaving Glamorgan to join us in 1999. Now it was my turn.

After we'd been presented with our trophies I was approached by Stewart Regan, Yorkshire's chief executive, a man I'd never met before. He told me that he'd spoken to Yorkshire's coach David Byas and that my name had come up as someone who might head up the planned restructuring of their cricket operation. He asked if I'd be interested and I gave him my mobile number. The conversation cannot have lasted more than a minute.

I was both flattered and intrigued, particularly about the management element the job would entail. I was starting to think seriously about life after playing and earlier in the year I'd applied for the chief executive vacancy at Sussex, which was eventually filled by Gus Mackay, and I was taking my level four coaching qualification. When I told Sam she seemed pleased that my efforts at Sussex had been recognised and urged me to at least meet them to see what they had to offer. If she had any reservations about the upheaval it would cause to our domestic life in Sussex she kept them well hidden.

I spoke to Regan the next day and arranged to meet 48 hours later in London with him and Yorkshire chairman Colin Graves. Things were moving quickly and for the next couple of days I could think of little else. I also knew at some stage I would have to front up with Sussex. My relationship with David Green, the chairman, was excellent and if the county had offered me some security beyond the remaining year on my contract I would have signed there and then. Sussex had paid me well of course, but I hadn't had a salary increase for six years during which time I'd helped deliver two Championships and a first win at Lord's in a one-day final for 20 years. I felt that if it had been up to David alone he would have given me the security I wanted but it was going to be a committee decision and I accepted that, at 36 and with my best years now behind me, others might not be so willing.

I lost count of the number of times I went to call David and bottled it. Eventually I spoke to him outside a fish and chip shop in Hassocks, somewhere he'd recommended to me funnily enough. I told him about the offer from Yorkshire and that it interested me, particularly the managerial element. He was shocked, as I knew he would be, but he graciously gave me permission to speak to Yorkshire. I should have been pleased but somehow I got it into my head that it was a sign Sussex were happy for me to leave when, as I was to discover, it was nothing of the sort.

Like Stewart Regan, I didn't know Colin Graves from Adam but he obviously knew Adams as he bounded across the hotel room to introduce himself as if we were long-lost pals. He outlined that the club's management were unhappy with the cricket structure at Yorkshire and that Geoff Boycott, who had been co-opted on to their board, had recommended a scenario where the captain called the shots on and off the field. Captaining Yorkshire on its own was not going to swing it for me, but the director of cricket role definitely appealed. I would be controlling a sizeable budget at one of the biggest clubs in the country. Yorkshire had endured some lean times since winning the Championship in 2001 but they were a much bigger county than Sussex. My father was from Yorkshire and when I left Derbyshire I'd hoped they might be one of the counties interested in signing me, but they weren't.

I gave my own ideas on how I envisaged things working and outlined how bringing in key personnel would be key to making it work. The more we spoke the more I warmed to the idea. Colin Graves and I got along fine and I formed the impression that anything I wanted they would agree to. The financial package was mind-blowing. I would be captain for 2007 and 2008 before becoming director of cricket full-time. After a meeting lasting nearly two hours we shook hands and I promised to make a decision in the next couple of days. My big mistake that day was not making sure everything we'd agreed in principle was subsequently put in writing.

The following morning I met David Green. When I told him the financial offer he was staggered. 'How can you turn it down?' I was to get similar responses over the next few days from other people I spoke to. I reiterated that if Sussex put a new three-year contract on the table on the same terms I was on I would sign in there and then. David was in an impossible situation. The best Sussex could offer was a year's extension with the option of another year after that. A few days later I met Pete and Ian Salisbury while I was doing more level four coaching modules at Loughborough and dropped my little bombshell. I respected their views and both told me to accept. No one could make a convincing case for me to stay. Sam and I and our family loved Sussex and we had put down some strong roots. It would be a massive wrench to leave but she remained very supportive and by the end of the week my mind was made up.

By now the story had got out in the press and I happily fronted up. I'd hoped that the adverse reaction it created from Sussex supporters might persuade the club to improve their terms but when I met with David he reiterated that their existing offer could not be changed. It was a very emotional moment and David could sense my unease. I e-mailed him just to make sure everything was in writing and he signed off his reply with, 'Everything that glistens isn't necessarily gold.' They proved to be prophetic words. A few minutes later, and an anxious fortnight after we'd first met, I rang Colin Graves to tell him I was accepting his offer. I went to see Robbo but could hardly speak, I was that upset. He just asked me to be sure I was going for the right reasons. When I told him the director of cricket role appealed more than pulling on a Yorkshire shirt he gave me his blessing. It meant a lot.

I wanted another meeting with Yorkshire, which was arranged for the end of October. The following day I would be unveiled at a press conference while Sam and the kids would be shown around houses by the club. We drove north on a thoroughly miserable day made worse by hold-ups on the M1. We finally got to Headingley after eight hours on the road and as we pulled into the ground I looked in the rear view mirror. The kids' faces were as miserable as the weather. Sam was still very positive but I could tell Georgia and Sophie were deeply unhappy at the upheaval that lay ahead.

The meeting with Regan and Graves didn't start too well. Regan told me that Michael Lumb was leaving to sign for Hampshire and Anthony McGrath was still insisting he wanted away as well. They told me there was no chance of Darren Lehmann returning as overseas player. I had asked for full control over the selection of his replacement but the next thing I knew Regan was telling everyone he had some great news – Younis Khan, the Pakistan batsman, had been signed for 2007.

I was stunned. What happened to the assurances I'd been given about overseas players at earlier meetings? Of all Pakistan's batsmen he was probably best suited to English conditions but I was concerned how much he would play because of international commitments. At that stage I was really beginning to have serious doubts but it felt as if I was on a conveyor belt and couldn't get off. We went through my proposals to overhaul the coaching structure but again Regan pulled the rug from under my feet. I wanted a first-team coach and physiologist with Steve Oldham taking over as senior bowling coach and Kevin Sharp looking after the second team. I also wanted David Byas's new role as head of cricket development more clearly defined. All fairly basic stuff I felt, but Regan dismissed my plan to bring in two new people out of hand. I got the impression that if it wasn't his idea he wasn't interested.

People who watched the press conference the next day on TV subsequently told me they could sense my unease. Ten minutes earlier Yorkshire had poured scorn on my plans to restructure the cricket operation and now I was expected to say how proud I would be to pull on the white rose. I fronted up as best I could and even then I felt sure we could compromise and sort everything out.

I headed back to Headingley the following week for more meetings, one of which was with the players in the indoor school opposite the ground. Previously the club had put me up in a nice hotel ten minutes from the ground where Sussex had always stayed. This time I was in the Headingley Lodge, which was about as soulless a place as you could get. I remember thinking that was another sign things weren't right. I ended up driving to the other hotel for a meal and a drink.

The meeting with the players went well. I'd already spoken to Michael Vaughan who was very positive about my appointment and I think I conveyed to the squad that this was the start of a great new adventure for them and me. The lads were quite quiet initially but eventually they fired off a few questions and I told them to call me during the winter if they had anything they wanted to get off their chest, good or bad. I think they left feeling positive. The same could not be said for me.

I think I slept about 30 minutes that night. I knew at the outset there would be some serious battles to be fought but now I was having some serious doubts about fulfilling all the roles I would be taking on – batsman, captain and manager. I'd done two well enough for nine seasons at Sussex but all three? What about my relationship with Regan and did I really feel, having met the players, that they could be my team? The doubts were crashing in. By 5am I was wide awake and feeling physically sick. All I wanted to do was be back with Sam and the kids and by 9.30am I was. As soon as I walked through the door Sam knew I couldn't go through with it.

Within an hour I was knocking on David Green's door. We'd kept in regular contact and he knew I was wobbling so my visit wasn't a huge surprise. When he told me coming back was definitely an option I thanked him and drove straight to the ground to ask Robbo whether I could come back. His face broke into a massive smile; he hugged me and told me of course it was. You cannot imagine how relieved I was to hear those words.

By mid-afternoon I had agreed the club's original contract offer, all I had to do now was phone Regan and give him the news. We spoke for no more than a couple of minutes and I hardly allowed him to get a word in edgeways. I explained that my change of heart was the best decision for my family and me and that I wanted to finish my career in a Sussex shirt. He was stunned and asked if a face-to-face meeting with Colin Graves might salvage the deal. I told him I would happily talk to Graves on the phone. Regan knew my reasons and I was sure he could easily convey those to his chairman. That phonecall never came. Fortunately, I had never signed a contract.

It was the hardest decision of my career, but now a decade later I have no regrets. It was the right move at the time and still is. I had underestimated just how big an undertaking it was that I had initially committed to. Would I have been too much for Regan? Probably. I would certainly have questioned his decision-making more than he was used to. Colin Graves was a grafter who worked 24-7 to improve Yorkshire cricket and his efforts have paid off in recent years with the success they have enjoyed. Unfortunately, when it came down to it, I could not offer him, or Yorkshire, the same level of commitment. There was only one shirt I wanted to be wearing when I finished my playing career.

# 14

# End Of My Era

OF the three Championships Sussex won, 2007 was undoubtedly the hardest, and not just because of the way it finished as we hung around for hours at Hove, slowly getting drunk, while we waited on the outcome of Lancashire's game against Surrey at The Oval.

Between 2003 and 2007 we had used 29 players in the Championship with eight players involved in all three title wins: myself, Mushtaq Ahmed, James Kirtley, Jason Lewry, Murray Goodwin, Richard Montgomerie, Robin Martin-Jenkins and Mike Yardy.

They had been the foundations of our success in 2003 and 2006. In 2007 we used 18 players with five of those playing in four games or fewer. We had been lucky in 2003 and 2006 to get through relatively unscathed in terms of injuries but 2007 was different and by the time we faced Worcestershire at Hove in the final game we were down to our last 13 fit players.

A sign of what lay ahead came in the opening game at Lord's when Mike Yardy, on 99, had his finger shattered by Steve Harmison in the annual curtain-raiser between the champion county and a strong MCC side captained by Alastair Cook, who made a hundred in the first innings. Yards missed two months of the season and at various stages of the summer we were without key players like Jason Lewry, Murray Goodwin and Rana Naved.

Mushtaq was still an outstanding performer and his 13 wickets in the Worcestershire finale took him to 90 for the season and made him leading wicket-taker for the fifth successive year. But by 2007 he was starting to struggle physically and facing the prospect of knee surgery, which he accepted might mean the end of his career. It had been a troubled few months for Mushy, stemming back to the death of Pakistan coach Bob Woolmer from a heart attack during the World Cup in the Caribbean in March. A couple of days later he was implicated in some ridiculous story in the Pakistan media which claimed Woolmer had been poisoned by a drink of champagne from a bottle teetotal Mushy had given to him. When he arrived back in Sussex he was as low as I've ever seen him. He laughed off the speculation but was desperately upset by Woolmer's death. He had brought Mushy into Pakistan's coaching set-up and they got on very well.

As well as the injuries and other distractions, for the first time since 2003 we were seriously affected by England call-ups. On the one hand I was delighted that our success had been recognised and it was a proud moment for all of us when Peter Moores, promoted to the role as England's head coach, gave Matt Prior his Test debut against West Indies at Lord's and Matt responded with a brilliant century. We were trying to save a game against Surrey at the time at Hove and I remember the final session of the third day being played in front of a near-deserted ground as all our supporters crowded around the bar in the pavilion to watch Matt's big moment.

In addition, Mike Yardy was now a regular in both T20 and 50-over formats, Luke Wright made his England one-day debut against India in September (and scored a half-century) and both he and Prior were joined by James Kirtley in the squad for the inaugural World T20 in South Africa in September. International call-ups hadn't really been a major headache for us before but we always knew it could be an issue, especially as Pete was in charge and knew the potential of our players better than most.

When we reported back in April I wasn't sure how the squad would react to me following my dalliance with Yorkshire during the winter but I need not have had any concerns. I think, to a man, they were all relieved the status quo had been maintained. Better the devil you know I suppose and in 2007 I can't remember either Robbo or I ever had a serious conversation about who might eventually succeed me. I guess Matt Prior would have been in our thinking but his elevation into the Test team ruled him out. For now though, it was business as usual. Seemingly the only refuge for Mushy from all the hoo-ha surrounding Bob Woolmer in those early weeks of the season was on the field itself. He took ten wickets against Kent, one of his favourite opponents, as we won our opening game easily but then we had another horror show at Edgbaston, losing in just seven sessions to Warwickshire, and produced an even poorer performance at Canterbury in the next game as we lost successive games by an innings for the first time in a decade.

After the events of the previous winter I'd been a bit softly-softly with the squad but after we were beaten by Kent I laid into them to try and get them re-focussed. Initially, it didn't look to have made much difference. Against Surrey at Hove Mark Ramprakash, who always did well against us, made 266 as he and Mark Butcher put on 403 and we followed on despite making 365 in our first innings. Fortunately, in Murray we had a batsman capable of batting like Ramprakash for long periods of time and he scored 119 and 205 not out while I made an unbeaten century in the second innings as we saved the game.

It was a big turning point for us. We won three and drew three of the next six and then headed to Aigburth in Liverpool to play what I consider to be the best Championship match I was involved in during my career against our old rivals Lancashire. On our previous visit there 12 months earlier Lancashire bullied us to defeat inside two days and when we arrived we knew the club wicket would definitely produce a result. This was a real heavyweight contest. Although we didn't have Luke Wright, who'd hurt his groin the previous week when we were forced to play on a sopping-wet outfield at the Rose Bowl against our old friends Hampshire, the team was as strong as it could be. Lancashire's line-up wasn't bad either and included Andrew Flintoff and Muttiah Muralitharan. The three days produced the most intense cut and thrust with Chris Nash, who was now establishing himself as Richard Montgomerie's regular opening partner, Murray Goodwin and Mike Yardy all getting crucial runs for us. Lancashire's target was 242 and I brought Mushy on in the fourth over to try and get us an early breakthrough. The turning point came when I held what I consider to be the best catch of my career in the slips to remove our old nemesis Stuart Law. My reflexes, even at 36, were still pretty good and we won the game by 108 runs.

Durham were now our biggest rivals. We had a pretty good record at the Riverside and went into the penultimate match of the season on a high after thrashing Yorkshire by an innings at Hove to return to the top of the table. Another win would have clinched the title with a game to spare but the bus back down the A1 was like a scene from *Casualty*. Saqlain Mushtaq, whom we'd signed earlier that year when he got his UK passport, and Mushy were both hobbling and every time the coach went over a bump in the road the only noise was Rana Naved howling in pain after he'd badly dislocated his shoulder colliding with an advertising board as he tried to prevent a boundary. Rana was in a terrible state when it happened and it was very distressing for the rest of us. An ambulance came on to the outfield and the game was held up for 45 minutes. We lost by nine wickets and went into the final match facing a massive test of our resolve. As well as Rana, Murray Goodwin had flown back to Australia because of a family bereavement and there was no Prior, Wright or Kirtley either.

I guess we were fortunate in the three years that we won the Championship that none of our opponents stretched us in the match when we clinched the title. Worcestershire had already been relegated and once we'd negotiated the new ball on a really slow deck I felt we were capable of getting a big total. We managed 532 despite no one making a century (six of us got past 50 and Robin Martin-Jenkins was out for 99). When Worcestershire batted we showed both patience and resilience to bowl them out for 213 and then 305 and by Saturday lunchtime the game was won. A few days earlier Richard Montgomerie had told me he was going to pack up at the end of the season to take up a teaching job and it was fitting that he was sent into retirement with another trophy. During my career I played with fewer selfless cricketers than Monty. He was a brave and fearless opening batsman and later in his Sussex career adapted his game to play a lot of important one-day innings for us as well. And, of course, he was the best in the business crouched under his helmet at short leg. Fielding there takes a lot of courage but Monty loved it because, as a non-bowler, it meant he was always in the game. And if I was ever stuck on a clue in the *Times* crossword, he'd always help me out having completed it a couple of hours earlier. I say non-bowler, but he did have the pleasure of getting Kevin Pietersen out at Trent Bridge in 2003 when the game was meandering to a draw!

That last afternoon at Hove was a surreal occasion. When a long season finishes the first instinct of any cricketer is to have a drink so most of us spent those next few hours getting slowly pissed in the changing room. Lancashire's game at Surrey was on TV but we had no access to the pictures so it was a case of refreshing the score on the internet and listening to the cheers of the crowd outside. Surrey had dominated the game for three days and eventually set Lancashire 489 to win in four sessions. They had begun the last round of games six points clear at the top and, not having won an outright title since the 1930s, were desperate to make history. Surrey kept chipping away but when Lancashire reached 431/7 and needed just 58 more I thought they were going to do it. Dominic Cork was going well but then Sajid Mahmood and Gary Keedy got out and finally, just after 6pm, Robbo – who was monitoring the game through his parents watching on TV – erupted. 'Cork's out!' We'd won the title by just four and a half points. Just like 2003, the celebrations started in the dressing room and spilled over into the Sussex Cricketer and continued long into the night. In a way it had been an unexpected triumph. After the Durham game I felt Lancashire were going to win so it made our success that bit sweeter.

To be honest, it should have been another double-winning year. For the first time we'd made it through to T20 Finals Day in style, losing only two of our group games and then defeating Yorkshire easily in the quarter-final at Hove. It was easy to see why we were regarded as favourites to win the competition. Luke Wright had been in blistering form with the bat, we had Matt Prior back and in Mushy, Rana and Saqlain we had a brilliant attack. But when we met Kent in the semi-final we were guilty of complacency. Chris Nash and Murray Goodwin smashed 60 in the first five overs but after Nashy got out we folded, and were bowled out for 140 with two balls unused. Kent bowled really well but our shot selection was haphazard to put it mildly. Rob Key then made a very fine half-century and although we took it to the last over Rana, in particular, lost his nerve and bowled four no- balls. The fact Kent went on to win was little compensation and while all this was going on I was having to deny more rumours and speculation, this time linking me with a return to Derbyshire in a playing and coaching role. There had been contact, but I still believed that my future after I'd retired would be at Sussex.

It had been a gruelling summer and we all relished the chance to let our hair down. It took me a month or so to recover from the physical and mental strain but I soon turned my thoughts to 2008. It had been 1968 since a side won three Championships in a row and I seriously thought we would be the team to beat again. As well as Monty, we no longer had Rana or Saqlain but we'd brought in Rory Hamilton-Brown from Surrey, Corey Collymore, who was a very steady and consistent bowler in English conditions, as a Kolpak and we nearly had Ryan Harris, the Australian fast bowler as well. In fact, we did have him – for one game. He had a UK passport and played in the curtain-raiser against MCC and bowled very well. But then literally minutes before I had to hand in the team-sheet for the opening Championship game against Hampshire at the Rose Bowl it was announced that he had signed back home for Queensland, and would only to able to play for us as the overseas player, the slot which was still filled by Mushy of course. I was ordered by Gus Mackay to remove him from the team and a few hours later he was saying his goodbyes. It was a real shame, bearing in mind what he subsequently achieved in his career.

It was a relatively young side now with four old stagers in me, Murray, Mushy and Jason Lewry and at the start of my 11th season as captain I felt rejuvenated, probably because I also knew it would be my last in charge and that we had identified in Mike Yardy my likely successor.

I was conscious of the need to have some succession planning in place. We had integrated a lot of younger players into the team and they all hugely respected Mike as someone who had, like most of them, come through our junior system and made the most of his ability. I knew he would do the job a lot differently to me but as the 2008 season wore on I began to realise that it was time for that to happen. My race was run and the same could be said for a few others. After 476 Championship wickets in five years, Mushy retired. He'd already had one knee operation and when we played Lancashire at Hove and lost badly he bowled 33 overs virtually on one leg, hobbling to the outfield between overs but still summoning the energy and verve with ball in hand to take his last three wickets for Sussex. It was such a shame that no one at the time knew it would be his last game for if anyone deserved a special send-off at Hove it was Mushy.

I had spoken both to David Green and his successor as chairman, Jim May, about a role for me at the club once I'd stopped playing but there wasn't really anything on the table, which was what I half-feared. I felt that some of the Sussex committee wanted to make a clean break from the Adams era anyway, which was fair enough. Their view seemed to be where would this strong character, who had been a powerful figure at the club for more than a decade, fit into the future? There's no room for sentiment in professional sport and I understood that, but I was very disappointed when I realised there was nothing for me.

On the field 2008 turned out to be very hard, particularly in the Championship. We only survived after drawing our final game against Yorkshire. I'd had a difficult year with the bat, scoring 431 runs in 14 games – another sign, perhaps, that I was coming to the end. In the last game I made a duck in the first innings.

Matthew Hoggard was captaining Yorkshire and when I went out to bat in the second dig their players formed a guard of honour for me. Adil Rashid was bowling and I promised him that if he gave me one to get off the mark I would have a dip. He bowled me a full toss on leg stump which I just about crabbed to square leg for a single and then I hit three sixes and scored 35 off as many balls. Every year after you play your final innings of the season at home you walk off to a standing ovation but this felt different. I was very emotional and came off with everyone in the ground standing up. By then I'd already confirmed that I would be stepping down as captain, but at that moment it was still my intention to finish the last year of my contract with a return to the ranks and the opportunity to play with freedom and enjoy myself. And I also quietly hoped than in 12 months that opportunity to remain at Sussex might have presented itself.

Before the Pro40 decider against Nottinghamshire I'd told the committee of my decision to step down as captain and recommended Yards as my successor. I knew he would have massive support inside and outside the dressing room and I later found out that before the game at Trent Bridge he'd gone round to everyone in the team, imploring them to find that bit more at the end of a long season so I could go out in style having lifted yet another trophy.

Nottinghamshire had batted first and got to 227/7, more than we'd have liked to chase on a used pitch that was taking spin. My main memory of my last one-day innings for Sussex (I made 24) was facing Graeme Swann, who was spinning the ball hard, and struggling just to lay a bat on the ball. We lost wickets regularly and with ten overs to go were 130/8, needing 98 off ten overs. The plan was to announce I was stepping down on Sky Sports after the game but as I sat in the dressing room with Notts poised to win the title I decided I would delay the announcement for a couple of days, as I didn't want to take anything away from their achievement and celebrations.

We'd brought the whole squad up to Nottingham so our balcony was packed. So I sat in the back room watching the game on TV with the dressing-room attendants. I was sitting on one of the washing machines behind the door when Paul Franks's wife popped her head around the door to make sure they had the champagne on ice. She didn't see me at first and apologised profusely, but I told her that they could have ours anyway.

I'd seen Murray play several fantastic innings over the years in pressure situations. He was our go-to batsman and someone we could rely on in a crisis but his effort that day surpassed anything else I'd seen. With Mohammad Sami offering him fantastic support at the other end he began to eat into the target. There's no doubt the Notts lads thought they had won the game and by the time they realised otherwise we'd got to the last over, which would be bowled by Charlie Shreck, with 16 needed. They took 12 off the first five balls so the equation was now simple enough – four to win. Because of the delay between real-time and the TV coverage the ball was already sailing over the boundary as I watched Shreck complete his run-up to the crease. All I remember after that was a massive cheer from the balcony and that familiar feeling of being buried under a mass – and with all the boys there it really was a mass – of celebrating team-mates. What followed was a mixture of sheer unbridled joy, relief and sadness. I lifted the trophy and announced a few moments later that I would be stepping down at the end of the season. Letting go of something that had defined my career and become my life and not just mine but my family's as well was a more painful experience than I'd imagined it would be.

A few weeks later I took a call from Gus Mackay, who had left his post as chief executive earlier that year to join Surrey in a newly-created role as managing director of cricket. There were still a few Surrey legends on the coaching staff with Graham Thorpe as batting coach and Alec Stewart having a wider coaching and consultative remit. Alec had spent a few months with Sussex as part of our coaching set-up when he retired as a player but The Oval was his spiritual home. Gus knew how I operated and I guess when he made that call he had it in his mind that it might not be a bad thing to have at least one familiar face with him as he tried to turn Surrey around.

He offered me the job of professional cricket manager. I didn't accept at first, although I was absolutely thrilled to be offered the post, because I wanted to do some research. From what I could gather after speaking to several individuals in the game, some of whom were closely attached to Surrey, it wasn't a job that people were queuing up to take. In hindsight I should have guessed what lay ahead when I went to interview and was told that the other person they were keen on, Andy Moles, had phoned Gus that morning to say he'd been offered a role with New Zealand and wasn't available. Instead of advertising the post again, or taking more soundings, I was offered the job there and then.

So it might have been a poisoned chalice but there was never any chance I would turn Surrey down. How often do opportunities like this come along, especially to someone new to coaching and management? Although some of my confidants had reservations no one told me not to take the job. I spoke to Jim May and Mark Robinson and although they were disappointed they were totally supportive. I had a farewell dinner with the Sussex players and backroom staff and after ten years and 11 seasons that part of my life was over.

I spent my entire playing career operating to the mantra of no regrets but, looking back seven years later, I now accept that it was too early for me to leave Sussex.

## 15

# Captain Turned Coach

I KNEW what I was walking into at Surrey as 2008 had been one of the worst seasons in their history. They failed to win a Championship game and were relegated to the Second Division. Alan Butcher's long association with the county had ended when he was fired at the end of the season as coach and I realised that the squad needed to be massively overhauled. The only batsmen who finished that season with 1,000 runs were Mark Ramprakash, who was as consistent as ever and had scored his 100th first-class hundred that season, and Scott Newman, the left-handed opener.

Their recruitment policy seemed scattergun at best, so much so that halfway through the summer they brought Chris Lewis out of retirement to play some one-day cricket seven years after he had last played for Surrey. They had a bad injury record so that area of the cricket operation needed to be addressed as did the overseas player situation after Matt Nicholson and the West Indian Pedro Collins, who was a Kolpak registration, had flattered to deceive and they had finished the season by employing Shoaib Akhtar in a desperate bid to win their final three games and climb out of trouble. By that stage of his career, though, the Rawalpindi Express had hit the buffers.

So major surgery, rather than a bit of tweaking here and there, was required. In short I was brought in to make some tough decisions and while nobody at Surrey, least of all Gus, hid the fact that a lot of hard work lay ahead I was just thrilled to get the opportunity. I only envisaged what might happen if I could get things right and turn it around rather than the consequences of failure.

I made mistakes during my four and a half years with Surrey and the critics of my time at The Oval, and there were plenty of those in the committee room and among the supporters, would argue that I did well to last as long as I did. In defence, I would contend that someone with far greater coaching and management experience than I would have struggled to turn things around. And remember, we did win promotion back to the First Division and Surrey's first one-day trophy at Lord's since 2001. Compared to previous years of underachievement at The Oval, I am proud of those accomplishments.

If you look up the word 'club' in a dictionary, you could accurately apply its meaning to somewhere like Sussex where there is a real togetherness among the players and people behind the scenes. I don't believe there is a county in the country like Surrey where so much emphasis is put on the six or seven days a year when The Oval stages international cricket. That's the priority and everything else revolves around that. I would never use it as an excuse for performances on the field but for the first two years a lot of my time was spent trying to move Surrey cricket a bit closer to the centre of the operation, with only partial success.

When the Test was on the ground would be out of bounds for ten days beforehand and in 2010 four of our first five Championship matches were at home, three of them at The Oval. It meant half of our home fixtures had been played by mid-May when, ideally, you wanted as many home matches as possible in the second half of the season when The Oval traditionally favoured spin bowlers.

I had countless meetings with the commercial and financial directors at the club and when I argued that Surrey cricket needed to be given more prominence their argument was that it was international cricket that paid for the biggest playing budget of all of the 18 counties. When I arrived in 2009 I was told that the playing budget was a whopping £2.3m. The problem was the ECB were introducing a salary cap in 2010 and £500,000 had to be trimmed from the wage bill.

Paul Sheldon, the chief executive with whom I always had a solid relationship, and Gus Mackay gave me three very clear directives. They wanted a Surrey team to be competitive across all formats; they wanted more international recognition for their players; and they wanted a clearly defined pathway from their junior squads through to the first team. In other words, I had to compete with 17 other counties, all of whom regarded beating Surrey in whatever the competition as a feather in their cap and raised their game consequently. This had to be done while losing our best players to England and at the same time bringing youngsters through. It wasn't an impossible challenge and I must stress it was one I was very keen to take on. I was being well paid and there was a good performance-related element to the three-year contract I signed when I joined but the first year was far more difficult than I'd expected as we tried to regenerate and refresh the squad while trying to be competitive on the pitch.

And throughout this, and for the rest of my time at Surrey, there were people at the club desperate for me to fail. I won't even give my sternest critics on the bloated 20-strong Surrey committee the satisfaction of name-checking them but even when we got promoted and won the Lord's final in 2011 they were not prepared to enjoy the success. They could never get around the fact that someone from outside the county was heading up their cricket operation. At a place like The Oval, where there are reminders on every wall and in every corridor of the many great Surrey and England players, it was impossible to get away from the past. I felt a prisoner of it for a lot of my time at the club.

My predecessor as coach, Alan Butcher, had been sacked at the end of 2008 after Surrey failed to win a Championship match so you could say our record in 2009 was an improvement, although I didn't see winning one game in the Second Division as anything to shout about. Neither was finishing bottom in the Pro40 League with two wins.

Mark Butcher had been a fantastic servant for Surrey but his knees were hanging by a thread and he managed just five Championship games before he was forced to retire halfway through the season. I'd played a lot of cricket against Butch during my own career and I admired him greatly. He was a fantastic batsman, capable of playing some wonderful innings for county and country, and when he was in charge of the side he captained us intelligently and was always prepared to gamble to get a result. But that final year can't have been easy for him. Not only was he struggling physically but our bowling attack was nowhere near good enough. We used 21 bowlers in total in 2009 but between them in the Championship they took 184 wickets. Jade Dernbach was emerging as a young seamer of real potential and was leading wicket-taker with 37 but he lacked support. Andre Nel, who should have been the focal point of the attack, missed five games through injury and Chris Jordan only played eight matches because of back problems. Our West Indian Pedro Collins was a disappointment although I had some sympathy for our bowlers, particularly at The Oval where the wickets that the groundsman at the time, Bill Gordon, produced were pretty flat. They turned a little, and Chris Schofield and Murtaza Hussain, who had taken the last Lancashire wicket when Sussex won the title in 2007, did okay but we rarely looked like bowling teams out twice.

Michael Brown, who had been recruited from Hampshire before I arrived, and Stewart Walters led the side in Butch's absence and senior batsmen like Mark Ramprakash, who was still going strong even as he approached his 40th year, and Usman Afzaal both scored heavily. But in search of short-term solutions we signed guys like Jimmy Anyon and Richard Logan on loan and although both tried hard in hindsight it was a mistake. We only had four Surrey-born players on the staff as well, and although this had been the case before I arrived it was sometimes used as a stick to beat me with. And as I soon discovered, when the flak was flying, it was mostly in my direction and not at Graham Thorpe, Martin Bicknell or Alec Stewart, three Surrey legends who were on the coaching staff. There's no doubt in my mind that Alec coveted my job and, with his history at Surrey, it would have been a popular appointment. But Alec is a smart guy. He looked at the situation in 2009 and thought, 'I'm going nowhere near that.' A lot of the mess had been cleared up by the time he did get the top job four years later.

At the end of 2009 we had a clearout which was a pretty unpleasant time for me but I knew it was necessary pain, especially if Surrey were to move forward and I was to get anywhere close to meeting the three criteria laid down by the management when I arrived. In particular, we needed to appoint a new captain. Neither Brown nor Walters were secure in their own positions in the side so I began to look outside Surrey at alternatives. One target was Rob Key, who'd done a good job at Kent and was still a wonderful batsman. He'd always enjoyed playing at The Oval and we spoke to him but he made it clear that it wasn't the right time for him to move. A captain from abroad was not an option because I wanted our overseas player to be a frontline spinner.

I'd been introduced to Roger Hamilton-Brown, Rory's dad, by Ian Salisbury. It was early autumn and we had been due to play golf together but it poured with rain and instead we sat in the clubhouse talking shop. One of my clearest memories of Rory when we played together at Sussex was of a one-day game when he ran up from third man at the end of an over to propose a field change. I remember thinking at the time it showed a bit of character even though I'd probably ignored his suggestion. Roger said he was happy at Sussex, where he'd made his maiden first-class hundred at the end of the previous season. But

I felt he would get more opportunities at Surrey, where he had played all of his junior cricket, and I believed he had leadership potential, even at the age of 22 and with just eight first-class games under his belt. And I knew he was a talented player, who would improve our batting in all formats while his off spin would give us another useful option in one-day cricket.

He'd left Surrey because the pathway from junior cricket into the first team wasn't there at the time and, of course, this was one of the criteria I had been asked to instigate. The more we got chatting the more Roger, at least, warmed to the idea that his son might come back. When golf was cancelled we reconvened later that day in London and he assured me that my idea had some merit. I knew there were obstacles in our path, not least the reaction in Sussex when their former captain, now in charge of their main rivals, came back and pinched one of their most promising young players.

But the more I thought about bringing Rory back the more it made sense. I knew I would have to spend a lot of time with him, far more than any other player in the squad, because as someone with as much relatively recent captaincy experience as myself I would try to pass on all knowledge as he wanted. I wanted to build a much younger squad and I thought that element of the dressing room at least would look up to him. He had a strong Surrey background of course and that was one of my main arguments when I presented the case for Rory as our next captain to the committee.

In truth, I was expecting them to turn down the idea because of his age and lack of experience but in all my time at Surrey it was the proposal that met with the least resistance. When I finished outlining my case there was silence in the room for a moment but after that the mood was totally positive.

They knew, as I did, that it represented something of a gamble but I outlined a vision of Rory leading a vibrant, young Surrey team competing in its rightful place with the bigger counties on a regular basis for trophies. I think a few of the committee members were a bit shocked to be honest. It looked like something out of leftfield but when Richard Thompson, who was chairman-elect at the time, gave his approval the mood was completely supportive. All we needed to do now was sort things out with Sussex.

They made things difficult,, as I knew they would, and tried hard to persuade Rory to stay. We were given a 48-hour window to talk to Rory, the problem being that he was in Pretoria with the England development squad! So I flew overnight to Johannesburg, got a cab the next morning from the airport to Pretoria and after Rory had finished training we sat down over lunch. All we did was talk cricket, and specifically Surrey cricket. It was clear from the start that he still regarded Surrey as 'his' club, even though he'd established himself as a popular member of the dressing room at Hove. At the end he told me he wanted to be the next Surrey captain and although the announcement provoked the response I expected from Sussex they knew they were fighting a losing battle once he'd told them that the opportunity, a bit like the one I'd been offered a year earlier at The Oval, was too good to turn down.

Compensation with Sussex was agreed and when Rory was unveiled at a press conference at The Oval just before Christmas he spoke very impressively. He had some captaincy experience, most notably with England

Under-19s, which was something a few of those doubting the decision in the media conveniently chose to ignore but we went into 2010 feeling very optimistic, although I knew that bringing in Rory was not the answer to all of our ills. There would be another year of pain before we finally started to make progress as a squad.

We suffered a blow before a ball was bowled. Having lined up the Indian leg-spinner Piyush Chawla, who had made a real impact with Sussex in 2009 when he finished as their leading wicket-taker despite only playing six games, the Indian Cricket Board refused to sanction his release to play county cricket. We were left scrambling around as the best overseas players, had already committed themselves to other counties. Iftikhar Anjum and Younis Khan both had stints but were largely ineffective. Steven Davies, whom we recruited from Worcestershire, settled in very quickly though and in 2011 he formed an effective opening partnership with Rory. But in 2010 the top order was a real problem for us. In the end we tried nine different opening combinations, our options limited by injury to Michael Brown. Arun Harinath battled hard but didn't really break through on a consistent basis and we were still far too reliant on Ramps, who scored 1,595 Championship runs that summer, nearly twice as many as anyone else.

Jade Dernbach had another good season and one of our other recruits who attracted criticism when he joined us, Chris Tremlett from Hampshire, did well after overcoming injuries at the start of the season and finished with 48 wickets and a place in the England squad.

Jason Roy was also starting to emerge, initially in one-day cricket, and, as I expected, the younger guys in the dressing room reacted well to Rory. He made some mistakes and some of his decision-making had me tearing my hair out but he'd have flashes of inspiration too and I could see that he was growing into the job, although by the end of 2010 he was running on empty physically. He couldn't believe I had been captain of Sussex for 11 seasons! Some of the more experienced players had their reservations and Andre Nel was openly critical of Rory's decision-making at times and when he left halfway through the season there weren't too many tears shed.

Pakistan had been England's Test match opponents that summer but the game lasted just three and a half days and the aggregate attendance of 72,000 was well down on previous Oval Tests. As the economic recession began to bite Surrey also experienced a drop-off in T20 attendances, which had traditionally attracted a big element of corporate hospitality clientele. The result of all this became painfully clear at the end of the season. Having announced record profits on the back of a successful Ashes summer in 2009, now Surrey was bracing itself for big losses and the only way of stemming them was to cut back staff.

Towards the end of the season I turned up as usual at The Oval for a training session to find a lot of the staff, with whom we shared the same offices, in tears. Word was filtering out that everyone was being invited to a meeting on the top floor. If you were being asked to go to the chief executive's office your job was safe, but your role might be different. If your destination was the finance director's office you were getting your P45. Nineteen people were made redundant that day, including Gus, whose position as managing director was among those to go.

Although our performances in one-day cricket had improved, four Championship wins and a seventh-place finish in the Second Division hardly made me bulletproof and when I headed into Paul Sheldon's office after encountering a visibly upset Gus heading in the opposite direction I feared the worst.

I felt relieved when Sheldon told me I was still in a job, but my responsibilities were changing. My title was the same but I was now being asked to cover all of Gus's duties with regard to professional cricket, including managing the playing budget and presenting a detailed plan to the board outlining Surrey's future, as I saw it. At least I would have Ian Salisbury as my coach, a development which I definitely saw as a positive. I felt I had a strong ally in the ongoing battles with the committee, who had welcomed Rory's appointment but were unhappy at the rate of progress we had made in his first year. I would still have day-to-day contact with the team of course and I guess it looked as if, with more responsibility, I was actually in a stronger position. But I wasn't sure, with more on my plate, I could do everything the job now entailed to the best of my ability.

Paul Sheldon eventually left too and his replacement Richard Gould, who, like me, had come from a relatively small county in Somerset, had been in the job for more than a week before we had our first conversation. Almost his first words to me were, 'In my opinion, you're the best young coach in the country and I want to give you as much support as I can. How can I help?' Immediately he put my mind at ease. I told him two things. The contracts for Ian and I were due to run out at the end of 2011 and I wanted an indication as to whether they would be renewed. And I also told him I needed some space to do the job and when he asked what I meant I didn't hold back. I told him I was fed up having to constantly fight fires with certain people on the committee, who two years after I'd arrived still resented me because of my Sussex background.

We held any number of member forums during my time at Surrey and the same old faces, who thought they spoke for the majority of the members, would moan about anything. On one occasion I think I got the blame when the toilets in the pavilion stopped working during a Championship match! Most of my main critics would base themselves just below the dressing rooms at The Oval, in earshot of the players if they chose to listen. I'm not sure if they ever worked out that I spent most of my day in my office, which had a much better view of the square high up in the pavilion. They were a small bunch (I used to call them 'the minority') but felt they had the ear of the high-ups. When I spoke to members myself, particularly those based outside London, they were much more positive. They knew the situation I'd inherited wasn't great and they could see progress being made, albeit slowly. I compared it to my first three years at Sussex when we had to reach rock bottom before climbing again. Richard was very supportive at this time, backing me in public and then giving Ian and I two-year contract extensions. Of course I knew I had to deliver at some stage, and that the minimum requirement during those two years would be promotion, but at least we could put our plans for 2011 into place without fear of getting the sack.

Rock-bottom for us in 2011 came at Canterbury in August. We lost heavily to Kent and at that stage were seventh in the Second Division, 57 points off the leaders. I thought we were making progress though. Two of our winter recruits, Zander de Bruyn from Somerset and

Tom Maynard, a player we'd recruited from Glamorgan, had been pretty consistent, Rory and Steven Davies had become a settled opening pair and Tim Linley, a left-armer who'd had a season at Sussex when I was there without getting too many opportunities, was on his way to taking 73 wickets. We had four games to go and had recruited Pragyan Ojha, a slow left-armer from India, for the run-in and although I felt we would finish strongly I must admit that getting the two wins and two solid draws I felt we needed to finish in the top two would be a tall order.

We ended up winning all four, thrashing Leicestershire by ten wickets, Northamptonshire by 333 runs, Essex by 109 runs and then, in the final game of the season at The Oval, we beat Derbyshire in eight sessions. It must have been written in the stars that we'd go up because everything just clicked into place.

The aggressive cricket, which had seen us win ten of our 12 group games in the CB40 one-day competition, was transferred into the longer format and little things went our way too. Against Derbyshire we lost our eighth wicket still needing 18 runs for maximum batting points with only Tim Linley and Ojha, neither of whom had any great batting prowess, to come. But they hung around with Stuart Meaker and we reached 400 with four byes and eventually totalled 468. Tom Maynard had made a brilliant century and now our bowlers got to work, dismissing Derbyshire cheaply twice with Ohja, who finished with 24 wickets in four appearances at less than 13 runs apiece, the match-winner we felt he could be.

Surrey were back where we felt we belonged in the First Division and thanks to a comprehensive win over Sussex in the semi-final we had a Lord's final to look forward to a few days later against Somerset. That night was the first time I felt overwhelming backing for me among the supporters and behind the scenes at the club. Yet there was still a discordant faction on the committee who, even in this happy moment for Surrey, found it hard to return the toast when I raised a glass in their direction in the pavilion bar afterwards because another opportunity to lever me out had gone.

That night I told Sam that even if we won at Lord's I was going to resign. She had to talk me out of it, 'If you go, people will say you never see anything through. You had the flirtation with Yorkshire and now this. You need to build your reputation. You can't see it but the players respect you and they need you.' I still wasn't convinced but I told her I would think again after the final.

Our one-day cricket that year was brilliant and I just sat back and enjoyed the ride. We decided from the start to play with freedom, to enjoy ourselves and see what happened. I knew that even if one of our stroke players didn't come off in a certain game someone else would. We got on a roll in the CB40 and by the time we lost our last group match we had already qualified. We totalled more than 250 in seven of the 12 games and smashed 311 against a decent Hampshire attack at Whitgift School. We had a clear gameplan and I knew it would take a special performance from Somerset, who had a reputation for choking in finals, to beat us at Lord's.

We would do anything to get an advantage, however small. On the day of the final I sent our fitness coach Ashley Wright (Luke's brother) to the Nursery Ground to set up our cones for warm-up over as big an area as possible. We had no intention of using such a large space, I merely wanted to disrupt their preparation. I respected their coach, Andy Hurry, a lot but I thought if I could make him tense it would make his players tense. They had lost their last four one-day finals and earlier that season had thrown away the T20 final at Edgbaston when chasing a very modest Leicestershire score.

When I got to the Nursery Ground I could see they were pissed off. I went up to Andy. 'Is there a problem?' I asked. To Andy's credit he didn't make a song and dance about it but while their squad fretted over their preparation I got Ashley to gather up all the cones and we just ran a small session in a tiny bit of space before going on to the main ground so the bowlers could sort out their warm-ups and we could do some catching and fielding practice. Did it make a difference to the outcome of the game? Probably not, but I was pleased. My strategic brain was working and as a coach I felt I was improving, a bit like the team, with more experience.

I enjoyed the next few hours far more than I expected, and certainly more than when I'd captained Sussex against Lancashire five years earlier. Despite losing the toss we always seemed to have control. There was a bit of rain around and it was the day Jos Buttler announced himself to the wider cricketing audience with a fabulous innings of 86 from 71 balls. Jade Dernbach had been on England duty the previous day in Cardiff and only got to the hotel at 2.30am but he bowled superbly, taking 4-30 including the wicket of Buttler. There was a bit of rain at the start of our reply and we lost a couple of early wickets but Rory played what I will always regard as his best innings for Surrey that day, a calm and composed 78.

Others like Tom Maynard, Chris Schofield and Matt Spriegel chipped in and we reached our revised target of 186 with 15 balls to spare to win by five wickets. It was Surrey's first trophy since 2003.

I will always remember the moments after we'd won when we did the traditional lap of honour around the ground. The ground was only half-full but they all seemed to be Surrey supporters and as we walked round Tom sprinted over to me, jumped on my back and gave me the biggest hug. 'Thanks Grizz,' he said. 'This is what we work for and this is what we want more of.'

Would I have left if we'd lost to Somerset? Possibly. In the end, though, it was the support and positive feedback I got from the players, both on that evening at Lord's and in the days that followed, which persuaded me. I couldn't walk away. We were back in the First Division, which was where everyone felt Surrey belonged, and we'd put some silverware on the table. It would have been hard to leave, far less explain that in the midst of the celebrations I still felt I was being constantly undermined by a small but vociferous element of committee members at the club.

I knew things would come to a head some time down the line on that score but as we started preparing for 2012 I was excited about the future. We had players in the England set-up, both in the Test and one-day teams and the development squads, youngsters like Zafar Ansari and Rory Burns emerging, and we'd won some trophies. I felt we had met the criteria laid down by the club a couple of years earlier.

We recruited that winter from a position of strength. I felt we needed some experience to cover for the likely absence of key bowlers with England and in Jon Lewis we identified someone who was still excellent in English conditions and who would enjoy a new challenge at a relatively late stage of his career. As I anticipated, the bar was raised in terms of what the club expected from the team now. The chairman, Richard Thompson, talked enthusiastically about winning the Championship and I genuinely felt we had a chance, especially if we could avoid injury. We had a good group of seamers that we could rotate if necessary and I wouldn't have swapped our top six for any in the country.

Yet before the season started things began to unravel. I'd had a couple of conversations with Tom, who'd been on the England Development Programme during the winter. He was unhappy because the coaches were messing around with his technique. We'd also got reports back that Jason and Tom had stepped out of line at a preparation camp at Loughborough. I put it down to the normal high spirits everyone had at their age and trusted the England management would deal with it.

Rory had played in Zimbabwe and New Zealand during the winter. There was more pressure now we were back in the First Division and expected to challenge for the title and it quickly became clear to me that Rory had raised the expectations he had of himself as well. He'd played in the First Division and knew there was a big step up from the cricket he'd experienced in his first two years as captain. Would he be able to bat with the same freedom at the top of the order against better new-ball attacks for instance? We had some good chats in pre-season and he needed a bit of reassurance but I just sensed that he was feeling the pressure of his high-profile position.

Within two months of the season starting we were all plunged into the most awful tragedy imaginable, the death of Tom Maynard.

# 16

# Tom

MONDAY 18 June 2012. Sophie was up at the crack of dawn, excited about her first trip away with her school. As we were gathering her stuff together I noticed a missed call on my phone from Richard Gould timed at 6.50am.

No message. I thought it was a bit strange but carried on, figuring if it had been important he would have left a message. As I was getting ready to take Sophie to school he called again.

'Morning Richard, everything okay?'

'Well, no.'

'Right, what's wrong?'

I could tell in his voice straight away. He explained that he had taken a phonecall from the British Transport Police a few minutes earlier.

A body had been found on the line near Wimbledon underground station.

'They think it's one of our players.'

I don't know how long it was before Richard spoke again, probably only ten seconds. But it felt like a lot longer.

'They think it's Tom.'

When Umer Rashid drowned on Sussex's pre-season tour in 2002 I really struggled to come to terms with his loss. We all did. Does anyone have the right mechanism to deal with something like that? Somehow we got through and when, a year later, we won our first County Championship the memory of a lad who would, had he lived, probably been celebrating that moment with us was the first that we toasted.

Now it was happening again.

Richard hung up and promised to call back when he had confirmation. I went back into the house where Sophie had finished packing her suitcase and was desperate to get to school to start her big adventure.

Sam was making tea but as soon as we made eye contact she knew something was wrong.

It had only been a couple of weeks earlier, during Surrey's match against Sussex at Horsham, that Tom and the rest of the team had been at our house for a barbecue. Sam loved Tom, so did the kids. I went outside with Sam and repeated the conversation I'd had with Richard. She burst into tears and then stood in silence for a few minutes.

We tried to act as normally as we could for Sophie. I dropped her off at school and was heading home again when Richard rung to confirm the awful news. I don't cry easily but I did that day, all the way back to the house and then when I saw Sam.

As parents, our first thoughts were for Sue and Matt, Tom's mum and dad. More tears.

Richard rang back. He'd kicked into his management role by then and gave me a job to do. Could I ring the other players and anyone else who knew Tom well? The last thing any of us wanted was for Tom's friends to find out the news through the media. I told him I would, but only after he reassured me that Matt and Sue had been spoken to first.

Thirty minutes or so later, the first person I called was Dean Conway, who'd watched Tom grow up while he was Glamorgan physio and Matt was their captain. Dean was in shock. Every time I looked up a number on my phone contacts and dialled someone whose name I recognised the reaction was the same. Tom? Dead? Are you absolutely 100 per cent positive?

By mid-morning the news was out, thankfully after all his team-mates and close friends had been told. Rory Hamilton-Brown and Jade Dernbach took it worst, as I knew they would, but Rory suggested that the squad come together at his mum's house in Wandsworth later that day. I drove to London in a daze and for the rest of the day we sat around, consoling each other. Rory was broken. Some ties are even stronger than family and he had lost his soulmate.

I guess some people deal with grief by hiding themselves away. My instinct was to do what I'd always done; step forward and lead.

Of course we were not trained to deal with a situation like this but there were practicalities to consider. Those next two or three weeks were awful. At times I felt close to breaking point. And the question I and everyone at Surrey no doubt asked themselves a thousand times was, 'Could we have done more?'

A few weeks earlier I was doing a lap of the ground at New Road, Worcester, with Gordon Lord, the ECB's head of elite coaching development, and feeling as comfortable and settled as I had at any time during my time at Surrey. Promotion and the Lord's cup final victory had at least bought me some time with my critics at the club and Gordon said he felt my own coaching career was moving in the right direction and that I might be given more responsibility during the winter of 2012/13 within the ECB's coaching structure.

Although we hadn't started the season in a blaze of glory we were doing okay. We had beaten Sussex in the Championship and then lost by just three runs to Middlesex at Lord's. I felt the squad was evolving nicely. Experienced guys like Mark Ramprakash, Jon Lewis, who had settled down very quickly at his new county, and Zander de Bruyn were the solid, reliable core which enabled the more expressive players like Tom, Steve Davies, Jason Roy, Rory and Jade Dernbach to play their natural, attacking game.

Tom had started the Championship season well. He made runs against Sussex and on a difficult pitch at The Oval against Worcestershire had shown another side to his game. He only scored 34 in the first innings but the conditions were extremely tough and the gutsy way he approached the task demonstrated to me that, as I knew from the first day I worked with him, he could adapt his game. A few weeks later at Worcester he and Rory put together a partnership of 225 in 44 overs that showcased the aggressive and entertaining way we wanted to play our cricket. Tom scored a career-best 143 as he and Rory matched each other shot for shot. It was exhilarating to watch. Two best friends, having fun playing the game they loved. A special time.

At the beginning of June we moved on to Horsham to play Sussex, a fixture I was looking forward to for the obvious reasons and also because it would mean four nights in my own bed. Sam and I decided to hold a barbecue for the players and their wives and girlfriends on the first night. We had about 35 guests and it was a lovely evening. I've still got pictures of Tom relaxing with Sam and our girls and enjoying himself.

The following evening Tom, Jade and Rory had gone for a meal after play. Afterwards, Rory and Jade headed back to the team hotel near Horsham but Tom drove into Brighton to meet an old school friend. A few hours later, as he was walking along the seafront, a car that had mounted the kerb hit him and he was flipped on to the bonnet. He was fortunate just to escape with a badly bruised shoulder and some cuts to his face but it didn't look good the next day when he had his arm in a sling and was unable to field.

When I heard what had happened the explanation didn't feel right. The press had got hold of the story so I fronted up as best as I could but during the rest of that game I met with Tom, Rory, Jade and others on an individual basis, and on more than one occasion, to try and get to the bottom of what happened. They all assured me that Tom's version of events was correct.

We lost the game, so the scheduled committee meeting at The Oval early the following week was not something I was particularly looking forward to. I knew there would be calls for Tom to be disciplined so before leaving for the meeting I rang Jade Dernbach, who had gone off to play for England, again. 'Look Jade, I've got to go to the committee tonight and present an account of what happened last week. Are you absolutely sure that what happened is 100 per cent the truth?' He assured me it was and the club duly fined Tom.

We had no hard and fast rules about what was out of bounds during a match. There was certainly no curfew in place. We trusted the boys to be sensible but Tom accepted that there are certain situations, which present themselves, which should not happen and he had no problem with the fact that he would have to be punished. As I drove home from the meeting I was just glad that the incident had been put to bed. We were in the middle of an intensive period of preparation for the T20 Cup, a competition which I felt would play to our strengths. The opening game was a few days away and I was now looking forward to fine-tuning our plans with Tom and the rest of the players.

The following day Ian Salisbury pulled me to one side before training. I hadn't seen them but he had been alerted to several pictures on social media of Tom, Rory and Jade in a nightclub in Brighton the evening Tom had been hit by a car. Richard Gould and I pulled all three into a meeting and they were all heavily fined. Of course I was disappointed that they hadn't been truthful with me in the first instance. We knew they had to have the opportunity to let off steam and it certainly wasn't a lecture about morals and responsibility we handed out when we spoke to them. These players were old enough to know where the boundaries were. Had they come clean in the first place we might have been able to handle it without the committee getting involved. Tom felt hard done by but, like the rest of us, all he wanted to do was draw a line under the incident and concentrate on cricket. Richard finished the meeting by saying, 'Let's be thankful you weren't more badly injured, Tom.'

After Tom's death, the club conducted its own rigorous internal investigation. The findings showed the squad to be as hard-working, responsible and well-managed as any in the country. It also revealed what we later were to be informed of by the players themselves – that a small minority were pushing the boundaries too far. I trusted the players and felt there were enough mechanisms in place within the team environment that if something had been going on I would have found out about it and so would everyone on the coaching and support staff, either through our own investigations or if a member of the squad had tipped us off. You can't keep a lid on certain things in such a closely-knit environment as a cricket team, living out of each other's pockets for six months of the year.

We started the T20 campaign well, winning our first two games while Tom recovered from his injury. Our next match was against Kent at Beckenham on Sunday 17 June and after training the day before Tom came over to me. 'I know I've let you down and I'm sorry. I want to play tomorrow and make it up to you.' I wasn't sure because Tom was not 100 per cent fit and changing a team that had won its first two games didn't sit right with me either. However, there was overwhelming support from his team-mates that he should play. Against my better judgement I relented and Tom played. We lost the game and Tom struggled, scoring seven off 17 balls.

Our next game was the following Wednesday. It had been a difficult few days but I was upbeat when I addressed the squad afterwards. 'Look, get a good night's sleep, take tomorrow off to recharge the batteries and then we will train on Tuesday and talk about ways where we can improve as a team and progress as individuals.' That night Rory, Jade and Tom met up in one of their favourite restaurants to reflect on the past few weeks and toast Jade's selection for the England one-day squad. We would never see Tom again.

\* \* \* \* \*

Throughout my career as captain and coach I can honestly say that I never came across anyone who was more universally liked than Tom Maynard. In any team you have players who bring different things to the group. Senior players have experience and wisdom, youngsters the energy. There are the carers, who will put their arm around you and encourage you when times are tough but also guys who will try and rein in team-mates who are going too far. I think Tom had a bit of all those characteristics. We absolutely loved him and I know the Glamorgan lads felt the same.

Tom was laid to rest in Cardiff Cathedral in front of hundreds of friends, family and team-mates. We did his memory proud that day and I remember emerging from the church into the warmth of a summer's afternoon feeling a mixture of emotions.

Of course it had been a very difficult day, but it was also a wonderful celebration of Tom the cricketer and Tom the human being. Everybody who spoke that day did so with courage and paid their own fitting tribute, but the overwhelming theme was just how much Tom was loved by all. The rest of that season was tough for all of us, but I was proud of the way I handled the situation. For the next few weeks I was at The Oval on a daily basis, dealing with the players and, of course, wrestling with my own emotions. Jade needed time away, which he was given, and other players wanted time out too. Some reacted differently and threw themselves into gym work and net sessions. Everyone had a different way of coping.

Physically and mentally I was struggling. Sam had taken Tom's death very badly so when I did spend periods at home I was trying to support her as well. We were like a couple of ghosts. One afternoon at The Oval Richard Gould saw me and insisted that I take a break. Initially I resisted because I felt my place was with the players but he wouldn't take no for an answer and said Ian Salisbury also needed time out.

Ian felt the same as me, mentally and physically drained, and thought it was a good idea. We had two Championship games coming up, against against Warwickshire and Durham, and we decided that I'd take the team at Durham and he would be in charge at Edgbaston, against his former county. So I went off while the team played the game but when news leaked out of my absence all hell broke loose. My critics at The Oval were having a field day, the keyboard warriors who spent all day on a Surrey internet forum vented their spleen. Richard rang me and gave me the option of coming home early from my week away. I flatly refused and told him he would have to front up and back the decision publicly, especially as he had made it in the first place. When Ian found out about all the stick I'd got he revised his decision and decided to stay with the squad for the next match, a decision which put me in a difficult position to say the least.

We knew at some stage we'd have to get back to playing cricket again. Rory was told to take as much time as he wanted but it was only four days after Tom's death that we reconvened at Chelmsford to try and pick up the pieces of the T20 campaign. The first home game since his death was ten days later at The Oval. It was a horrible, dank, drizzly evening and the ground was only about a quarter-full. The lads were playing from memory although gradually things started to return to some sort of normality. At Guildford in early July, Kevin Pietersen scored a blistering double hundred that he dedicated to Tom. It was certainly the sort of innings Tom would have been capable of playing.

When I got back from the break I had renewed energy for the season run-in, and I also had clarity on what was required. I gathered the squad together at Durham and spelt out exactly what was needed to stay in the First Division of the County Championship. I always felt with the group that when they were presented with the exact scenario of what was required from them over a series of matches, whatever the format, they usually responded positively. And they nailed it. By the time we arrived in Liverpool for the final match of the season we'd already secured safety and relegated our hosts, Lancashire.

Rory had attempted a comeback and played but perhaps we should have insisted he take the rest of the season off. It wasn't until the final game, against Lancashire at Liverpool, that we talked for any length of time about what had happened. He told me he had spoken to Sussex about the possibility of making a clean break and resuming his career in an environment both he and I knew would be ideal for his rehabilitation. I didn't want to lose him, but after Tom had died I sensed it was the end for Rory's Surrey career as well. He'd grown as a captain and as a cricketer over the previous two years but Tom's death had completely overshadowed everything. I told him I would support him if he wanted to go to Sussex and Richard Gould agreed. At the end of the season he left for Hove but he was never the same player again and retired early in 2015 because of a persistent wrist injury. For Rory, a light went out the day Tom died. Scoring runs in that carefree, attractive way of his would never be the same again without his best friend. As for Jade, Tom's death affected him just as much. Now he is battling away to save his career and I wish him every success in that. Rory and Jade will carry a burden for the rest of their lives over what happened to Tom. They are not responsible for his death. Only Tom will know why he made the decisions he did on the morning of Monday 18 June 2012.

Three years on Surrey appear to be recovering from what happened which is good to see, but what a terrible waste it was, not only of a young life cut off in its prime but also for the club. That season we had a fantastic opportunity with a young, dynamic and exciting squad with a progressive attitude that was capable of taking Surrey to the top in all forms of the game. And knowing what was coming through in the development squads, with the likes of Dominic Sibley and Tom Curran, made me seriously believe that once established at the top of the domestic game we could dominate for the next ten or 15 years, as Surrey sides of the past had done and just what you would expect from a big, well-resourced county.

I try to keep in regular contact with Matt Maynard, especially now he is back in the county game with Somerset. I was also very humbled when Matt told me after Tom's death how much his son loved me and the way I was helping his career develop. For everyone at Surrey the aftermath of Tom's death was an awful time, but nothing compared to the loss Matt, Sue and the rest of Tom's family must deal with for the rest of their lives. I wish them all well and hope they are comforted by the many wonderful memories of their son that we all have.

A few months after his death I talked about what had happened at that time with Jade. He said he, Rory and Tom felt almost invincible. There they were, three good-looking lads living in one of the best cities in the world, fit and strong and playing the best game in the world and getting well rewarded for it. 'We were living the dream weren't we?'

# 17

# The Next Chapter

TOM Maynard's death was the beginning of the end for me at Surrey. After what had happened, it was only a matter of when rather than if the club got rid of me.

I had a conversation along those lines at the start of 2013 with Richard Thompson, the chairman. He was very candid, which I appreciated, and told me they would not look at me being at the county beyond 2015. I knew that every coach, whatever the sport, has a finite shelf life. In a strange way I admire those who could continually reinvent themselves and be sufficiently motivated to stay in their roles for years and years. Personally, I'm not sure it does either them or their club any good and if you look at most of the major sports now, including cricket, the top coaches tend to do two- or three-year cycles, even if they are successful, before they move on.

When Surrey's two Richards – Thompson and Gould – came in they made it abundantly clear that their long-term planning involved Alec Stewart being involved in a full-time role at some stage. That future was now. At the end of 2012 if I had told the club that I would be happy for Alec to take on my role as team director and that I would revert to first-team coach, with Ian Salisbury moving on, I'm convinced the club would have agreed. But I was loyal to Ian. I had brought him to Surrey to work alongside me and we came as a pair. I certainly wasn't going to force the issue. If Surrey wanted to make changes they would have to instigate them.

Alec had already been around, but in more of an advisory role. Of course, he was a massive figure in Surrey cricket whose views were sought at all levels of the club's management, both on what was happening on the field and in other areas of its operation. But he was in the same situation as I find myself now. He had no central full-time cricketing role. At that time he did media work and was an ambassador for Clydesdale Bank, who sponsored the 40-over competition then. I found him to be a great sounding board. He came in occasionally to work with the team and it was helpful to have a different viewpoint on things. As players we'd always got on and he was around for two of the biggest moments of my career. He was in the Surrey team when I made my Championship debut for Derbyshire in 1988 and, of course, we'd been England team-mates in South Africa in 1999. We then worked together at Sussex when Mark Robinson brought him in to mentor Matt Prior, who idolised Alec. I always felt I had Alec's backing, right up until the day I was sacked.

Another big figure at the club was Mark Ramprakash, who'd been the rock of Surrey's batting for more than a decade. When I arrived, he was still a really good player and, in my mind, the best technical batsman of my generation. When I played you only saw him at close quarters two or three times a season and during my Sussex days he always seemed to get runs against us, often big scores as well. But it was only when I worked with him closely that I began to appreciate just what a wonderful player he was, the way he worked out bowlers' strengths and weaknesses and adapted his game to different match situations. At the end of his Surrey career he played with some very good players but also some average ones as well, who he made look better than they actually were because when he was in full flow no one was bothered too much about who was batting at the other end. For a while his runs covered up a lot of the fault lines in our batting.

I loved the challenge of coaching him. Actually, coaching is probably the wrong word. I guess advising him is a better description of our relationship. My job was to create the environment where he could excel and after I arrived I felt I did that. I found it interesting that when he retired he admitted that batting was much more fun than being in the dressing room. The junior batsmen in our squad often felt intimidated by him. I'd had an interesting conversation with someone close to the team just after I arrived when we talked about Mark. 'You'll never win anything with Ramps in the side,' I was told. I argued strongly that he was wrong and I wanted to prove him so but they turned out to be prophetic words.

In November 2010 Mark suffered a bad knee injury playing football. He was going to miss the start of the 2011 season and, at 42, I thought it was better for the longevity of his own career that when he returned he should concentrate on four-day cricket. So, when we won the Lord's final that warning I'd been given turned out to be spot on. We had played brave, high-risk cricket and, at that stage of his career, Mark was doing anything but. He'd battled all throughout 2011 after returning to the team but he couldn't recapture the consistent form he'd had for virtually all his career. To my eyes he looked laboured at the crease and was leaving balls outside off stump that he would normally have put away to the boundary.

I'd been in exactly the same situation at the end of my career. The signs are there when you can't do things on a cricket field or with a bat in hand that were once second nature. Mark continued to struggle at the start of 2012. By then he was playing on reputation alone, which was no good for us in terms of our development as a team but also a bonus for the opposition because Mark was no longer the dominating presence of old at the crease.

After Tom died I was convinced Rory Hamilton-Brown would not be coming back so we had lost our Nos. 3 and 4. My view then was that we needed to find out if guys like Rory Burns, Zafar Ansari and Arun Harinath could make the step up from the second team. I argued again that we had to give them a long run in the side. At the end of it, we would know just how much – or how little – recruitment we would need to do for our batting unit. Mark's future then came up for discussion and it was decided unanimously that we would not offer him a new contract. Yours truly was given the task of passing on the news to Mark.

That was a conversation I wasn't looking forward to, but I was honest. His first response was, 'What does Alec Stewart think about this?' Alec, of course, had been part of the decision-making process and maybe it might have been easier for Mark to accept that his career was drawing to an end if Alec had told him instead of me. Anyway, all I wanted was for Mark to leave the game on his terms. If that meant one more Championship or even one-day appearance, which we could publicise in advance as his final game before retirement, then I promised him I would make it happen. A few days later, in July 2012, Mark called a press conference and announced his retirement there and then. Of course, I was portrayed as the villain of the piece because I'd been the person to give him the news. All the usual suspects – former Surrey players, committee members – lined up to have a pop at me without knowing the facts. I would have loved Mark to bow out with one last big flourish at The Oval in front of an appreciative crowd. It was his decision to retire in the way he did and his decision to only tell half the story of his departure when he did so.

Mark's retirement left us short of experience and so the idea to bring in Graeme Smith as captain did make sense. He was still one of the best players in the world and his experience and presence would bring some stability to the dressing room, which we needed after the traumatic events of 2012. When he arrived, he had a very positive effect on the team. He kept things simple and was quite autocratic but because of his stature in the game the players couldn't help but respect him. When it was time to go to work Graeme switched into cricket mode but he was quite a relaxed, almost playful character away from the game. We spoke quite a bit about leadership. Having assessed the set-up at Surrey for a couple of weeks he told me that, in his opinion, he thought the coaching structure needed to be streamlined rather than expanded, which by the start of 2013 was the case with Alec now having more and more of an influence on decision-making. It was an interesting suggestion but one, if I'm being honest, I knew he had little chance of being able to implement.

There were others. At the end of 2012, when Rory Burns, Zafar Ansari and Arun Harinath were coming through and we knew we were signing Graeme I argued we didn't need another senior batsman and that we had to keep investing in the younger batsmen. So we signed 37-year-old Vikram Solanki, which I thought was a backward step. The decision to bring in Graeme meant the overseas slot was filled. I'd always contended that our first-choice overseas player should be the best available spin bowler and we should build the team around him and the captain. With that option unavailable we ended up bringing in Gary Keedy, who was 39. Like Vikram, Gary had a lot of experience but I wasn't convinced they were going to make the difference. And, of course, we went from being a young, dynamic side to suddenly one that was full of 30-somethings. The brave new era at Surrey now looked still-born. We would have gone down a different path if the decisions had been left to me, but by the start of 2013 they were being made as a collective.

Graeme was desperate to make an early statement of intent with the bat but in his first game against Somerset in the Championship at The Oval he scored just two. We then played Sussex and after making three in the first innings he scored 67 as we batted through the last day to save the game. We then met Middlesex at Lord's where he got a duck and 48 not out. I felt he was batting with his familiar authority in the second innings, a belief reinforced the following day when he scored an unbeaten 74 against Hampshire in our opening Pro 40 match. But he came off the field complaining of soreness in his left ankle, a problem that had dogged him before. He went to see the physio and later that night I was told that a scan had revealed some pretty serious damage. There was no time to formulate a plan for his rehabilitation. At the request of Cricket South Africa, he returned home that night, his Surrey career over before it had really begun.

We then swapped one legend of the game for another when Ricky Ponting joined us for a two-month spell. Ricky was absolutely brilliant. He could still play and produced a masterclass on his debut at Derby when he scored 192 not out. As a team, though, we had yet to win a Championship game when we arrived at Arundel to face Sussex in mid-June, although I did feel we had started to turn the corner.

The pitch was typically slow, but that was our most complete performance of the season to date and I'm convinced we would have won the game had we not lost the first day to rain. On the second day Richard turned up at the ground with Alec Stewart and his agent Alan Smith, the former Crystal Palace manager. I didn't think too much about it – there was a former players' reunion going on organised by the Professional Cricketers' Association which they were all attending but I took the chance to do a couple of circuits of the ground, first with Richard and then Alec. I asked them both the same question. 'Look, is my job under threat?' Both said categorically that it was not. I told them that I was quite bullish about our prospects for the rest of the season. I knew we wouldn't win the Championship that season but we had spent a month planning the Twenty20 campaign and I was very confident we would do well in that competition. We certainly had the players who would relish the format.

A couple of days later I was sacked.

Richard phoned me and requested a meeting at The Oval. 'We need to have a conversation about your employment,' were his words. I don't know what surprised me more, losing my job or losing it a year to the day since Tom had died. To his credit, when I pointed this out to him Richard was very contrite. Within 25 minutes of our conversation it was all over the media. That's how Sam found out. Richard said that he and the decision-makers, whom I assumed to mean Alec, felt that the pressure both Ian Salisbury, who was also sacked, and I had been under had become intolerable and was being felt by the players too. As I expected, Alec was to take more of a hands-on role with support from Stuart Barnes, the bowling coach who had been brought in at the start of 2012. To a man, every player in the squad rang me that day. They could have been doing it because it might have made them feel better but I sensed from the conversations I had that they were genuinely disappointed that Ian and I had gone.

Time is a great healer of course, but even now five years later I still argue that Surrey acted in haste. For the first time that season we had a week without any cricket coming up where we could take stock and move forward. During the Arundel game I genuinely felt for the first time since Tom died and Graeme Smith had left that we were moving forward. Surrey's argument was that the break gave them time to shuffle the pack. I knew they were going to get rid of me eventually so what difference would three months have made? If they had told me that I'd run my race and would be replaced at the end of the season I would have been fine with that. It would give me time to start thinking about my own future and also incentivise me to make sure

Surrey finished the season strongly, not least because if I left them in a good position it would not do any harm to my own employment prospects.

Later that week I finally managed to have a conversation with Alec. He explained that when we had spoken at Arundel he wasn't aware that he would subsequently be part of a conversation where my future would be up for discussion. He told me that the decision to fire Ian and me had been unanimous. So, what had happened in the hours between our chat on the boundary, when he assured me my job was not under threat, and the subsequent meeting? I felt betrayed. Like me, Ian hasn't been able to get a county post since then but he is a fine coach and doing great work with the England disabilities cricket team.

Our good friends, Ray and Kerry Fine, took us off on holiday, the first proper break I'd had during the cricket season for more than 25 years. When I got back I went to The Oval for the last time. I saw Richard but found it tough to speak to him. I reiterated that I thought we'd have a good run in the Twenty20, because of the preparations we'd already made, but that we would get relegated in the Championship. Sure enough, we reached the final of the Twenty20 but went back down to the second division.

Look, as I've already mentioned I know every coach has a shelf life. In hindsight, I should have followed my instincts and left on a high after the success at the end of 2011. But I have never backed away from any challenge during my career – it's just not in my nature. I always feel there is a solution and a workable way forward.

I guess I did well to last at Surrey for as long as I did considering the hostility in some quarters to my appointment in the first place. There were some good times too, don't get me wrong. The Lord's final win was one of the highlights of my career and to see some of the young players who came through or were emerging from the Academy during my time as coach develop into good Surrey cricketers, including Jason Roy, Zafar Ansari and the Curran brothers Tom and Sam, is gratifying even now. Another experienced player, Gareth Batty, did a solid job to get them back into the first division of the County Championship and Michael Di Venuto, an old team-mate from the early days at Sussex, is doing well as head coach working under Alec, who is director of cricket. Although I was disappointed to lose my job there, I still have a soft spot for Surrey and am proud of what I helped to achieve.

I was desperate to get back in the game as soon as I could but the trouble with county cricket is there are only a limited number of jobs. I was invited to interview for the post of elite performance director at my first county Derbyshire. Initially the role held a lot of appeal, not least because of my links with the club. I thought I interviewed well but when I came out of the room I bumped into Graeme Welch, who was also in the frame. I thought we'd have made a good pairing but Derbyshire were left with an interesting dilemma. If they wanted a fresh start they would go for Graeme; if they wanted someone with experience then I'd have got the nod. In the end Graeme got it and he did a good job at a club not as well resourced as so many of the other counties until he left in 2016 to work for Leicestershire before returning to Warwickshire, where he'd had so much success as a player, to be their bowling coach. In hindsight not getting the Derbyshire job was probably a blessing in disguise for me. It was too soon after Surrey for me to get back in the saddle.

Preparing for the interview got me thinking deeply about my own coaching ethos and how it had evolved over the years. The basis of my presentation to Derbyshire was that the fewer people involved in decision-making the better because there are less conversations to be had, fewer opinions to canvass and therefore more time to do what I love most which is working with players, whether that's as a head coach, assistant or in a specialist role.

When I left Surrey I lost some identity because people didn't know where my strengths lay. Was I a team director, manager or coach? That was my own fault because when I switched roles at Surrey, I allowed myself to be drawn further away from the team. They wanted me to take on a more directorial role because it would have made me easier to replace with Alec further down the line. But I have always preferred to be in shorts and a tracksuit, in the nets trying to make players better.

The former Australia coach John Buchanan once explained that a coach who focussed solely on winning wouldn't be in the job long. It was a statement that really bothered me, but in the county game now I think a lot of coaches have the same mind-set because they are more concerned about the longevity of their own careers. Yes, you have to develop players but primarily players have a responsibility to develop themselves. It can't always be down to the coach who, these days, find themselves primarily tasked with creating an environment where players can perform at their best. I think there are too many counties who are satisfied with low expectations, even using the excuse that there are only three trophies to win. That doesn't sit right with me. I'd rather not bother entering than go into a competition thinking I can't win. It's difficult because the two-divisional split means only nine teams can win the Championship and in the second division there are four or five counties who we can all name who would struggle to get promoted. Instead, they focus on trying to win one-day trophies and increase revenue and exposure that way, providing a pathway for their players into the England set-up. Leicestershire and Northamptonshire are the best two examples. That business model works for them but it is still gratifying for me, as someone who loves four-day cricket, to read even now that the players regard the Championship as *the* competition to win.

One of the most enjoyable periods of my career in the game came in the spring of 2014 when I was asked if I would join Sri Lanka's tour of England in a consultative coaching role. Graham Ford, who had just led them to success in the Twenty20 World Cup, was heading to Surrey and his replacement, Paul Farbrace, was about to be named as assistant to the then England coach Peter Moores. The new coach, Marvan Atapattu, was taking a team to England and I was asked to help in all areas of coaching and preparation and offer advice on English grounds and conditions.

When I was approached I was on the verge of taking a totally different direction in my career. An opportunity to get heavily involved in a food business promoting a Sussex-based product was on the table but when Sri Lanka got in touch I had no hesitation in accepting. I guess it showed that my passion still lay with coaching and cricket. I had a fantastic six weeks, culminating at Headingley when Sri Lanka beat England with one ball to spare to clinch their first series win in England. It was a privileged insight into how an international team works and how some of the best players in the world operate.

I am proud of my input into what was a very successful tour, although I won't deny that plotting England's downfall was something I struggled to come to terms with. When the players were cavorting on the Headingley balcony I found it difficult to join in, although inwardly I was delighted, especially when the captain Angelo Matthews said afterwards that he couldn't understand why the best coach in England was working for Sri Lanka!

At the start of the tour Marvan led a team meeting and I was surprised that there was no interaction at all with the team. Of course there wasn't much you could tell guys like Kumar Sangakkara, Mahela Jayawardena and Lasith Malinga, all legends of the modern game, that they did not already know but afterwards I asked Marvan, who was pretty new to coaching, if he'd considered involving the players more. I asked if I could work with the bowling group alongside the bowling coach Chaminda Vaas, who was a lovely guy but who struggled with his presentation skills. We went through a plan and I asked him to trust me that it would work. When the group met, Chaminda said a few words by way of introduction and then invited Lasith to explain his plans for the various English batsmen to the rest of the group. When I arrived in the room Lasith looked as if there were a million other places he'd rather be than in another team meeting but within a minute or so his whole body language changed. He was scribbling all over the flip chart like a mad scientist as he explained how he would try and get the different English batsmen out. Chaminda, the team analyst and I just sat at the back. It was brilliant, you could feel the energy in the room. The feedback to Marvan was positive and that is how meetings were conducted for the rest of the tour. Marvan would prime the players in advance that he wanted them to lead the discussion and it worked wonderfully well.

I threw myself into the tour, not least because of the opportunity it presented to put myself back in the shop window and slowly I began to get more involved in the decision-making. We won the Twenty20 and one-day series but the focus was always on the two Tests. Before the first Test at Lord's I told Marvan and Angelo that we had to bat first if the pitch was firm and the sky was blue, no matter how much grass there was on the wicket. Don't look down look up at Lord's was the old adage. I felt that for us to win the game we had to bat first so we had Rangana Herath, our quality left-arm spinner, to bowl at them in the last innings. There was always the chance that we could get rolled over cheaply in the first innings but we had a batting line-up that was good enough to get 500 in the second dig when the pitch had flattened out. So, of course, Angelo put England in to bat! For the first hour it did all sorts and then it flattened out. We would have lost but England delayed their declaration too long and Sri Lanka saved the game by the skin of our teeth on the last day with nine wickets down.

The wicket at Headingley was greener and it was overcast. I felt the brave option again was to bat first, although it was 60-40 this time. England won the toss and put Sri Lanka in but I was delighted that when he was interviewed at the toss Angelo admitted he would have batted first – he'd come around to my way of thinking! We dragged it back on the third day to restrict England's lead to 108 and then made 457 in the second innings with Angelo scoring his second century of the tour. That put

England under massive pressure. We timed the declaration right, took four wickets on the fourth evening and then won the game despite a magnificent hundred on the last day by Moeen Ali and some brave resistance by James Anderson.

Despite winning the series Marvan had to re-apply for his job and I was asked to apply too. I'd love to have been his assistant but was told it wasn't an option. I then got a call to say I was on a shortlist of five and that I'd be contacted about interview arrangements. Five minutes later I was called back. I was no longer on the shortlist, was thanked for my interest and before I'd got a word in edgeways the conversation was over! A shame, but I'm pleased that Marvan is still in the job because he and the rest of the guys there were great to work with. If the opportunity arose again in the future to be part of Sri Lanka's set-up I'd have to give it serious consideration.

Later in 2014 I was asked by Mick Newell, who was Nottinghamshire coach at the time, to conduct a root and branch study into why the county weren't developing their own home-grown batsmen. For five or six weeks I watched a lot of cricket, from under-13s to second XI, before presenting my report. I enjoyed the work and I hope some of it will be implemented because it's a shame that a county with such a strong tradition of bringing through their own have largely imported batting talent since Samit Patel came on to the scene a decade or more ago.

Such is the transient life of a coach for hire that a few weeks after running the rule over Nottinghamshire's age group teams I was in the heat of a South African summer, working for the Netherlands in the second division of the World Cricket League. It was the start of an association with Dutch cricket that would endure for the next three years and nearly ended with me putting down roots in Amsterdam as their full-time coach.

Back in 2014, Roland Lefebvre, against whom I'd enjoyed some good battles when he played for Glamorgan and Somerset, made the initial contact. We met at an ECB coaching convention and he asked me if I would get involved, working alongside their young South African coach Anton Roux. Anton had only played a handful of first-class games but over the next few months I saw what an impressive young coach he was developing into. He made a few mistakes, but he did a lot of things right.

After a training camp in Pretoria we moved to Namibia for a week-long World Cricket League tournament where the aim was to qualify for the first division. The focus of Peter Borren, the captain, and his players seemed to be merely on making sure they finished in the top two to secure promotion. My challenge to the group was to win the tournament and secure the Netherlands' first trophy for 14 years. To the delight of everyone, we did that by beating Uganda in the final group game and then defeating the hosts in the final.

In the summer of 2015 I linked up with the Dutch boys again for the Twenty20 World Cup in Scotland and Ireland. I liked the set-up in so much that there wasn't a big backroom staff and it meant the players have to step up and take more responsibility for their own performances. Of course, with part-time cricketers you can get fluctuations in form but Peter is tactically one of the most innovative captains I have come across in my career. He's very creative in a lot of what he does and although we had a few ups and downs we came good when it mattered, winning our last two group games and then beating Ireland in the semi-final. The final was washed out which meant we shared the honours with Scotland but we had got through to the finals in India where we would take part in a qualifying competition to try and get into the main tournament.

It is one of the biggest frustrations of my coaching career that we didn't get to play with the big boys in India. We were in a good position to win our first game against Bangladesh but ended up losing by seven runs. When our next fixture against Oman was washed out we were heading home, a victory over Ireland in our last match nothing more than a consolation prize.

Having won the World Cricket League our other challenge, along with the T20 World Cup, was to claim the 13th spot in the one-day international rankings and improve the chances of going through to the next 50-over World Cup in England in 2019. You play your rivals in two ODIs as well as a four-day match in the Intercontinental Cup. For a time, the incentive was that the eventual winners would gain Test recognition from the ICC but when they realised that only Afghanistan and Ireland had the necessary infrastructure they awarded it to them instead and Ireland are due to play their first Test match against Pakistan in 2018.

In September 2016 Anton got a great offer to become No.2 to the head coach at Otago state in New Zealand and left his role with the Netherlands. I was asked to take over as interim head coach, an easy decision as I knew the boys pretty well by then. In February 2017 we headed to Hong Kong, after a training camp in Dubai, to play them in two 50-over matches and an Intercontinental Cup game.

I prepared as if I would be offered the job at the end of it although we knew Hong Kong would be no pushovers.

So it proved in the four-day game. They dominated for three days, leaving us a day to bat out with only five second-innings wickets in hand and chasing 507 to win. But Ben Cooper and Pieter Seelaar both made unbeaten hundreds in an unbroken stand of 288 to save the game. It was an extraordinary performance and I sensed that the squad really moved forward that week. Before, there had been pockets of brilliance by the team like beating England at Lord's in the T20 World Cup finals but those four days suggested to me that we were laying some really solid foundations for our development. We took the confidence into the 50-over games and won them both, Peter Borren leading the team as well as any captain I have come across during my career. Home wins over Papua New Guinea and Namibia sealed 13th spot, but by then my involvement with Dutch cricket was over.

They asked me to become head coach but it would have meant a full-time commitment to living in Amsterdam. At my interview, I pitched them a model similar to the way Phil Simmons has run Ireland based on modular team time where you have the squad together for three or four intense weeks, training and playing proper games in guaranteed weather abroad, as opposed to more sporadic sessions with the guys at the indoor facilities back in Rotterdam. They listened, and offered me the chance to stay on as consultant to the new coach Ryan Campbell, the former Australia player, when he took over in April 2017 but I felt after three great years it was time to step away.

By then my coaching journey had, literally, taken me back to school.

Friends of ours, Adrian and Judith Batchelor, were at a dinner with John Green, the headmaster at Seaford College near Petworth, and my name came up in the conversation when they chatted about cricket provision at the school. John gave me a call and after meeting him and the director of sport, Anthony Cook, in the winter of 2015, I was offered a part-time role coaching cricket.

As its name suggests, the college was originally in the Sussex coastal town of Seaford. When the government requisitioned it during the Second World War they moved to Worthing before settling at their current home in East Lavington in 1946. I remember thinking how impressive the place was when I met John and Anthony for the first time. The drive up from the road to the main building is a mile long and all I could see on either side were rugby, hockey and football pitches. Seaford College has always had a strong tradition in rugby. John played for Saracens and when he went there he was keen not only to uphold that but also make them stronger in other sports, including cricket. The list of old Seafordians who played top-level cricket runs to one name – Adrian Jones, the former Sussex and Somerset fast bowler – but the environment for that to change is definitely in place.

Early in 2017 I was offered a full-time role as head of cricket, although I coach in other sports and also work to try and get some of the alumni more engaged with their old school. As for coaching kids, it obviously presents different challenges but the foundations are the same. If you can instil good disciplines you are halfway there. We spend time doing technical work, but that's no more than 30% and involves teaching them the fundamentals. Primarily I want them to enjoy the game. Most of the pupils don't remember my career. I was regarded as an explosive batsman but I don't remember playing too many ramp shots, even at the end of my playing days, so it's quite refreshing to see kids in the nets expressing themselves in this way and playing without fear. They love range hitting but, as I keep telling them, trying to hit sixes does increase the risk of being caught in the deep. They find it hard to believe sometimes that you can hit the ball along the ground to the boundary as well!

I love my work at Seaford College but I can't deny that the urge to work in elite coaching is still strong. In May 2016 I had been offered the chance to take over as head of Ireland's Academy but after a successful interview with their performance director Richard Holdsworth and coach John Bracewell I changed my mind 48 hours after they had announced my appointment, although I hadn't signed a formal contract.

I don't regret the decision but I know I messed up. In my desire to get back into mainstream cricket I didn't do my due diligence. It would have involved uprooting the family to Dublin, which would have been a greater financial burden than I first realised, as well as interrupting Sophie and Mollie's education at a crucial time. Those weren't deal-breakers on their own but it was a different job to what I came away from the interviewing expecting it to be, with less pure coaching and a lot of time going around the country trying to build the infrastructure at club and schools level. Perhaps I didn't listen hard enough or ask the right questions at the interview.

These days, the question I'm asked more than any when the conversation turns to cricket is, 'Why aren't you working for Sussex?' When the county made the decision in October 2017 to get rid of Mark Davis after two years in the job, there was inevitable speculation linking me to the vacancy. And I did have a long chat with the chief executive Rob Andrew. In the end they chose Jason Gillespie, who had such a successful time when he was coach of Yorkshire. Fair enough and I wish him every success, although it will be fascinating to see if giving Jason a seven-month contract will work. Anyway, as far as Sussex is concerned my door is always open.

In 2017 an unimaginable hole was ripped into our family after we lost my brother David, at the age of just 49, and our dad John in the space of a short few months.

David was in Bournemouth for some meetings about his successful sports drinks business. He arrived at the hotel with his colleague around midnight and was found the following morning at the bottom of the stairs. It appeared that he had either blacked out or fallen – we will probably never know. His washbag was propping open the door to his hotel room which suggests he was heading to reception or to his car because he'd forgotten something. It happened in March and nearly a year later the inquest into his death has still not taken place.

David still played cricket in Derbyshire to a very good club standard and had played 99 games for MCC. At a recent MCC dinner they touchingly awarded the family a commemorative 100th cap as he was due to play his 100th game just a few weeks after his untimely death. I was really touched by the many messages I received from people in the cricket community. There isn't a day when I don't think about him and those early times growing up and when we played against each other while trying to earn a contract with Derbyshire.

He had travelled to Bournemouth that day from Southend where my dad John was in hospital. He'd been treated for lymphoma cancer some five years earlier but then a routine check-up found another growth in a particularly inaccessible place. He was told he could have an operation, although there was no guarantee that they would be able to get to the tumour, or take his chances. He decided to have surgery and whilst initially all looked good a couple of weeks after the operation he was back in hospital suffering from multiple organ failure. As the first born, David always had a closer affinity to Dad and had to make a frantic journey back from Dublin after I'd phoned him to say the consultants had given him very little chance of survival.

But, the fighter that he always was, he did recover somewhat but David's death knocked Dad for six. He was able to spend a few more weeks at home before he passed away in July. He had been back in hospital to undergo another operation and as they were taking him down to theatre I rang him. The nurse answered the call and I asked how he was doing. 'Tell him I'm bloody dying!' was his response. Typical Dad. Typical Yorkshireman. Always straight to the point. I think he knew that day that he didn't have long left. Again, the family were really moved by the tributes, particularly from Southend United FC, where he spent 15 years as chief executive from 1984–99, and the town where he enjoyed his retirement.

You don't realise how big a part someone plays in your life until they are no longer there. That is certainly the case with Dad and David. My mum has come down to Sussex to live close to us and we stay constantly in touch with David's wife and children, but it has left a very big hole in all our lives, especially as we lost them in the space of just four months.

I still love cricket, although I resist virtually all invitations to play the game these days. My other sporting passion in tennis. In fact, I'd call it more of an obsession these days. Sam had played a lot during her early years and joined a country club a few miles from our house in West Sussex called Wickwoods. For my 42nd birthday she bought me a tennis lesson. I wasn't that keen initially and for the first ten minutes I was under-cutting every shot, just as I would have done on the squash court. The coach stopped me, we went back to basics and slowly I became hooked on the game. I had found another sport that gave me everything cricket did. As well as the physical element, there is a tactical and mental aspect too. I started playing in the fourth team and gradually rose up the ranks and eventually made my debut in the firsts. I play three or four times a week and occasionally team up with Sam, although we do try and avoid it for the sake of marital harmony!

Cricket has been my life ever since I first picked up a bat in the back garden at Whitwell with Dad, Mum and David. I have always encouraged my girls to enjoy their sport and I'm as proud as any parent would be at the progress my eldest, Georgia, is making with her cricket. She is now captain of Sussex and coaching full-time at the Aldridge Academy in Brighton, a purpose-built facility and home to the county's women's and girls' teams. Although she was in the ECB's Academy and is regularly involved in squad sessions with the England team, now coached by Mark Robinson of course, she hasn't quite broken through at the highest level yet. But I'm sure she will. She is extremely dedicated and the exposure she and so many of those who aspire to play for England get by playing in the Kia Women's Super League, where they come up against some of the best players in the world, can only stand her in good stead. Georgia and her partner now have their own flat in Brighton and she is loving life. We still see her every Sunday for lunch, or when she comes home on Wednesday afternoons to raid our fridge!

Sophie's love isn't cricket but ponies and she's completing a gap year at Handcross Park as a student teaching assistant before embarking on what I'm certain will be an entrepreneurial career after a double distinction in business studies. I'm also very pleased to say that my youngest girl, Mollie, has got the bat and ball bug and is in the Sussex under-11 squad. She has taken a shine to wicketkeeping.

And then there's Sam, my rock for 26 years of marriage and many years before then as well. She is the most incredible person I have ever met. She has kept things together and put up with the highs and lows that being married to a professional sportsman entails without complaint. In times when I have struggled she has been strong and likewise when things have been tough for her I hope I have been the support she needed. I have been very lucky in so much of my life so far, but never more so than the day I met Sam. She took David's death particularly badly, because they had always been close, and I was so grateful to have her alongside me during those difficult months in 2017.

We've had a terrific journey, though, and I'm looking forward to what the next stage involves.